EVOLUTION OF HINDU ADMINISTRATIVE INSTITUTIONS IN SOUTH INDIA

EVOLUTION OF HINDU ADMINISTRATIVE INSTITUTIONS IN SOUTH INDIA

S. KRISHNASWAMI AIYANGAR

GYAN

Published by

Gyan Publishing House
5, Ansari Road
Daryaganj, New Delhi-110002
Phone: 011-47034999, 9811692060
E-mail: books@gyanbooks.com

Distribution Network
gyanbooks.com
India, USA, Canada, UK, Australia, France

ISBN : 978-81-212-3371-2 (PB)
First Published, Madras, 1931

2nd Impression 2020

Printed at: Gyan Press, Delhi.

Evolution of Hindu Administrative Institutions in South India
Author: S. Krishnaswami Aiyangar

Sir William Meyer Lectures 1929-30, Madras University

EVOLUTION

OF

Hindu Administrative Institutions in South India.

BY

Rao Bahadur

S. KRISHNASWAMI AIYANGAR, M.A., HONY. PH.D.,
Honorary Correspondent, Archaeological Survey of India,
Fellow of the Asiatic Society of Bengal.

PUBLISHED BY THE UNIVERSITY OF MADRAS.

MADRAS :
PRINTED AT THOMPSON & CO., LIMITED.

INTRODUCTION

The University of Madras invited me to deliver the Sir William Meyer Lectures in History for the academic year 1929-30, and the following pages contain the lectures and the material upon which the lectures were based. Sir William Meyer was a Madras civilian, and during his stay in Madras was associated with the University for a number of years. His interest in University education was great, and he carried that interest in his retirement. The lectures instituted at the University here are the result of a bequest that he made for the purpose, and the lectures were actually inaugurated two years ago.

Having accepted the invitation, it was a matter of some difficulty to choose an appropriate subject for the occasion. The choice has had to subserve two ends;—it must first be sufficiently attractive to a general audience; and secondly it must be acceptable, as far as may be, to the tastes and inclinations of the founder. One might almost say Sir William's partiality was for administrative history. He translated a work on British Administration in India by Joseph Chailley, a treatise expounding the British administration of India as it appeared to a talented Frenchman. Sometime before he left India, while yet serving the Government of India, he delivered a lecture to the United Service Institution in Simla, under the presidency of the then Viceroy, Lord Curzon, on "How Rome would have governed India". An administrator of eminence as he was, and showing such interest in the British administration of India, I thought it quite fitting that the Sir William Meyer Lectures delivered by me should bear on the administrative institutions of India. India is too wide in area and would be too vast even otherwise to be dealt with as a whole, having regard to the advance made in the study of the subject as a whole. At the present stage, the problem could be attacked only in blocks. South India and the administrative institutions that she developed in the first 1500 years of the Christian era under Hindu rule, constitute a distinct division of the subject. Almost at the outset of my work in this line, very near thirty-years since, I made an effort to reconstruct the Chola Administration from the inscriptional material then made available. At the time the first volume of South Indian Inscriptions, 3 parts of Vol. II and the first part of Vol. III were all that had been published. We have now six volumes available. The last three contain only the texts. The actual inscriptional material accessible now may be about five to six times what we then had. An attempt at a fuller picture of Hindu Administration in Tamil India has become possible. The following lectures therefore attempt to pass in review, in the light of this vast material, what the administrative ideas and ideals had been, and what the actual institutions were that had developed to give practical effect to these ideas and ideals of administration.

After the lectures had been delivered and the manuscript had reached its final form, I read with pleasure a work named "Loyal India", consisting of a survey of seventy years of British administration from

1858 to 1928 by a distinguished official of the India Office, who had had unrivalled opportunities of studying the development of the British Administration from the inside. The author who entered service in the India Office, and had opportunities of serving on the personal staff of the late Lord Morley, observes "One who was behind the scenes during those years, pregnant as they proved to be with world-history, may be excused for believing and desiring to proclaim his conviction that here, in a reversion to counsels of that temper and to the orderly procedure then adopted, is to be found, if anywhere, the safe line of advance towards the establishment of a true and lasting Commonwealth of India." Admitting that the study of the problem is bewildering in its variety and complexity to the Western mind, and almost despairing of understanding the Indian mind, he records his faith that "if Englishmen are to continue to serve in India, or even to trade there, the attempt must be made". With a view to this understanding he writes the book, the purpose of which is best explained in his own words. "Without entering into the deeper mysteries of Indian thought and feeling", he proceeds to observe that the key to tolerance and mutual trust between Europeans and Indians is to be found in the community of service in the cause of the uplifting of the weaker sections of humanity, which in the past had successfully built up an empire out of diverse peoples almost discordent in their modes of life and thought. He is hopeful that "India, under divine providence, has before her, as a self-reliant, self-respecting partner in the British Commonwealth of Nations, as glorious a future as she had behind her a splendid past; and it may be a happier future, when more of the mists of prejudice and passion shall have cleared away." In that faith he sets about his work, and in striking out a method, he came to the conclusion that the "essentials would be best apprehended by a brief examination in turn of, first, the native Indian theory of government in ancient and modern times, so far as it can be ascertained from authentic sources; next, on certain historic documents issued by the British Royal House constituting the Charter under which the rights and liberties of the peoples and princes of India are proclaimed, guaranteed and safeguarded; thereafter to outline, as simply as possible, the structure of the existing constitution and trace its gradual growth". What he says regarding native Indian theory of Government is to the point here;—"What, then, is the Hindu conception of soverignty? In other words, what are the attributes that are looked for in a ruler? If the example of other peoples is any guide—as of course it cannot fail to be—the answer to these questions must be sought not in formulas of the political platform and the Press, but in current songs and sayings that are in the mouths of the common folk and mould their thought and daily life and conversation; it must be sought, too, in the ancient scriptures, the Epics, which display Hindu political ideals functioning, as it were, or in the ancient Sanskrit Books of the Laws, of which there are now many adequate translations."

* * * *

"The Hindu conception of soverignty, unlike other features of Hinduism, is simplicity itself; it is Kingship, Monarchy, the rule of one person, Autocracy; and all that complicated system of checks and balances—Legislature distinguished from Administrative authorities, Judicial from Executive, and so forth—upon which the mind of Western Europe and America prides itself (and not without good cause) as the most efficient instrument of government yet devised by the wit of man, the system known as "representative government", is, in essence, repugnant to Indian thought. This is not to say that some adaptation of it may not be both possible (it clearly is that, as the history of recent constitutional reforms in India shows) and even desirable. But it must be recognised that to the teeming millions of the Indian peasantry Britain's attempt to introduce the machinery of democracy is, and, it would seem, must remain, a stone of stumbling and a rock of offence." It will be seen from the above that for a correct appreciation of the constitutional needs of the country two things are essential, namely, an understanding of the native Indian theory of government, and secondly the evolution of the British Administration in India. While providing a fully documented series of charters regarding the second, the author has perforce to leave the first part of it unattempted. If the following lectures based upon a mass of material, much more reliable than the kind of documents to which reference has been made, supply the need in any degree, the choice of the subject would have been justified even from the practical present point of view. This is the more so, as the documents from which the administration of the Hindus of this part of the country is built up are in their nature, official documents, and are very far from being merely indicative of the ideas underlying the prevalent inner notions of government. These are documents that lay down in so many words how the administration was actually carried on, and, coming as they do from various sources and by the mere chance escape from the ravages of time, they have a value of their own, which perhaps official documents drawn up of set purpose could not lay claim to.

While holding that the Hindu conception of soveriegnty is a monarchy, which he equates with autocracy, the rule of one person, the author adds the caution "let it not be thought, however, that the ideal Hindu sovereign is a tyrant of the type, such as the great political thinkers of ancient Greece depicted and held up to obloquy—Common-sense alone should suffice to prove the futility of such an idea." A perusal of the following pages, particularly lectures from 3 to 6 will clearly demonstrate that we are not depending upon common sense alone for this position. While in form the Hindu government may be described as a monarchy, and even an autocracy, and while it may readily even be conceded that the Hindu monarchy had autocratic powers for application in times of emergency, the actual use of the power was made in a way to satisfy the exacting demands even of a pure and complete democracy, not only in form, but more completely in spirit, and that is what is really wanted, not the mere form of it; and, if democracy is exotic to India and has to be introduced into the country, the aim ought rather to be to introduce the democratic spirit and a democratic administration of the governmental functions, rather than a mere arithmetical exhibition of democracy. It is hardly necessary to point out that a literal going back to the centuries when this system worked with success is an impossibility. Circumstances have so far changed, and so radically, that a swing back to the second millennium is impossible. It cannot transcend the wit of man to bring into any form of administration the actual democratic spirit that can carry on the administration for the benefit of the masses as a whole, not in the form of the paternal autocracy, or a worse bureaucracy, which would blatantly claim the special guardianship of the masses as against the classes, but certainly in the more genuine form of democracy, where the classes and the masses alike have their influence at least for general initiation and active correction, if not the actual carrying out, of measures of beneficence to the people as a whole. The actual details of a constitution satisfying these ends can hardly be built up except by a careful examination of how they worked in the past. Even the notion that Representative Government is repugnant to Indian thought, would on closer examination be found to be wide of the truth. The principle of representation was understood and acted upon. It is with a view to the possibility that some little useful light may perhaps be gained from the past that the following lectures were designed, and nothing more is expected of them than to serve, however inadequately, this particular purpose.

It is hardly necessary to take up space to expound the scheme of the course. The ideas prevalent and the ideals in regard to government are expounded in the first and the second lectures, and the *disjecta membra* regarding the administration from the earliest times, of which we can gain a glimpse are collected together and studied as far as may be in the chronological order with a view to gaining an idea of the tendencies of these institutions. This is done in the following three lectures. The last one exhibits cursorily the changes that had actually come into the system of administration owing to stress of circumstances arising out of the Muhammadan invasions. How these institutions were affected, and what efforts had been made to preserve these administrations from collapsing are indicated, though briefly. A similar study of other blocks of territory in India exhibiting perhaps differences of features would be necessary to complete the picture, and it is hoped that efforts would be made to supply this as occasion offers.

I acknowledge with pleasure the assistance rendered by Mr. V. R. Ramachandra Dikshitar, an old research student of mine, now Lecturer in the Department of Indian History and Archaeology at the University of Madras, for having verified references in the first and the second lectures, as he has in his own way covered the ground in his "Studies in Tamil Literature and History" published since the lectures were delivered, and "Hindu Administrative Institutions." I have not thought it worth while burdening the lectures with extracts from the authorities. Those of the readers that may not be willing to go to the originals for reference can find many of them collected *in extenso* in the works of Mr. Dikshitar referred to. I also acknowledge here my gratitude to the Syndicate of the University of Madras for having done me the honour of this invitation, and for thus giving me the chance of presenting these lectures to the public under the auspices of the University.

S. KRISHNASWAMI AIYANGAR.

"Śrīpadam", Mylapore,
18th February, 1931.

CONTENTS.

ERRATA.

P. iv. l. 2 from bottom, for *soverignty* read *sovereignty.*

vi. 2nd para l. 2, for *soveriegnty* read *sovereignty.*

8. l. 23, omit 'he'.

19. l. 11, read 'Madurai-k-Kāñji' for Madurai Kānji.

23. *Footnote* read 'Jáyaswal,' for Jayaswall.

33. l. 8, and last but one line, read 'Purushārthas' for Purushartas.

36, l. 6, read 'Arthaśāstra' for arthaśāstra.

48, last but one line:—read 'upadha' for upadā.

49, l. 2, read 'upadha' for upadā.

50, l. 8, read 'Madurai-k-Kanji',

l. 9, read 'Śilappadhikāram' for Śilapadhikāram.

54, l. 4, read 'Mātsya-nyāya' for Mātsaya-Nyāya.

70, l. 19, read 'Śilappadhikāram' for 'Śilapadhikāram'.

83, l. 15, omit 'Pavittiri'.

114, l. 15, read 'unoccupied' for 'unoccuped'.

333, para 2. l. 7, read 'Kampili' for Kampli.

376, last but one line, read 'bureaucratic' for beaurocratic.

ADMINISTRATIVE INSTITUTIONS OF SOUTH INDIA

LECTURE I

South India—a separate political entity.

South India, geographically not quite a separate region; historically is much more so. At the beginning of the historical period, reference to South India proper were, in Sanskrit literature, Dakshiṇāpatha and Dākshiṇātya, vague and not specifically referable to this part of South India. Increased knowledge from Kātyāyana onwards, and fairly complete knowledge of South India in the days of the Arthaśāstra and periods subsequent down to Patanjali. In the earliest South Indian sources, South India seems synonymous with Tamil land. Tamil land distinctly markable as the country south of a line drawn eastwards from the mouth of the Kalyanpuri river on the West Coast down to a little way to the south of Nellore. The Kalyanpuri river in its lower course and Pulicat Lake along its northern border may be regarded as marking the country. Tamil authority and influence claim to have extended as far as the Vindhyas and sometimes even up to the Himalayas. The Tamil land is Tamil Aham. To the Sanskritist, it is Dramiḍaka, corrupted by the Greek geographers into Dimirike. Dimirike on the West Coast coming immediately past the south coast of Āryaka, a clear indication of the distinction between the Aryan land and Tamil land. Tamilaham divided into the three kingdoms and a number of chieftaincies. Very early, it seems to have assumed the form of four kingdoms, the fourth being Drāviḍa country proper, that is the Tamil Tonḍamanḍalam depending upon Kanchi. In the earliest literature that we know of, we find the three kingdoms in existence separated by a number of outer rulers of smaller divisions. The number of these chieftaincies varied from time to time. Five seems to have been the number that persisted. We have reference to eleven, sometimes even fourteen of these petty kingdoms.

Their ordinary character; generally autocratic, military rule. In the kingdoms things were a little better, but still the traditions of tribal chieftaincies, the norm. The rule of the king modified by the existence of a council, a council of ministers. Five great bodies; the significance of this group. Another group referred to as the eight groups. The general character of rule; paternal administration tempered by the existence of the council and of a fairly effective opinion. Analogy to the early northern institution of Ratnins.

ADMINISTRATIVE INSTITUTIONS OF SOUTH INDIA

LECTURE I.

South India a separate entity.

South India is a term which can, and is often used to, include the part of the country south of the Vindhya mountains. In that sense, it may be taken as synonymous with the term "Dakshiṇāpatha" in early Sanskrit literature. Gradually both the terms acquired a narrower meaning. Dakkanobades of the Greeks got limited in its application to what is known in modern times as the Dakhan, in contradistinction to the farther south, South India properly so called. In modern parlance, therefore, Hindustan, Dakhan and South India indicate the three divisions of the country: Āryāvartta of Manu,[1] between the Himalayas and the Vindhyas, or Hindustan of modern times; Dakhan, the territory between the double frontier of Vindhya-Narmada on the north and Tuṇgabadra-Krishna in the south similarly marks the Dakhan; the region south of this is what is known as South India generally, as distinct from both the north and the Dakhan. This is in full accord with the history of the country.

South India in Historical Periods.

The earliest reference to South India in Sanskrit literature is in the Rig Veda itself, which contains the term Dakshiṇāpatha.[2] In later literature the term Dākshiṇātya[3] also gets into use. The first term Dak-

[1] II. 22.
[2] Ṛig Veda X. 61:8.
[3] IV. 2:98.

shiṇāpatha seems intended vaguely, as if to say the southern roadway, without perhaps any definite comprehension of the farther limit thus indicated.[1] It is a region extending southwards indefinitely, probably beginning with the Vindhyas or a little farther north. Within quite historical times the centre that marked the various divisions: north, south, east and west, seems to have had a starting point somewhere on the borders of the deserts of Rajaputana where the now vanished river Sarasvati had its mouth. This is known to Sanskritists as Vināśini[2] as having been destroyed by disappearance in the sands. We do come across references in more historical literature to Māhishmati[3] constituting the centre of division between the north and the south. Māhishmati is on the Narmada and is identified with Māndhāta, more popularly known as Onkarēśvar, about sixty miles south of Indore. Panini is responsible for the reference Dākshiṇātya, meaning the southerner. Even then the term seems to be used with the general significance attached to the term. From Kātyāyana onwards the knowledge of the Sanskritists extends, and in the scholia of the latter there is an indication of knowledge of the south perhaps even beyond the limits of the Dakhan. That would be nothing strange since the Arthaśāstra contains references to the more distant south, and particularly to a class of pearls described as Pāṇḍya *Kavāṭaka*.[4] This term Pāndya Kavāṭaka

[1]Compare the terms Andhrapatha and its equivalent Vaḍugavaḷi, distinguished as East and West; also Taḍigaivaḷi in South Indian inscriptions.

[2]See Ramayana IV.—Chap. 40—VS. 18—20: Govindaraja and Tilaka's Comments on Śloka. Also Manu II. 21.

[3]Rajaśēkhara: Kāvyamīmāmsa. Intro: p. 24 cf. his Balaramayana also. See his Bhuvana Kośa for fuller information.

[4]Book II—Ch. XI for Tamraparṇika and Paṇḍyakāvāṭaka.

means the door of entry into the Pandya territory, and may refer to the sea that washes the country on the southern coasts of the Pandyam kingdom;—at any rate it must refer to the sea, as pearls could be acquired nowhere else; and pearls are given a character according to their colour, quality and various other features, but named after the locality where they are found generally. Among the Tamils however, there is a difference of nomenclature. According to one set of authorities, the southern boundary of the Pandya kingdom is the sea; but according to earlier authority,[1] it is sometimes described as a river, Paharuḷi, from which probably the classical Paraliya[2] for the southern coast took its origin. In early Tamil literature there are references to a certain extent of land, south of where Cape Comorin is at present, having got submerged in the sea. Without going so far as to identify this with the hypothetical Lemuria, it may be possible to refer this to an encroachment of the sea of a moderate character within historical times, although we have no means by which to assert this as a definite statement. This knowledge continued, and the great commentator on Panini, Patanjali, the author of Mahabhashya,[3] indicates a knowledge of the south, which is far more thorough. He has a reference to the land of Kerala and his reference to Kanchi shows intimate knowledge. At the dawn of the Christian era therefore the knowledge of South India among Sanskritists had extended to take in the whole of the peninsula to its southern end of the present time at least.

[1] Śilappadhikāram 8. ll. 1—2; & 11, 10—14; Tolkāppiyam Sūtras 649—50 & Pērasiriyar's commentary thereon.

[2] Schoff's Periplus. p. 46.

[3] Bom. Gaz. I, Pt. ii, pp. 138—39.

Tamil Sources.—

In Tamil literature, however, the earliest available reference marks the borderland of the Tamil region at Vēngaḍam or Tirupati.[1] Apart from the actual reference in the Tamil grammar, Tolkāppiyam, in the introductory Sutra, there are casual references in literature to the language changing when one passed Tirupati.[2] There is an actual definition which marks the northern boundary as the region of the Vaḍuhas.[3] The term Vaḍuhar is analogous in formation to the Kanarese Baḍaga whom we meet with in the Nilgiris, and means in its origin nothing more than the northerner. But to the Tamils of modern times, Vaḍuhar means the Telugu people, and Vaḍuhu means the Telugu language. In the class of literature comprised in the eight collections we come upon references to these Vaḍuhas and the frontier of the Vaḍuhas (Vaḍuharmunai).[4] Vaḍuha is there applied indifferently to both the Telugus and the Kanarese people. A chieftain described as the chief of the western country (Kuḍanāḍu) is referred to under the name Erumai.[5] In one passage, he is described as the great son of the Vaḍuhar,[6] which means nothing more than that he was king of the Vaḍuhas. The northern boundary therefore of the Tamil land took into it Tirupati as a salient point, but seems to have extended a little farther to the north as the region round the Pulicat Lake is described as territory under

[1] *Vide* note 8 above.

[2] Kuruṁtogai 11. Māmūlanār. Ibid Aham 211 & 31.

[3] Tolkāppiyam Sūtra 650 and Perasiriyar's Comment. See quotation from Sirukāppiyanar.

[4] Māmūlanār: Kuruṁtogai 11 and Puram, 378; and Aham 374,

[5] Māmūlanār: Aham. 14 & 115. [6] Aham. 115.

the rule of a Tirayan, whose capital was Pavattiri and whose hill was Vēngaḍam or Tirupati,[1] and the territory itself is actually described as Kākandi in Pavattirikkottam submerged in the sea, which is identifiable with the town Reddipālem in the Gudur Taluq of the Nellore District.[2] Kākandi, it must be remembered, was the ancient name of Kaveripaṭṭinam which the capital is supposed to have taken from an early ruler Kakandan.[3] The northern region was named Kākandinādu because of the traditional conquests and the civilising of that region by the Chola Karikāla.[4] When exactly it was swallowed up by the sea and how much of territory was actually submerged are details of which we have no information. The Tamil land then had comprised all the country south of a line drawn westwards along the northern Pennar from its mouth with a slightly northern bend to the mouth of the Kalyanpuri river marking the boundary between North and South Kanara.[5] This would correspond roughly with the boundary which is traceable from references in the Rock Edicts of Asoka which mark off countries directly under his authority and those under his influence, and the territory with which he had to negotiate on terms of diplomatic equality. The Tamil kingdoms are referred to as among the last class, while some of the people capable of identification with some of the Dakhan peoples are included among the second class, that is, those under

1Aham. 85 & 340.

2Nellore Ins.: I. 441 ff.

3Manimekhalai XXII. ll. 37—38.

4Paṭṭinappālai. ll.

5V. A. Smith—Asoka. p. 115 and Early History of India 164 and 340—41.

his influence, if not directly subject to his authority.[1] In Tamil literature itself we seem to get two seemingly inconsistent definitions of this northern boundary. One stops short of the line indicated above. Another seems to take the boundary to the Vindhya mountains themselves.[2] This latter reference need not be interpreted as strictly accurate, because according to the Tamils just past the northern boundary of their land extended the great forest Daṇḍaka of the Sanskritists called Daṇḍāraṇyam by the Tamils, and which extended almost up to the Vindhya mountains. Daṇḍakāraṇya being regarded as no man's land[3] it may be taken to be an ordinary stretch of language to regard the Tamil land extending as far north as the Vindhyas. There is a set of references, however, which takes the boundary up to the Himalayas themselves, and this must frankly be regarded as a stretch of the poet's imagination at certain periods of Tamil history when Tamil authority was widest in point of extent. The generic reference is to a set of Tamil rulers having implanted on the face of the Himalayas their insignia (*lānchana*).[4] There is one reference to a Chera ruler who is described as Imayavaramban, he whose northern boundary was the Himalayas.[5] This may be taken as a poetical hyperbole which may have had its origin on a raid that an early Chera might have undertaken to the distant north, as almost a similar reference is found in the

[1]Rock Edict XIII.

[2]Padiṟṟuppattu 88, pp. 2 & 3.

[3]Padiṟṟupattu, vi. padigam.

[4]Manimekhai 28. 104.; Padiṟṟuppattu. II.; Puṟanānūṟu 59.; Silappadhikaram 28.

[5]Padiṟṟuppattu. II.

inscriptions of the Rāshṭrakūṭas under Govinda III[1] and of the Pallava Simhavarman II to a similar march up to the Himalayas. We can, as a matter of fact, trace in this case, the march of the Rāshṭrakūṭa army and actions fought by them in Allahabad and farther north perhaps as far as Kanauj itself. The statement is that he implanted his emblem on the Himalayas. Under the classical references in Tamil literature we are not enabled to satisfy ourselves by tracing out vestiges of such a march.

Tamil Aham.

Leaving the more extensive frontier out we are brought to the *terra firma* of history when we come to the term Tamil Aham in Tamil literature. Tamil Aham would simply mean the home or land of the Tamils, that is, the country of the Tamils. It is described as having the sea for its boundary, neglecting for the moment the northern, which has not the sea boundary.[2] It is when they come to a precise reference to this northern boundary that they refer to Danḍaka in a certain class of references as constituting the northern boundary,[3] the Vaḍuha frontier in a number of others,[4] the Vindhyas themselves in one or two.[5] The general reference, however, is to the northern boundary being marked by Danḍaka. These we get from references to the Chera ruler, who drove away herds of cattle from the no man's land of Dandaka to

[1]Sanjan Plates of Amoghavarsha, Ep. Ind. XVIII, vv. 22 & 23. Amarāvati Pillar, Ins. of Simhavarman II, S.I.I. 32, ll. 33-34.

[2]Silappadhikāram 25. 165 & 2. Padirṟupattu. I. I & II. Padikam.

[3]Padirṟuppattu. VI.

[4]Kuruṁtogai. 11; Aham 211 & 2.

[5]Padirṟuppattu IX. 88.

Tondi on the West Coast and given the herds away in gifts to Brahmans.[1] This is clearly confirmed by references in classical literature, and Ptolemy makes the particular reference that just past the boundary of Āryaka on the West Coast referred to as 'the Āryaka of the pirates' we come to the region of Ḍimirike on the West Coast. This Ḍimirike is no other than Tamil Aham. From Tamil Aham to Ḍimirike seems a far cry phonetically, but it does thus happen. There is an intervening link that is lost and when that is supplied, what seemed unintelligible to begin with, becomes quite clear. If we could call back to the mind that the Sanskrit word Dramiḍaka came out of Tamil Aham, we can understand the Greek Dimirike. So Tamil Aham equalls Sanskrit Draviḍaka.

The northern boundary of the Tamil land as defined above answers exactly to the border line between Āryaka and Dramiḍaka of Ptolemy. The Periplus states clearly that the country in the interior set over against the coast of what is now known as the Northern Konkan, was a country of the great forest,[2] Danḍaka of Indian sources, So then we come to this that what we call in modern times South India comprised the land south of the line of, say, the 14th degree of north latitude marked by the Asokan edicts and constituted the Tamil country, making Tamil Aham synonymous with South India.

Divisions of Tamil Aham.

Tamil Aham is divided, according to the Tamils, into the three kingdoms—"the far-famed three", of

[1] *Vide* note 28.

[2] Schoff's Periplus—Secs. 42—66.

Chola, Pandya, Kerala, and a number of chieftaincies which varied from time to time owing to historical exigencies. At one time these latter appear to have been five,[1] at least the more famous among them. Those that claimed suzerain power over the Tamil land claim a sort of a right to wear a garland of seven crowns.[2] This reference is found peculiarly in a number of poems celebrating Chera rulers, and this feature is referred to in regard to them. The famous Pandyan victor at Talaiālangānam claims to have defeated the two kings and five chieftains constituting the identical seven. This means no more than that he won a victory and thereby imposed his authority on the whole of the Tamil land, the Tamil land other than the kingdom of the Pandyas having been divided among the two other kings and the five chieftains.[3] The number of chieftains however varies. We have references to eleven, at one time and to fourteen at another,[4] which probably included some of the minor chieftains usually not of sufficient rank for the distinction, having achieved greatness and being numbered among the more important. That seems to have been more or less the general division of the land during the period covered by the class of literature generally known as the Śangam literature. There is another reference, however, in the Tolkāppiyam, which mentions the four

[1]Aham. 36 and Madhurai-Kānji. [2]Padirruppattu I. 14 & 16.

[3]*Vide* note 33 above. [4]Aham 135.

lands.[1] The commentator interprets it as meaning the four kingdoms of Chola, Paṇḍya, Chera and the Toṇḍamaṇḍalam, known to the Sanskritists in later times as the Draviḍa country proper. The reference is worthy of consideration in some detail. The actual reference is that a certain classification of writings obtained 'in the land known under four names, and included within the boundary of the far-famed three.' This means that the well-known three, Chola, Pandya, Kerala ruled over practically the whole of the Tamil land; but what are the four names by which this land was otherwise known? One commentator Pērāśiriyar is content with saying that the country comprised within the four names is synonymous with the Tamil land. The expression literally rendered may be taken as perhaps the four boundaries. He objects to that interpretation pointing out that the Sūtra does not take it upon itself, in the context, to define the boundary, but merely to indicate what was the accepted practice of the Tamil land; while the other commentator Nacchinārkiniyar gives the actual divisions, Malaimaṇḍalam, Soḻamaṇḍalam, Pandyamandalam and Toṇḍamaṇḍalam in the four divisions. The four divisions must have been under the three kings

[1]Śeyyul, Sūtram 391.

பாட்டுரை நூலே வாய்மொழி பிசியே
யங்கத முதுசொல் லோடவ் வேழ்நிலத்தும்
வண்புகழ் மூவர் தண்பொழில் வரைப்பி
னாற் பெயரெல்லையகத்தவர் வழங்கும்
யாப்பின் வழியதென மனார்புலவர்— (391)
மரபேதானு,
நாற்சொல்லியலான யாப்பு வழிப்பட்டன. (392)

as the Sūtra lays it down. The next following Sūtra of the same work states that 'this sevenfold division of Tamil' composition obtains 'in the four kinds of language.' What are these four languages, or four kinds of language (Nār-chol)? Here again the commentator Pērāśiriyar seems to accept the division noun, verb, adjunctive words and connectives, the four grammatical divisions of words. He would accept even the division, the natural Tamil, Tamil as modified for one reason or another, frontier Tamil that is Tamil modified by contact with other languages, and the northern language or Sanskrit. Here again Nacchinārkiniyar regards the first divisions into four as being divisions recognised by grammarians of the first of these, Ordinary Tamil, and therefore the reference here to four kinds of language must mean the latter four of Pērāśiriyar. The whole discussion is as to what forms of the language are appropriate for composition in Tamil literature, and they come to the conclusion that it is appropriate to compose in any of 'the four dialects of the language' provided the one is not confused with the other.

It may be noticed here in passing that some critics show an inclination to be hypercritical in regard to commentators and their commentaries, based on a misapprehension. Added to the misapprehension is an underlying notion that they were particularly interested in distorting truth and manufacturing facts. This is a criticism, the responsibility of which is very grave. The critic who would make this remark is under the heavy responsibility to prove his charge, and, as a necessary preliminary, to make out a *prima facie* case for fabrication of facts. This responsibility is hardly felt and never adequately discharged by this class of critics. In each particular instance a motive must be established for this straying away from the truth; and unless this is done as a preliminary, we shall not be warranted in acquiescing in the grave charge. The really more important part is this; that with respect to many of our works, particularly works thrown in the form of sutras, such as the Tolkāppiyam is, for instance, the implication always is there is the commentary from the very beginning. The Sūtras by themselves are not intended to be self-explanatory, as in their nature, they can hardly be. These are composed in the form of mnemonics for being got up to aid the memory. These will carry no meaning unless it had been explained beforehand, and therefore wherever Sūtras are written, a commentary is presumed. The commentators that write it make their commentaries on the traditionally handed down commentary, adding, altering, amending, as circumstances call for them in the process of the growth of language and of the literature. Taken therefore as such, all the matter that they introduce are not necessarily composition of a later period, although they might have been committed to writing at a later period. This is particularly the case where, whether it be general literature or literature that has been thrown in the sūtra form, the meaning of the text is not self-evident. Very often it is not, and an underlying allusion or reference has to be understood to make any intelligible meaning out of it at all, and to this extent the traditional interpretation handed down must be accepted as such.

The term Tamil Aham may be interpreted literally as the homeland of Tamil, or more simply Tamil land. This Tamil land during the period of classical Tamil literature seems to have been divided into three kingdoms only, the fourth Tondamandalam of Nacchinārkiniyar, having been during the period practically an appanage of the Chola kingdom. When this became the dominant part in the period following, the Pallavas who established an ascendency took pride in calling themselves 'Trairājya Pallava', which seems to be more or less a translation of 'the three-crowned kings' of Tamil India. Therefore then the recognised political feature of the country is the well-known division in three kingdoms.

The chieftaincies, we have had occasion to mention already, of varying number, ordinarily depended on one kingdom or another. Hence the common vogue to speak of the Tamil land as though it were composed exclusively of the three kingdoms alone. But that the Tamils themselves were aware of the independent political existence of the chieftaincies is recognised where writers of the period describe an overlord as wearing a garland of seven crowns, or when one of these is said to have carried a victorious campaign single-handed against the two other kings and five chieftains, again the proverbial seven. The seven of the latter are actually detailed as the Chera, Chola, Tidiyan, Eluni, Erumaiyūran, Irungō Vēḷmān and Porunan.[1] These are not the chieftaincies mentioned at all times. This is at the time when the dominant figure in South Indian

[1]Madurai Kānji lines 55—56 and 128—29. Also Aham 175 and 209.

politics happened to be the famous Pandyan victor at Talai-ālaṇgānam, that is, somewhat later than the period to which the famous seven patrons are referable. Besides the three kings, the seven patrons are Pēhan, Pāri, Kāri, Aãoy, Adikan, Naḷḷi, Ōri.[1] This last refers to a period somewhat earlier than the other. In another connection when the Tamil kings felt the necessity of bringing under control a chief on the northern frontier, they seemed to have felt the necessity for mobilising all the forces of the Tamil land, and in that connection, they refer to eleven chieftains and there is one allusion to fourteen.[2] The normal division therefore of the Tamil land is the three kingdoms, a recognised permanent factor with a fourth, which in the earlier period remained a dependency of the Chola kingdom, but soon established itself as a separate kingdom. At the same time this fourth division is always describable as a separate geographico-political entity, known by the name Tonḍamanḍalam. With the coming of the Pallavas into Kānchī, this Tonḍamanḍalam becomes a distinct political entity, and gets to be spoken of habitually as such.

Their ordinary character.

These Tamil states in this particular period show themselves to be generally monarchical in point of character whether they were under crowned kings or mere chieftains. From the class of sources from which we derive our information for this period, we cannot gain anything like an insight into the internal division

[1] Śirupān Aṟṟupaḍai 11. 84, 111. Puranānūṟu, 158.
[2] Aham. 135.

or devolution of political power. From all that we can make out of the general description that we get of these rulers and their character, they appear to have been more or less autocratic tribal chieftains who led the army on occasions of war and ruled the land during peace. They held their court, to which poets went in search of patronage, were usually well received and provided with all that they required during their stay, and dismissed with sumptuous rewards for the pains they bestowed in the exhibition of their talents in literature. Now and again we get a glimpse into the position of the court. Courtiers assembled, important questions were propounded sometimes, and consultations held. But the final decision seems to have still rested with the chieftain. Certain classes of people enjoyed the freedom to admonish the chieftain, and even kings, in respect of what they should do under given circumstances, and this privilege was utilised to the fullest extent. The privilege seems to have been given and freely exercised by learned Brahmans, poets of a high order and officials of certain character, and some of the elders of the land, generally those that constituted the Śishtas', the elite of the land. We come, however, upon one distinct reference where there seems to have been a recognised body, whose function it was to act the part of counsellors. These are not spoken of as merely individuals constituting the Board, but are generally referred to as constituting five distinct classes of ministers. We hear of this group of five generally only along with the monarchs. Probably the chieftains followed the example of the monarchs, and had a similar body to consult. These are spoken of as the *Aim-perumkuḷu,* which literally would mean the five great bodies of people. Along with these happen to be mentioned another group of eight referred to as *Eṇpēr Āyam* the eight great body of associates, *ayam* meaning a body or number. Uusually the term is applied to the attendants on a person, generally a distinguished woman: in other words, the feminine retinue of a queen or some such other distinguished person. These two groups, the famous group of five and the faithful group of eight alike, received each of them a double interpretation. The group of five is described as the Mahājana, the Brahmans, the physicians, astrologers and the ministers. This enumeration is followed by the general term that they constituted the Sabhā, or the Council of the king.[1] The second interpretation includes the following classes, the Amātyas (amaichchar or ministers), Purohitas (Purohits or priests), Sēnāpatis (generals), Tūduvar (ambassadors), and Śāraṇar (commissioners of information). These five constitute the great bodies of the king's councillors.[2] Additional light is thrown upon who these bodies were in certain passages of the Tamil classic Śilapadhikāram. When the Pandyan king died all of a sudden and the kingdom was for a moment without a king, the persons who were regarded as responsible for the safety of the kingdom during the interrugnum, were the five recited as Asan (Purohit), Perungaṇi (the great astrologer), Arakkaḷattu Andaṇar (the Brahmans in charge of courts of justice), Kāvidi (ministers in charge of accounts) and Mandira

[1]Śilappadhikaram. V. 157. pp. 147 and 167 (new edition). Pingalandai or Pingala Nighanṭhu V. 44—47.

[2]Ibid I.

Kaṇakkar (the learned that constituted the council).[1] In another connection this is slightly varied; but then it need not thereby be regarded as enumerating the whole body that constituted an actual group of ministers. A certain number of them happen to be mentioned along with a few others, who did not constitute the general body, but had charge of particular departments of work, as the actual work that had to be carried out related to those departments.[2] But what the group generally was is distinctly under reference in a passage of the poem Madurai Kānji, where the five are actually defined as a well-known classification including the ministers, purohits, the generals, ambassadors and the commissioners of information. These are not so mentioned in the text itself. The text actually speaks of the Kāvidi as a class first, and refers, in the lines following, to the four others who constituted the group of five, and they are all of them given the general character that they were people of unfaltering speech, that is, those that never swerved from truth and spoke it without fear or favour.[3] So it is clear that the group of five was a recognised body of people composed of five divisions and constituting a council. This clearly indicates that the other interpretation given, viz., the five bodies that constituted the people of the kingdom is not exactly what was generally understood by this group of five. The proper interpretation of the second list of five, that is the Mahajanas, Brahmans, the Maruttar, the Nimittar and Amaichchar may not seem quite clear, although it is possible to explain the

1Śilappadhikāram. 22. ll. 8 & 9.
2Śil. 26—40 & 41. 28 222—23.
3Maduraik-Kānji ll. 508—10.

Amaichchar as the chief body of ministers as a whole. The next one the Nimittar being the body of astrologers, the next one the body of Physicians, the other two being commercial folk and Brahmans attending court as representing the various communities. On a close analysis the lists do not seem to differ quite so much, as some of the divisions are identifiable. In any case, it is clear that the body that constituted the council was composed of five groups of individuals divided as given above, and they constituted the standing council of the monarch whom he was bound to consult on all questions of importance.

These five groups though they seem identifiable as shown above, do not appear to have been identified however by Tamil writers of authority. The two groups have been held apart and regarded as constituting two separate groups of five each. These ten together with the other group of eight to which we have adverted already, became the eighteen classes of officials employed by kings.[1] Therefore then we shall have to regard these two divisions as separate, one set being regarded as those that constituted the court, whereas the other actually those that carried on the administration, the former being a sort of an enlarged council on occasions, and the latter a regular set of ministers and executive officials. The Pingalandai, a lexicon of an authoritative character in Tamil literature, actually adopts this[2] and the eighteen divisions happen to be referred to even in inscriptions of a later time, and so the classification as stated above seems warranted by usage as well.

[1]Pingalandai. V. 47. [2]Ibid. V. 44—47.

Along with this group of five another group gets mentioned as the eight groups of Āyam, meaning eight groups of people in immediate attendance upon the monarch. Even here there is a double recital. The first of these seems to recite only those in personal ser vice constituting more or less the chamberlain and his staff, the men in charge of the unguents, the men in charge of flowers and dress and so on. We may take them to be eight sets of people detailed for separate items of duties contributing to the personal comfort of the monarch. The next recital has got very much more of an official colour. They are (1) the Karaṇikas (officials); (2) the Karmakaras (artisans); (3) Kanakaśuṟṟam (assayers); (4) Kaḍaikkāppu (guards of the palace); (5) Nagara Māndar (citizens of the city); (6) Paḍaitalaivar (commanders of the army); (7) Anaivīrar (men of the elephant corps) and (8) Ivuḷi Maṛavar (cavalry men). In this recital, it will be seen clearly that the eight groups constitute really the officials who are the mainstay of the monarch. We see therefore that this includes the civil officials, those engaged in the industries, those in charge of the currency, and the citizens of the city as a body. The rest of them are guards in immediate attendance and the different arms of the army. Broadly therefore they could be divided into civil and military administration of the state.

ஐம்பெருங் குழுவு மெண்பேராயமும்
வெம்பரி யானை வேந்தற் கோங்கிய
கருமவினைஞருங் கணக்கியல்வினைஞருந்
தருமவினைஞருந் தந்திரவினைஞரும். (மணி. 26. ll. 37-42.)

If the groups were ever allowed to take part in the administration, even as counsellors who could be consulted on matters of great importance, it could not have been but by some process of representation, whatever that process may have been. It is hardly necessary that it should have been elective, although we have nothing to warrant the conclusion that the elective principle was unknown, as we shall see more clearly later. But here the point is that apart from their taking part in festivities when these could assemble in crowds, if they took part in any orderly procedure apart from festivities, these could have played their part only by a process of representation of some kind or other. That point receives emphasis when we consider it along with what actually was the nature of the previous five groups. Even in respect of these a sort of selection, or even election, seems necessary. Except in regard to one or two, the other groups must be in some number and they could not all be represented on occasions of consultation. Therefore either the king must have selected the more important, or there was a customary arrangement in which certain kinds of officials actually represented the interests of the body as a whole and offered advice when consulted by the king.

Before passing out of this discussion, we must note here that, in connection with the coronation of kings in the Vedic period and the periods immediately following, a certain number of people took part, even a ceremonial part, and they were known as Rājakrit, king-makers. These are generally described as Ratnins (jewels). The early Vedic ceremonies seem to demand the active participation of this group of eight to make the ceremony of coronation complete, and the ceremony is called *Ratna Havis,* offerings by the Ratnins, and these are the commander of the army, the Brahman priest, the Kshatriya, the queen, the court ministrel, the Gramani, head of the towns, the chamberlain, the officer in charge of the treasury, the collector general of the revenue, the Accountant-General, the master of forests, and the chief courier according to one recital. The number differs. Sometimes it is fourteen.[1] We do not know a number more than fourteen as far as the Sanskrit sources go, and if the groups recited be considered, it will be found that there is a certain amount of overlapping between the eight and the five of the Tamils that we have already noted. But the total among the Tamils is made up to eighteen, and in this grouping the queen, either the chief or any other, does not figure, whereas in the Sanskrit sources these do play their part, and a rather important part. It would be difficult in the circumstances, therefore to suggest that they were identical. But the similarity however is striking. The importance of these groups among the Sanskritists consisted in their approval in the actual choice of the king and participation in the ceremonial making of the king. In the Tamil sources, however, there is not the faintest hint of anything like that kind of an important position given to these people, although there are vague hints here and there of some of them having taken a part. As far as we are able to proceed on the information available to us, it would be much better to regard the two as separate, and not perhaps identifiable. We come therefore to this result, that the

[1]K. P. Jayaswall Hindu Polity pp. 20-21.

states that constituted Tamil India, particularly the kingdoms, showed an organisation for administration, which seems to vest all the power in the king or the chief, this power being tempered by the existence of an influential council composed of representatives of the larger bodies constituting the kingdom as such and capable therefore of bringing to bear the pressure of opinion upon the doings of the monarch· It must be remembered that the making of the law was not the function of the king. It is at least, we have nothing in the Tamil organisation as far as we can see, not provided for as a function of government. Probably it was only customary law that was administered, and custom got modified in the usual way without any direct process of legislation. Therefore the duties of the king, with council or without, did not include the making of the law, but only the administration of it. If we should label a government such as this in the terms of modern political science, the earliest Tamil administration, of which we gain a glimpse is of the character of paternal rule by the monarch tempered by the existence of a council and of an efficient means of bringing public opinion to bear upon acts of administration. With this as a beginning we shall see how the actual administration developed in the centuries following, and attained in process of time to a perfection, which is strikingly modern about the end of the first millennium after Christ.

APPENDIX TO LECTURE I

On Prince Chēra of the elephant-eye, once thrown into prison by the Pāṇḍya, Victor at Talai-ālangānam.

O! descendants of ancestors! whose praise all the varied inhabitants of hills and mountains, of forests and country, bounded by the southern Kumari and Northern Mountain, and the Eastern and the Western Sea, sing in one voice; who had earned this high praise by removing all afflictions of evil and by holding a righteous sceptre, by maintaining themselves on their share of the fruits of the earth, and by administering unswerving even handed justice; and whose wheel of authority rolled unobstructed over the whole of this vast region! The warrior lord of the inhabitants of cool Tondi of broad fields, mountain borders, wide coast strip covered with bright white sands, the fruit-bearing plantain, the trees of which are bent down with the heavy bunches of fruits, and whose clear canals of back water are decked with flowers of bright red colour like fire! Like a great tusker-elephant, which, going about in thorough neglect of enemy activity, had fallen into the great dug-out made for capturing elephants, not having seen the artificial covering over it, digs up the side of the pit with its strong tusks and gets back to the herd by the use of its strength; so have you, having got into the enemy's hands for lack of adequate watchfulness against enemy stratagem, returned to the great body of your own relations and friends, and received great praise for your achievement. Those of your enemy kings whose vast kingdoms and great wealth you had taken possession of before this misfortune befell you, knowing as they did that they would get back all that by gaining your goodwill and esteem, yet raised aloft their banners of rebellion and hoisted their flags on their tall ramparts with adjoining dense forests and extensive moats. Having done so they have now lost heart, and are reconciling themselves to the idea of surrendering their all to you, feeling as they do there is no appeasing your rising displeasure at this wanton act of theirs. O great one! I have come to see you, singing of your great valour thus exhibited, and your great glory. Your armies in their varied order resemble a succession of clouds; your vast array of elephants resemble hills, and bees are building their hives on them in that feeling; your great army strikes terror into the enemy and resembles the sea itself; and clouds (of dust) gather above it (as if) to carry some of its water. Your great war-drum roars like thunder, making poisonous cobras drop their heads in fright. A great king of the westerners thou art whose unfailing generosity knows no end.

(*Puṛam.* 17. Kurungōḻiyūr Kiḻār).

II

POLITICAL IDEAS AND IDEALS.

General idea of a king—Poems of the Śangam collection—Tolkāppiyam-Kuṛaḷ Ideal of Kingship—No discussion of society and state or origin of kingship, as in Sanskrit—Kuṛaḷ polity follows the Artha and Dharma Śāstras. Does not go into the details of the former—Kuṛaḷ based on previous work on the subject—obviously the Arthaśāstra of Kauṭilya—Kuṛaḷ divisions—Araśiyal, Angaviyal and Oḻibiyal—Seems to follow Arthaśāstra division—Rāja and Rājyam—no notion of the Sapta-prakriti or Saptāngam constituting one unity—Otherwise follows more or less closely the Arthaśāstra division of functions—more like the Smritis than Arthaśāstra in character—Society based on Dharma—the pursuit of dharma, artha, kama and moksha implicit—narrower idea of Trivarga-Muppāl—life through existence on earth—a general treatise on how to lead one's life effectively cannot give the specialised treatment to Artha like the Arthaśāstra—there is more similarity to Dharma Śāstra generally—the Kuṛaḷ ideal, a monarchical state—definite reference even to the five groups of ministers and the other groups of faithful assistants in administration—the Kuṛaḷ polity reflects social life, but does not present a full or complete picture of political organisation—No discussion of the theory of Society or the origin of the State idea.

LECTURE II.

POLITICAL IDEAS AND IDEALS

I

General ideas of a king.

In the last lecture we concluded, on a general examination of the literature bearing on the subject, that society in Dravidian India was composed of classes and groups of people, and was governed by an organisation monarchical in character. The monarch exercised his power for the preservation of order in society and for whatever was considered the most important function of state administration, namely, doing justice between man and man, and whatever was necessary to ensure the prevalence of that justice as a matter of habit.[1] He generally took counsel of a certain body of people who assisted him both with counsel before action was decided upon, and in the carrying out of such action when action had been decided upon. This whole body is described by a term which is generally applied to relations in Tamil, blood relations. The word *Śuṟṟam* applied alike to those immediately in attendance upon the king and their assistants, as well as to those relations of his who enjoyed the privilege naturally of being close to him, as it were. So therefore we seem to begin here with a constitution monarchical in character evolving from out of tribal chieftaincies into something very much more advanced than a simple patriarchal tribal

[1]Kuṟaḷ, 40-8.

chiftaincy. The reference in the Maduraikkānji, adverted to already, makes it clear that the ministers assembled regularly and were expected to speak, and often spoke, what they considered the best course of action to take without the slightest fear, as though it was duty that they had to discharge, and as though that duty was being habitually, regularly discharged. This comes out from a number of stray references, references of a very casual character, that occur in a number of poems in the collections known to Tamil scholars as the Śangam collection.

Poems of the Śangam collection.

This collection is composed of a number of works which contain poems by various poets composed at different times and on different occasions, for various purposes, but having one feature in common mostly. They are poems addressed to individuals more or less from whom often-times appreciation and reward were obtained for the composition. Hence the usual classification, poets and patrons. These poems are given the form generally of a poet going to court, reciting his poem before the assembled court and winning the applause of the assembly for the composition; he received usually sumptuous rewards from the patron concerned. From out of a whole mass of poems like this, selections were made of those that offered the best illustration for a particular mode of composition. In other words, in the estimation of those that collected these poems on the criterion of the subject matter, they served best to illustrate, one or more modes of expression either of inward feeling or outward action.

Naturally therefore the collection was made at a particular time, and the poems are all of them of a time anterior to that. They reflect naturally the life of the times to which the composition may presumably be referred. The Śangam tradition is well recognised by the commentators, particularly Pērāśiriyar and Nacchchinārkiniyar, and even by an earlier editor, Nīlakanṭhan of Muśiri, the editor of the commentary of Kaḷaviyal, a poem ascribed to Śiva himself, originally commented upon by Narkīrar the Śangam celebrity, committed to writing and handed down in the present form by Nīlakanthan of Muśiri, coming twelfth in teaching succession from Narkīrar himself. What we are able to glean from this collection is in conformity with the duties ascribed to kings in the Tolkāppiyam.[1]

Tolkāppiyam ideal of a king.

According to this standard treatise, the duties ascribed to the king are like the six duties ascribed to the Brahmans, and the six ascribed to the other two classes of society, five, viz., learning, sacrificing, giving in patronage, protecting the people and punishing evil doers. It will be found that the first three out of these five happen to be the same to the ruling class as to the class of Brahmans. The correlative to these three, viz., teaching, performing sacrifices for others and accepting gifts given, constitute the other three functions of the Brahman, which functions are considered inappropriate both to the king and the other two classes. The peculiar feature among the duties of kingship is, protection which necessarily involves

[1]Tolkāppiyam Purattiṇai 75.

punishment. The one involving the other naturally leads to the notion that the king is the protector of the realm.[1] Often-times he is spoken of as such, all the others of his duties being regarded more or less implicit in this. The first, learning, is the essential qualification for his being able to do this duty. The second one, getting sacrifices performed, was generally with a a view to the welfare of society. As protector of society, it becomes one of his functions. The giving of gifts is usually for the purpose of promoting learning or for performing sacrifices, and thus advancing the welfare of society again, as without it progress in society and the proper understanding of the aims of social life are not likely to be brought home to the people. These three therefore constitute the necessary accessories for the efficient discharge of his duty as protector. It was already stated that punishment follows as a correlative if he has to take upon himself the responsibility of protecting society from harm. This harm may happen to society from inside as well as outside, both of which alike will have to be met by appropriate punishment. But punishment as a term is generally confined to punishment administered to those disturbers of society, who constituted a part of the society itself, and does not apply, although in a more generalised sense it can, to enemies of a society external to it. Protection therefore involves as a consequence punishment. Thus then the grammatical definition agrees more or less with the definition of

[1] Majjēt trayī dandanītau hatāyām, Sarvē dharmah prakshayēyur viruddhāḥ, Sarvē dharmaschās'ramaṇamhatāsyuḥ, Kshātrē nashṭē Rajadharmē purānē M. Bh. XII lxii 28.

Āpayan kuṇṛum arutoḻilōr nūlmaṛappar kāvalan kāvānenin. Kuṛaḷ 560.

royal duty as one finds it scattered through literature. There is a class of poems in the Śangam collection which has specific reference to the description of the duties of the king. One class particularly deserves attention in this case. There is one mode of expression called *Araśavāhai,* which is intended peculiarly to express the shining virtues of an illustrious monarch. The poems may be somewhat idealised, but they do reflect, and are actually meant to reflect, the existing state of the institution at the time. They give us a general idea of what a good king was expected to be and to do. There are such poems in Puṟanāṉūṟu which give an idea of what a good king was expected to be.[1]

Apart from these general references, there is a more formal treatise, the greater portion of which is devoted to a regular discussion of kingship and government.

The Kuṟaḷ.—

The Kuṟaḷ of Tiruvaḷḷuvar is a work which has to do with life as a whole, as it were. It is a book of aphorisms, which lays down how exactly one should conduct himself to lead the good life, if we may say so; in other words, it takes it upon itself to teach people how to follow the *Dharma* in this world, *Dharma,* the maintenance of which is the peculiar charge of the king and the following of which is equally the duty of every human being. *Dharma* is a term which is very difficult of definition as the historians of India have always felt it to be, particularly where Asoka speaks of it in his

[1] Puram. 17

Dharmalipi. Expressions of a similar character lie scattered throughout this discussion, and that is what Sanskrit inscriptions mean by the word *Dharma* as well.[1] The position is made worse when we speak of *Dharma* in general; we seem to be including in it another *Dharma* as opposed to *Artha* and *Kama.* Sanskritists recognise four supreme aims of existence, *Purushartas* as they are called. They constitute the four *Dharma, Artha, Kāma, Mōksha.*[2] These are represented by the corresponding Tamil terms, *Aṛam, Poruḷ, Inbam, Vīḍu.* Of these four, the fourth is the ultimate object of achievement, and is really the supreme object to be aimed at. The other three constitute the means by which this supreme end can be attained. Since the last of them *Moksha* or *Vīḍu* does not consist in the achievement of anything on this earth, it is excluded as not capable of being regularly definable in words, and therefore a narrower definition of life is adopted constituting the first three. These are the actual pursuits of man on this earth below, with a view to the attainment of the fourth in the hereafter. Works therefore that lay themselves out to teaching people how to lead the good life confine themselves therefore to these three; apart from books there is also a general recognition of these three classes constituting the motives that govern, or that ought to govern, action in life. This the Sanskritists call *Trivarga* in contradistinction to the four *Purushārtas;* and the Tamils have a classification exactly like it in the *Muppāl* and, as such, distinct

1 Dharmaprāchīra bandhaḥ, of the Samudra Gupta inscription. Dharmamahārāja of the Early Pallava inscriptions.

2 Artha Śāstra. II. 15. Kāmandaka. I. ii. 14.

from the fourth. The work Kuṛaḷ is otherwise known by the term Muppāl, because it treats of the *Trivarga, Dharma, Artha* and *Kama,* or as the Kuṛal itself has it *Aṛam, Porul and Kāmam.* This is not peculiar to the Kuṛal. The Tolkāppiyam itself recognises that the three constitute the matter to be dealt with in literature, and the fourth is taken out of its scope.[1] While others hold that since the fourth is attainable by the appropriate discharge of the duties laid down under the other three, an adequate treatment of these three, necessarily includes the fourth. The second seems not to be universally accepted; but that hardly matters for our discussion.

Kuṛal is a work composed of chapters of ten aphorisms each, and there are 133 such chapters, each one of which deals with a particular topic of the subject. Of these chapters 2 to 38 bear upon *Dharma* or *Aṛam.* The seventy following chapters 39 to 108 bear on *Poruḷ* or *Artha,* the remaining 25, 109 to 133, being devoted to *Kāma* or enjoyment. The seventy chapters constituting the second division form practically a Tamil Arthaśāstra dealing with the acquisition of that which is desirable, its retention and proper application with a view to the achievement of the ultimate object of existence. This is almost the kind of definition that Kauṭiliya gives his Arthasastra.[2] The third division of twenty-five chapters relates to Kāma or enjoyment, and is dealt with in two divisions, *Kaḷavu* and *Kaṛpu,* the two main

[1] Seyyul 418.

அந்நிலைமருங்கினறமுதலாகிய

மும்முதற்பொருட்கு முரியவென்ப.

[2] Book XV. 1.

divisions of the Tolkāppiyam. But the Tamil grammarians including the author of the Tolkāppiyam, have other divisions which here get to be included in the second main division. In other words, of the two main divisions the enjoyment of love in company is regarded as the first division; and the reminiscences of such enjoyment when the lovers are away from each other constitute the second division in which the other sub-divisions of Tamil grammarians are included. That is the way of treating the subject according to the commentator, who follows the practice of the Sanskritists. Our concern is not with that particular. While that which pleases the senses—and in this is included the pleasure that may legitimately be derived from the satisfaction of the senses—alone constitutes this particular division, excessive indulgence is as a correlative condemned and the exercise of discipline is insisted on even in respect of this particular division. Therefore legitimate enjoyment forms part of a disciplined life, and thus, in an ethical code, this forms an integral part.

Reverting to the political division, the seventy chapters are divided into three main divisions: *Araśiyal, Angaviyal* and *Oḻibiyal;* in other words, chapters relating to (1) kingship, (2) to the limbs of the kingdom, and (3) whatever else concerns the kingdom, but not included in the other two. The Tamil author here takes the first to be synonymous with king, the second synonymous with those instruments that go to make the power and greatness of the king conceived as six constituent parts. Whatever is comprised in royalty and the exercise of the power implied in royalty that is not included in the personal qualities and duties of the king, and the duties that his surroundings have actually to carry out, get to be dealt with in thirteen chapters, which in English may be put down as miscellaneous. In the arthaśāstra the main idea is the unified idea of *rule by a king,* or government generally; and what that is intended to convey is not the ruler exercising authority primarily, but what actually constitutes the dominion including the ruler to whom it is subjected. In other words the idea of state is held distinct from the idea of the mere territory over which a government exercises its authority. The Arthaśāstra and the *Smritis* alike take up first of all the idea of *Rājyam,*[1] and define it as composed of seven limbs, of which the king himself is one. That seems to be the prevalent notion, and we find the idea in vogue popularly as the term occurs even in inscriptions, in contexts where they mention the overthrow of a state completely. *Saptānga-haraṇa* involves the destruction of the enemy king completely and the assumption is generally, of all that went to constitute the king and the kingdom, by the successful enemy. The Kuṛal does not seem, on the face of it, to be familiar, with this notion, or if familiar, the author of the Kuṛal steers clear of it. It would be unwarranted to assert that the Kuṛal did not know this notion of the Arthaśāstra, or even of the Dharma Śāstras, since it follows the Dharmaśāstraic notion in other particulars. It suited Tiruvaḷḷuvar's purpose, and, perhaps served better in his immediate milieu, to

[1]Kāmandaka. I. 18-19 and Śankarārya's comment thereon.

treat of the king and the kingdom as it obtained in the Tamil country. There again he probably follows the Arthaśāstra lead, as both the Kāmandaka and the Kauṭilīya Arthaśāstra itself, countenance the division of Rāja and Rājyam,[1] while at the same time they could, for purposes of treatment of particular parts of the subject, take the whole as one. The Kāmandaka in its *Maṇḍalayoni Prakaraṇam*[2] (the 12th division), where the author has to deal with the state as a whole, in the midst of other states in their inter-relation, speaks of the ministers, subjects, fortresses, treasury and the army as the five *prakritis* or constituent elements. He later on adds along with these the sixth, *mitra* or allies, and the ruler himself making up the seventh, and constitutes out of these seven together Rājyam, according to Brihaspati, as he quotes it.[3] There Kāmandaka is simply following Kauṭilya. Kauṭilya begins with the united Rājyam consisting of the seven elements or *prakritis,* and later on, in a subsequent chapter, he comes to the same treatment as the Kāmandaka, and begins with laying down that Rāja and Rājyam constitute an abbreviated division of what is known as *prakriti,* and the division of Kāmandaka constituting Rāja and his allies as one, and the other five elements in its Rājyam, seem clearly intended. The Kuṛal begins with that division of Rāja and Rājyam, although it does not state it in the actual form; but the very first Kuṛal lays it down that that is the really sup-

[1]Kām. XII. Ch. IV. 1—2. Kauṭilīya Book VI. Ch. I.

[2]Ch. IV. 1—2.

[3]Artha. Śās. VI. Ch. i.

erior king, the king *par excellance,* who is well provided with the army, the people, the treasury, the ministry and the allies.[1] He would separate the Rāja from the other six *prakritis,* and make a division differing from the Arthaśāstraic arrangements apparently in isolating the king and associating the allies with the other *prakritis.* The notion that all the seven constitute one unity is what is found in Manu as well, where the expression used is *prakriti* or *angam,* synonymously.[2] Notwithstanding this apparent difference, the Kuṛal treatment does not seem to be really different from the Arthaśāstraic. There is another apparent difference in the recital of the constituents other than the king. The order in which they are presented in the very first Kuṛal under this section of the work is the army, the people, the treasury, the ministry and the allies. This order differs from the order of the Sanskritists. But as the commentator does actually point out, Tiruvaḷḷuvar does not necessarily differ from the arrangements of the Saṇskrit works. The difference in the order is due to exigencies of metre, the actual order of the Sanskrit texts being preserved in the treatment of the topics in the various chapters. The order of chapters follows the Arthaśāstraic division.[3] Hence we must hold that the Kuṛal arrangement of the topics does not differ from that of the Arthaśāstra.

But there is one point to which attention must be drawn. In the seventy chapters of the Kuṛal, the

[1]Ch. 39-1.

[2]Book IX. Ś. 294, 295, 296.

[3]Chaps. 64—108.

topics dealt with are all of them topics that are included in the general topics of the Arthaśāstra, and the chapters of the Kauṭilīya where the actual details of the administration are discussed are not taken up in the Kuṛal at all. That is, however, a feature not peculiar to the Kuṛal. The same omission of the really practical parts of the Arthaśāstra treatise get omitted in the *Smriti* works including Manu, and even Kāmandaka. While therefore we may say that the Kuṛal does not follow the Kauṭilīya in all its details, it has occasional remarks to offer upon even some of those chapters that are excluded from the general scheme. The difference, as it appears to be of a vital character, is due merely to the different plan of the work rather than to any difference in conviction in the authors. The Kauṭilīyan Arthaśāstra in plan is professedly a manual for the statesman who has to carry on the administration practically. The work is intended to be consulted by a man engaged in practical administration, and the hints offered are such as would assist a man so engaged; whereas the Dharma Śāstras, the Kāmandaka and the Kuṛal follow the other plan. They are content with merely laying down the general ideas that ought to subserve the conduct of government and do not go to practical details of the administration. In other words, the one is a practical manual for the politician, the other is a general book of instruction for the average layman, or the ordinary citizen.

How is this difference to be explained? Society, according to the Hindus, is based on *Dharma*, a general *Dharma*, not the first division of the four aims of existence. The members or groups constituting society-Hindu political science does not know of society constituting individuals, it does not even bring it into prominence that society was composed of families as in the Vedic age-consisted of groups, castes and communities such as Indian society has at present; and had therefore for the primary idea of social existence a society in which individuals and groups can pursue the plan of their life whatever that be, with a view to the attainment of the ultimate object of existence, according to the notions of each group of individuals and families. That is what is understood by *Dharma.* Each group, or individual, may plan out its life as men of religion, atheists or agnostics, and each one, man or group, can pursue life according to the particular plan of his adoption. The function of the state is to provide the means by which each individual or group pursued this life freely, but for the one limitation that, in the pursuit of any plan of life that each may have formed, it does not interfere with the freedom of its neighbours to pursue their own life their own way. That ought to be borne in mind in discussing Hindu polity, and this is what is understood generally by the term *Dharma.* This for the average Hindu is composed of the *Dharma, Artha* and *Kāma,* that is, (1) doing that which is good and unobjectionable; (2) the gaining of that which is worth having as a means to the higher ends; and (3) the application of that which has thus been acquired in the pursuit of happiness that is unobjectionable, and not demoralising to the individual or group. Society therefore exists for the pursuit of the *Dharma,* and a state comes into existence in society with a view to enable those constituting society to pursue this *Dharma* unhampered of those with whom their lot in life is cast[1].

It is this idea of *Dharma* and the pursuit thereof that constitutes the motive of social life, and the duty of a government as a necessary organ of society is to provide for the undisturbed pursuit of this Dharma on earth. This naturally would involve, (1) the laying down of a norm for that which is a good life, and the adopting of it in practice in the course of life, (2) the acquiring of the means by which that life would become possible, and (3) the application of that which has been acquired for the purpose of enjoyment, the enjoyment being such as would not offend the norm laid down in the first or turn out to be the misapplication of that which is acquired under the second, as either of these is likely to affect prejudicially the ultimate end. This is what writers on political science understand by the term *Svadharma,* and life, on the basis of this pursuit of *Svadharma,* is such as to provide for the pursuit of this *Svadharma* on the one hand and the government that ought to provide for this pursuit unmolested on the other.[2] Hence it is that the fourth of the main ends of existence, *Moksha,* is left out of treatment here. The scope of political science therefore narrows down to the three objects of pursuit in life, generally called (Sans: *Trivarga,* Tam: the three divisions or *Muppāl*). One of the characteristic names of the Kuṛal is *Muppāl,* and that is what is understood

[1]Manu. IV. 176.

[2]Mahā Bhārata. Śāntiparvan 63. 5 ff. Artha. Śas. I 3; also Wintertniz. On Dharma Śāstra and Arthaśāstra. Sir Asutosh Memorial Volume, Patna University.

exactly by the term *Trivarga,* both by writers on Dharma Śāstras and even those of the Arthaśāstra. Hence it is that both the Dharma Śāstras and the Kuṛal provide for this general life comprising these three objects, and therefore are content with merely laying down general instructions for the attainment of these three. The Arthaśāstra, on the contrary, lays itself out to treat of these three, but prominently of the second of these as subserving the ends of existence as a whole, and therefore taking into consideration in a subsidiary way the other two as well, with the result that the Arthaśāstra could deal with the one section in far greater detail than codes of ethics like the Dharma Śāstras and Kuṛal. A comparison of the divisions main and subsidiary of the Arthaśāstra on the one hand, and the Dharma Śāstras, the Kuṛal and even an abbreviated handbook of the Arthaśāstra itself, such as the Kāmandaka, shows the same general method and does not go into the details of administration that the Arthaśāstra actually does. It will be found that the divisions of the Kuṛaḷ in chapters follows to a great extent the general sections of the Arthaśāstra, and abbreviates the smaller section by combining the second and the third, and bringing them for treatment under one section for one thing. Secondly it passes over a certain number of *Adhikaraṇas* or main divisions as being too practical and detailed, and beyond the scope therefore of a general work. For instance, the Kuṛaḷ does not treat of the *Vyavahāra* section at all, although details of this topic here and there peer out in the treatment of the other sections. In point of revenue and revenue collection, the Arthaśāstra is about the most detailed, whereas the Kuṛaḷ adopts the Dharmaśāstraic method and merely lays down the general principles underlying governmental resources.[1]

It is just possible to take the view, and such view is taken and often-times vigorously urged, that the Kuṛaḷ is an original work, and is not indebted to any work, Sanskrit or other. The statement is several times made also that the Kuṛaḷ is a pure Tamil work and is entirely independent of Sanskrit. Both these are statements, which a constructive study of the question hardly justifies. These questions can be considered only by a careful study both of the Kuṛaḷ itself and of the Sanskrit works bearing on the subject with a view to noting similarities and dissimilarities, and arriving at a conclusion after a careful consideration in detail whether there is any possible inter-relation between the one and the other. The fact that the Kuṛaḷ is written in pure Tamil, that is, in Tamil which is not so much mixed with Sanskrit, is to a very great extent true, and that is not merely a characteristic of the Kuṛaḷ alone. That is equally the characteristic of the whole collection of works generally called the Śangam works. It marks a stage in the growth of the language when, as a vehicle of expression, it had more flexibility and richness than in later times, and much that would seem exceedingly difficult to render in pure Tamil now seems to have been ordinarily capable of being expressed in comparatively easy Tamil. There is a variety of diction and a facility of manipulation of the language as a means of expressing thought, which

[1]In only one chapter. Ch. 76.

one may say is not found to exist to the same degree in writers of a later period. That is only so far as the handling of the language is concerned. The writers themselves generally appear to have showed no disinclination when they could borrow either from Sanskrit, or from elsewhere, wherever they could borrow usefully. They could borrow, as all people with a great deal of originality often do, and so adapted what was borrowed to their own purpose that the borrowing becomes really beneficial and far from objectionable. That is the kind of borrowing that one meets with in works of this class of Tamil; but not the comparatively more narrow-minded, petty notion that the language must be self-contained. A language cannot be self-contained unless it makes an effort to contain within itself ideas in all departments of human life, and this width of knowledge could be acquired only by the use of experience—experience not only one's own self or of the group but of all human experience generally, the circle of humanity being wider or narrower according as contact with the outside world and communication admits of more or less intercourse. A careful examination of the Kuṛaḷ shows that it is not so free from knowledge of what is found in Sanskrit literature, nor is it so entirely free from the influence of Sanskrit diction. There are words in it even, that are borrowed from Sanskrit, and that is true not only of Kuṛaḷ, but of the whole class of this literature. The borrowing in this period, however, does not appear to be quite so much borrowing directly from Sanskrit, but seems to be through the Prakrit generally. The Sanskrit words therefore are hidden from view by the double transformation that the words have undergone, the transformation they attain to in the Prakrit form, and the further transformation that they had to undergo to suit themselves to Tamil usage. It is not necessary for this position that the words should have been all of Sanskrit origin and put into the Prakrit form. It is just possible that the words are originally Prakrit, but Sanskritised for purposes of classical use. That does not concern us in this context.

Apart from this question purely of diction, the parallelisms in subject matter are so many and so frequent that it would be taking too much upon ourselves to assert that in the subject-matter the work is quite independent of Sanskrit. The author of the Kuraḷ does not appear to have cherished the notion that his merit lay in his being completely independent of contact with the other culture: He seems to have cherished a very considerable amount of regard for that which was of use in the other cultures without sacrificing any of his regard for the language that he handled with so much facility and effect. He acknowledges his indebtedness in places explicity, not to mention those in which the acknowledgment is more or less recondite and not so readily seen. There are certain places in which he refers to *Nūl* in the text.[1] The term *Nūl* certainly does occur in several places and with different meanings. But in certain contexts it stands for the Veda and Vedic learning generally.[2] But there are con-

[1] 54. 3, 59. 1, 65. 69. 3. 75. 3.

[2] 56 10.

texts in which he undoubtedly refers to something far more secular, and he cannot refer to anything else than a work of political science of some kind. Unless it is possible for us to point out, if not actually quote, an actual pre-existing work on the Arthaśāstra in Tamil, we shall have to accept it that it refers to the Artha-śāstra-Arthasastra the well-known one, either the Kautilīyan, or its abridgment the Kāmandaka. Kuṛaḷs 683 and 743 are instances in point. The first occurs in the chapter on *toodu,* which word itself is a Sanskrit word, and institutes a comparison between the most efficient ambassador and the most efficient warrior, as it were. That ambassador is most efficient, who among the proficients in political science is the most proficient, as that warrior is the most proficient in the use of his javelin, who could give a good account of himself in a body of experts in the use of that weapon. There is no other science (*Nūl*) which is so essential and comes in handy for an ambassador than the science that treats of that particular subject, which forms an essential and integral part of political science or Arthaśāstra. The other Kuṛaḷ has reference to what ought to be the essential requirements of a fortress. There again the Kuṛaḷ has it that height, width, strength and rarity are the essential characteristics of an efficient fortress according to science (*Nūl*). The *Nūl* here could be no other than a work which lays down the instructions for the building of fortresses for military purposes, and that must be a work either on military science, or a science of which military science is an integral part. Here again we are face to face with the position that it could refer to nothing else than the Arthaśāstra.

Therefore then the Kuraḷ polity is one that applies to the society of Tamil India when that society had already become constituted on a basis offering analogies of no remote character to the society depicted in the Arthasastra. That is the view that comes out from the Tolkāppiyam itself notwithstanding the fact that the Sūtras of the Tolkāppiyam could not be explicit and detailed in regard to these, and the details have to be supplied by the commentator as no Sūtra in the whole range of Sūtra literature can be complete in itself and self-explanatory. It is undoubtedly complete in itself provided only when you understand the full extent of the implication of the technical language employed and what it is intended to convey, and that could be understood only by a man who has had the Sūtra expounded to him. This is an implication which is inherent in the character of the Sūtra itself. It is utter ignorance and want of understanding that could charge commentators with having imported ideas when they expound what is merely implied in the Sūtras; not that commentators are not up to importing their own ideas, or the original ideas that had undergone modification into their interpretation. They are actually expected to do so in regard to certain classes of works. But at the same time what ought to be borne in mind carefully is that the commentators are there commenting with a view to expounding the Sūtras primarily, as they were understood by those that first put them into that form, and indicate the changes that that original idea might have undergone in process of time. Where we find it necessary to say that a commentator has gone beyond his limits, the responsibility is undoubtedly ours to prove that that is a fact. We have no right to assume the fact that a commentator is a fraud who reads his ideas into the Sūtras composed centuries before his time. These remarks are offered here, as it is often asserted that Parimēlaḻagar's profound learning in Sanskrit is what is responsible for the affiliation of the ideas of the Kuṛaḷ to Sanskrit works. Not only that, but sometimes it is pointed out that other commentators do not always see eye to eye with Parimēlaḻagar in the interpretation of particular verses of the Kuṛaḷ. Ignorance of Sanskrit and the necessarily imperfect exposition of a Kuṛaḷ are not certainly features of higher authority. It is knowledge of what the Sanskritists have to say, and a comparison of the two in their contexts that really would lead to anything like a justifiable inference rather than the ignorance that would shut its eyes to all possible sources of light from elsewhere. Many of those passages would be obscure and hardly understandable unless you let into it the light that Sanskrit literature has to offer. This would become clear from verses in certain chapters which do not explain themselves unless the technical senses of certain words, for instance, are understood; and in some cases it is impossible to understand them without the aid of Sanskrit. We may refer particularly to Kuṛaḷ 501 as affording a very good illustration of this. There are numbers of other passages which are equally sound illustrations, but may not be quite so complete as this particular one, where without introducing the idea of the *Upadā* of the Arthaśāstrakāras[1] which is not unknown or quite so unfamiliar to ordinary people

[1]Arthasas. Bk. I Ch. X.

the passage can hardly be understood. The idea of the *Upadā* is explained in the Rāmāyaṇa, and occurs even in the inscriptions of the Guptas in the fourth century A.D.[1] as an idea that is familiarly known to all. Why should we deny that knowledge to Tiruvaḷḷuvar, and read his verses and understand them but imperfectly? This is hardly justifiable criticism.

The Kuṛaḷ ideal then, as projected in the seventy chapters constituting the second section, is a monarchical state as depicted in the Dharmaśāstras, and to a very considerable extent in the Artha Śāstra as well. As was pointed out above, the Kuṛaḷ begins with the notion of *Araśu,* that is, not in the style of the Artha Śāstra with the abstract notion of *svadharma* and the application of the *daṇḍa.* So it takes up the state, at the head of which there was a king. The qualities he ought to possess, the education that he has to undergo, and the discipline to which he has to submit himself are expounded, and then follows naturally the treatment of ministers and friends with whom he ought to associate, and the relations that he ought to admit to his presence. These are dealt with under the heads *amaichchu* and *śuṛṛam.* The word *amaichchu* is again a Sanskrit word coming through the Prakrit, one of which has a form of *amachcha* corresponding to the Tamil *amaichchar.* The whole body is treated as a group of ministers constituting various classes, the *Mantri, Purohita* and others of the Artha Śāstra. The Kural follows generally the same kind of division. The ministers and the relations are sometimes spoken of as

[1]Junagadh inscription of Skandagupta, F. G. I. No. 14.

those in immediate attendance, and the term *amaichchu* itself is expounded as those near about, on the formation of the word from a Sanskrit root. Where the Pingalandai[1] groups them together and gives them the common name *surram,* as the eighteen *surrattār* to which reference has already been made, it follows a recognised usage. Where therefore we find the Madurai Kānji[2] speaking of the five groups of ministers, and the Śilapadhikāram[3] refers to these five groups and the eight of the other section, and the Kuraḷ[4] more or less indirectly lays down who ought to constitute the *inam* (the ministers) and what their qualifications should be, what constituted the *śurram* and how far they ought to be allowed to influence the work of the monarch, it is following probably the divisions of the Artha Śāstra, and possibly what was the existing practice in Tamil India of the times. This will become clear when we remember that the Kuraḷ deals in a number of sections with what constituted the qualifications for ministers and what exactly a king was expected to do to secure the right kind for his service.[5] This is followed by a section bearing upon how exactly to treat those that are related to him and dependent upon him. In this treatment, he uses two expressions *inam* and *śurram,* which are synonymous in Tamil. But the author of the Kuraḷ, however, seems to make a distinction that when he speaks of the *inam,* he means the councillors, the ministers and those trusted servants

1 64. 8.

2 Above. p. 19. n. 3.

3 Above. p. 19 n. 1 & 2 and p. 21.

4 Chapt. 51-53.

5 Of Arthasastra I. 4—5.

in immediate attendance, and relatives generally. But he makes use of the word *śuṟṟam* for the last class alone. In any case, all the three groups are there and therefore the expression, "the five great bodies and the eight groups" of Tamil literature, have to be taken to be what was in the mind of the author of the Kuṟaḷ.

The Kuṟaḷ polity therefore not merely reflects the social life of the times but represents, more or less, faithfully the state of society and the arrangements for the administration of government at the time, and perhaps would warrant the inference that it is not a mere abstract book of aphorisms of merely theoretical value, but a work that reflects correctly the prevalent ideas and the practice to which those ideas gave rise in the department of political activity of the age. At the same time, it must be recognised, as was pointed out before, that it is not a full or detailed description of the administrative machinery of the times, being not an administrative manual. It will be noticed that what it lays down in the seventy chapters out of a total of 133 may be regarded, more or less as an accurate description of the general principles which ought to underly the creation of the administrative machinery for the carrying on of the government of a state such as an Indian state was conceived to be in the Tamil India of the time, or we might even say, in the whole of India of the time. There is such a similarity between the northern organisation and the southern as described here that perhaps it will not be justifiable to regard the one as entirely distinct from the other. Where this polity shows itself to be defective is, as was pointed out already, in the details of the general administration, while those relating to the local are practically absent. That is a feature not peculiar to the Kuraḷ; but it is a feature quite common to the *Smritis* and even Kāmandaka, a professed treatise on politics. The idea seems to be more or less that, except for a technical student, such general notions as are given in these treatises are ample and if further knowledge be required, it is for those that seek it to go to the really technical treatises, which deal with the subject in detail. Similarly those that wish to gain a complete idea of the administrative machinery by means of which the administration was actually carried on, must acquaint themselves necessarily with the details of the local administration before they can feel justifiably that they have gained a complete idea of the actual machinery of government. To do this, we have to go to the Arthaśāstra of Kautilya to fill in the details from a text-book or treatise, and we shall have to, as a supplement, make a close study or a fairly full survey of such details as we gain from the inscriptions both of Asoka and his successors, drawing even occasionally from such notes as we have from the foreign travellers who have left accounts of the administrative system of the Mauryan times. The Greek accounts and the Asokan inscriptions would, to some extent, supplement each other and give, not a complete, but an adequate picture of the administration, and the agreement between the details that we get from there and the Arthaśāstra are so close that we would perhaps be justified in assuming that such glimpses as we get in the inscriptions and the accounts of the foreign travellers reflect a society formed on the basis underlying the Arthaśāstra, and the Arthaśāstra polity therefore would give a more or less complete picture. Sometimes we still find that even the Arthaśastra does not go down to the full details, and these may be found in the inscriptions of a later period where we have them in some number and in full detail. There again we shall have to take it that the Artha Śāstra omission is not necessarily evidence of the non-existence of the institutions but may be due to the exigencies of a treatise, which has to conform to certain requirements which may necessitate the avoidance of details of too technical or too local a character. With these cautions we may project a picture of the political life of India, and the political machinery by means of which the aims of that life were attained, by a combined study of all these.

Before passing from this subject, however, one remarkable omission of the Kuṛaḷ has to be noted. The Arthaśāstra treatises generally and the political chapters of the Mahābhārata[1] alike begin the subject by a discussion as to the origin of society as arising out of the social needs of humanity, and then proceed to point out the need of a government for regulating that life. The discussion is on the subject society and state. They arrive at a state of society perhaps not altogether theoretically, although definite statements are not wanting that they regarded that society existed without an administrative guardian of some kind where people were expected to live together and respect the law.

[1]Śānti Parvan 582.

The preservation of that society becomes impossible, and that kind of a social life soon lapses into a life where might is right. This is what they describe as the *Mātsaya-Nyāya,*[1] the law of the fish, the bigger fish eating the smaller, the stronger oppressing the weaker and taking forcible possession of all that is worth having. In such a state of things they felt the need of a machinery, the function of which would be to regulate life, and to see that the real interests of society as a whole are not actually sacrificed to the interest of the stronger individuals: in other words, to see that social progress is not hampered by the pursuit of individual ambition. They therefore created consciously a kingship which came into existence either by the decree of providence at the request of the sufferers, or created by the voluntary agreement of the people among themselves, or by a compact between the people on the one side, and some one that was prepared to take the responsibility on the other. According to the first, Manu was ordained to give protection to society in return for his being placed beyond need for pursuing life and securing the wherewithal for himself and his family. There again it takes on the form more or less of a contract. He was to get a portion of the produce of the earth and all else from which a revenue was derivable generally by the processes of pursuing gain. That is the more orthodox view. The heterodox view, the Buddhistic view, for instance, frankly states that it was the result of a contract, the *Mahāsammata*[2] between the Ikshvāku kings and people generally.

[1]Arth. Śas. I. 13.

[2]Digha Nikaya III. p. 73.

Either way, this preliminary discussion both in the Mahābhārata and, in a somewhat abbreviated form, in the Arthasastra brings into view how the Hindus attempted to explain the coming of society into existence, and the creation therein as it were, of a state. The preliminary discussion of society and state, and the circumstances leading to the creation of the one from the other, are absent from the Kuṛaḷ which starts with the statement that there is a king and he has a kingdom to govern. The author indicates thereby clearly that he is more really concerned with the realistic description of a kingdom that existed rather than to trouble himself to expound how a kingdom or a state is a necessary organisation for the conduct of human life. This seems, however, implicit in what he says, and the whole polity of the Kuṛaḷ could not be well understood without presuming the background of the Arthaśāstraic or Rajanīti culture, as it is expounded in the Arthasastras and the Mahābhārata respectively.

II

THE KURAL POLITY.

The following abridgement of the Kuṛal polity may then be of interest to give an idea of what exactly the state was that was projected by the political chapters of the Kuṛal which may be regarded as an ideal presentation of what an actual state really was. According to the Kuṛal, he is the most excellent king who is possessed of an efficient army, a flourishing population, growing wealth, faithful ministers, dependable allies. These six make him eminent among kings. This lays down, as has been pointed out, the idea of the *Saptaprakriti*, as in the Artha Śāstra, Manu and Śukra, it does not deal with the *Saptānga* as such, but proceeds on the division for which there is warrant in these works on the principle of Rāja and Rājyam as constituting the more convenient kind of a division. The king was to see that he himself does not fall away from the path of duty laid down for him as protector of society, that he carefully removes that which is detrimental to the pursuit of Dharma or duty, and that he maintains himself in this position of high responsibility. This is an idea not peculiar to the Kuṛal itself. Even other Tamil works which lay it down that Dharma or duty is at the root of society, as for instance, the Puranānūṛu, (poem 55), set down that at the root of the valour of the king lies the pursuit of a path of virtuous duty. Once a king, he has to see to it that he creates fresh sources of income producing additional revenue for himself, collects what is due to him, provides for its safety and increase, and ultimately applies it to purposes which are worthy of that which constitutes the grand duty of the king. That king is counted among people a god, who protects the people and administers justice righteously. His duties therefore would resolve themselves into generous gifts to those in need, kindness to all those who come under his protection, unswerving justice and efficient protection to his subjects. The king possessed of all these four features preeminently, is the most illustrious among kings. The king that rightly understands what is acceptable to the people generally and adopts that in his life of action, possesses the right discernment among kings. This is noted as one of the essential qualities of an ideal king and the great dramatist Bhavabhūti puts it into the mouth of his ideal character, Rama, where he is made to say that for the sake of pleasing his subjects (*loka, Tam:. ulakam*), he was quite prepared to give up friendship, mercy, his own well-being and even his beloved Jānaki herself.[1] It would cause him no sorrow to give up these if only the world would thereby be pleased. The king ought to surround himself with friends, older than himself who have a thorough understanding of the nice details of the *Dharma*. The idea here is just exactly the same as is contained in Manu, Chapter VII, 11, 32-38. As the king's ministerial surroundings constitute his eyes, a king must choose only those that could be used as trustworthily as his own eyes. That king who is surrounded by worthy men, ministers and officials. and

[1]Uttararāmacharita. I.

do his duty acceptable to them can suffer but little from his enemies.[1] That king would destroy himself even without having enemies to do so, if he has not among his surroundings those that are not afraid of speaking unpleasant truths (Manu VII. 40). There is nothing that a king cannot achieve whose action is based on deliberation in a council of knowing ministers (Manu VII. 155-57). When action is called for, it is best that one takes action after due deliberation. Deliberation following action is useless.[2] Here what is stated has reference to the choice of the particular line of action on an emergency arising, and though put in general terms in the context, it has reference to the adoption of the means to the end on the lines laid down in treatises on political science generally. That is the adoption of the four kinds of means against an actual or possible enemy, viz., the familiar, *Dāna, Sāma, Bēda* and *Daṇḍa* or gifts, pacification, detaching possible allies, and war.[3] That is the most appropriate way for the proper maintenance of the treasury and application of that treasury which in gifts gives just what is necessary and adequate. This has reference to what is found clearly stated elsewhere in the Sanskrit treatises on polity as well as even Tamil texts, and has relation to the division of state revenues into four parts, of which two parts are intended for his own expenditure, holding one fourth as a reserve and applying the remaining part for these purposes.[4] When no hostile action is called

[1]Manu. VII. 39.

[2]Ar. Śās. I. 15.

[3]Manu. VII 106.

[4]Trikaṭukam. 21.

for, remain quiet like a crane listlessly waiting for the appearance of a suitable victim; when action is called for, see to it that it is quick and decisive as that of that self-same crane when the victim comes before it. This is clearly an injunction that one finds scattered through the Arthaśāstra, and is generally put down for one of those teachings of Kautilya regarded unmoral, if not immoral. Tiruvaḷḷuvar could hardly be accused of want of morality, not to speak of immorality. The minister is best chosen whose choice has stood the test of morality, worth, desire and fear of life. This has reference to the choice of the ministers and the staff of a king in attendance upon him, and what is said here and the chapter following in regard to this matter apply also to other officials. In this clearly the Kuṛal follows the teachings of the Artha Śāstra and what is said here in this particular verse has reference to the *Upadā* of the texts on Dharma, which as was remarked already, finds exposition in a work like the Rāmāyaṇa and was familiarly enough known in the days of the Guptas. An inscription of Skandagupta refers to his choice of a suitable Governor for the province of Gujarat, which at that time offered the most anxious responsibility among provincial governments. What the Kuṛal discusses in chapters 51 and 52 generally follows more closely than usual the injunctions of the Kautilīya.[1]

Chapter 51 begins with the statement that the minister is best chosen when the choice is made after testing him by means of ethical standards, impending

1 Bk. I. Chapter X.

danger to his religious faith, possible acquisition of wealth, attractive gratification of the senses and fear of life. It is only those who come out of these tests unscathed, that ought to be chosen. The twenty verses that constitute the two chapters follow the usual method of Tiruvaḷḷuvar, but cover practically the whole of the subject matter under discussion in the chapters relating to these topics in the Arthaśāstra even to the point of detail. Without going into too much of detail, this very chapter lays down that a choice without test, and suspicion of one that has been chosen, are alike productive of evil from the consequences of which escape would be impossible. The duties of a minister ordinarily are the increase of sources of income, the adopting of the means to make the wealth of the king grow quickly, and the removal of that which would diminish either of these.[1] His daily attention ought to be how to canvas these three ends. The country is not likely to go wrong unless the protecting hand of the administration goes astray The constant and unremitting attention of the king therefore is called for to see that those that carry on the administration for him do not swerve from the righteous course of action. That is the real relationship between king and Minister which continues unchanged even when the king suffers badly in regard to his prosperity. When old friends had fallen away from the king, and they return to friendship again for good reasons, the king ought to accept their services again on an examination of the motives inducing their return. Relaxation in effort does not lead to fame. This is the conviction of all

[1] Ar. Sas. I. 5.

sciences (not merely of the science of politics). A king is bound to pursue by all means in his power that which has been held up as the duty of the king. Such as neglect these will come to no good even in "the seven births."[1] The seven births here referred to are the various classes of beings and even inanimate creation, among any of which one could be borne. Of course what is recognised here are the recommendations laid down in the Artha Śāstra, and they are certainly detailed by the commentator. To interpret merely in general terms would prove to be quite unintelligible in the context. A king's righteous rule is that which is ever watchful to note the shortcomings of his officials, to punish these according to measure after deliberation with his council, and discharge his duty with strict impartiality. The righteous rule of a king stands at the root of the whole learning of the Brahman and at the root of morality alike.[2] It is not the weapons of war that bring victory to a king; it is the impartiality of his rule. A similar idea to the first gets expressed in the Maṇimēkhalai, a Buddhist work of a Buddhist author, where rendering almost the same idea, he puts it down that the religious observances of those devoted to ascetic penance and the chastity of women alike are under the guardianship of the ruler.[3] The Puṟanānūṟu expresses a similar sentiment to that of the second verse when it states in poem 55 that the valour of a king has its root in the morality honoured of old. The whole world is protected by a righteous king while he himself finds equally efficient protection in the righteousness of his rule.

[1] Ar. Śas. I. 19. [2] *Ibid* Bk. I. 5 & 6. [3] XXII. 208—10.

Where a king punishes people of evil propensities with death, he is doing just what a cultivator does when he pulls out the weeds from his cultivated fields. The king who oppresses his people by undue imposts is worse than an enemy, who makes killing the object of his campaign. Where a king fails to offer efficient protection there the very cow ceases to yield; and those whose duty it is to conduct the six[1] occupations forget their works of authority. The king that does not discharge his duties after due consultation with those with whom he associates himself for this purpose, and throws the blame on them when actions miscarry, is one whose prosperity will dwindle gradually and disappear. Commissioners of secret information, and knowledge of the science of government, are both of them the eyes of the king. Here the word used is *Orru,* which means a person sent out to inform himself and make reports of what is taking place confidentially, and is ordinarily translated spy. It is an unsuitable translation,[2] as according to the Artha Śāstra works as well as the Kuṛal itself, this class of people is included among ministers, and the qualifications which are necessary are something far superior to anything that may be expected of a spy. This class of people are sent out within and without while the actual spies are another class and are treated of separately. The author of the Kuṛal does go the whole length of the Artha Śāstra itself when he lays down in 586 that he is the best of

[1]Learning, teaching, sacrificing for themselves and sacrificing for others giving in gifts and accepting gifts are recognised as the six duties of the Brahman both in Sanskrit works and in the Tolkāppiyam. For a similar idea. See M. Bh. Śānti 68, 28.

[2]Ar. Śās. I. 12.

this class of people who, assuming the disguise of ascetics,[1] could get entry into the most confidential places of others, and will not give out the information gained even when put to the greatest pain. The only course of action in regard to these agents of information, by the king is to see to it that one of them does not know what another is about, and accept that information as correct only when three such separate informants agree in conveying the same report independently.[2] Just as a stock of a waterlily is longer or shorter, according to the depth of the water, so men are greater or smaller according as they exhibit more or less of courage and determination. That king who shows no relaxation in his effort rightly directed, will become at once ruler over all that the great God measured with his feet. Here the author points out that a king must be capable of great and unremitting effort, and one that is possessed of it in a large measure is likely to be a ruler of the whole earth—the whole earth, in fact, the whole universe described as that which was measured by the three strides of Vishṇu.

The above is a summary of the qualities that are essential to a king, what comes within the sphere of his action, how he has to carry action to effect, and what high qualities he is to exhibit in the course of this action together with the instruments that he should make use of in the successful carrying out of action such as he might have resolved upon. The author then proceeds to deal with the limbs of a state. As was already pointed out, Tiruvaḻḻuvar, unlike the Sanskritists, re-

[1]*Ibid* Ch. XIII. [2]*Ibid* Ch. XII.

gards the other six of the seven *prakritis* or *angas* as really the limbs of the state, having dealt with the king separately. He then proceeds to deal with them in the order of the Artha Śāstra, although in the first Kuṛal of this section, he recited them in a different order. The first section therefore deals with *Amaichchu* or ministers in a general sense. Those that constituted the ministry must be possessed of the following five qualities in a high degree: unswerving determination, efficient protection of subjects, great expertness in the sciences relating to government, fully developed understanding acquired thereby, and capacity for great effort.[1] Those that are possessed of these in a very high degree are those fit to constitute a ministry. That minister is the most dependable assistant to the king, who has complete knowledge of what actually are the duties of a king, who is possessed of learning to expound those duties in a persuasive way, and who has the capacity and discernment to select the best means in carrying out what has to be done. To the minister who combines a penetrating natural intelligence and has cultivated it by education in the science of polity, there is nothing that is really too difficult of understanding. Even where a king shows neither capacity to understand what others have placed before him, nor the discernment to understand it himself, it is still the duty of those near him to place before him what they consider is the best course of action. Here the term used for the minister is worthy of notice. The man near to the king is the Tamil periphrasis by which a minister is indicated, showing that the Tamil

[1]Bk. I. 9.

word *amaichchu* is the Sanskrit word *amātya*, and this is translated by the term *uḻaiyinan*, he who is near. Where a minister speaks, let him speak with knowledge of the capacity of those whom he addresses. There is no morality or worth superior to that. Here so much importance is attached to the proper method of offering counsel as the acceptance of good counsel depends upon its proper presentation. Where something has to be done, and the good minister placed it in proper form and order, the whole world will accept his advice with out question. No minister should do that which will not appeal to the intelligence of the cultured, even if his mother should suffer from hunger; that is even in a supreme moment of necessity he ought not to swerve from the path of rectitude. In the pursuit of action, a minister ought not to take it upon himself to do that which is likely to fail, and not to lose heart when that which was undertaken fails by chance. These two are the best methods of action for a minister according to the experts in the science of politics. In adopting a course of action, a minister has to take care that he adopts the course of war only when he has got a fair guarantee of success. Where this is impossible, he ought to adopt his action to suit the circumstances actually. Here Tiruvaḷḷuvar is actually laying down, when exactly the minister should adopt the last means of the four, the arbitrament of war. That has to be adopted only where he is certain of success. Where this is uncertain, other means have to be tried before proceeding to war. In adopting a course of action, a minister must have full consideration for the five elements constituting action, need of action, means for carrying it out, the instruments to carry it out, the time that is suitable for doing so, the kind of action that is useful and the place to be chosen.[1] He must have an eye to the end to be attained, to what might possibly intervene to prevent the attainment of what actually is to be gained when the end is reached. These he has to calculate beforehand in taking action.

He then passes on to that class of ministers, whose function is to be deputed as ambassadors, and lays down their qualifications very high indeed. That is what is called *Dutū* (ambassadors). The qualities that an ambassador should possess[2] are preeminently affection for his people and dependants, high birth, and other qualities that are attractive to kings. Those possessed of these qualities alone are fit for being sent out as ambassadors. Among these the best is he who has full knowledge of what he has to do before the king to whom he is deputed. He ought to be able to understand thoroughly the time suitable for conveying his message. He ought also to understand the circumstances, which would assure success to his embassy. He would make a success who considers all these beforehand on information, and proceeds to action. Here Tiruvaḷḷuvar in general terms includes all the three classes of ambassadors, described in Sanskrit works on the subject, viz., ambassadors, who can use their discretion and successfully acheive that which is good for their government. He mentions as the first the man who can use a good deal of his discretion in the carrying out of his mission. The man who has not to exer-

[1]*Ibid* Bk. I. 15 [2]*Ibid* Bk. I. 16.

cise that amount of discretion but is merely to convey that which he has been previously tutored to convey would be the second. But the man who actually carries the very message by means of a letter would be the third. By referring to the first class here as the best, he implies knowledge of the other classes as well. An ambassador must achieve the object of his embassy, even if it should involve, in the course of its carrying out, his own death. Ministers ought not to keep away from kings, nor ought they to get too near him in familiarity; but ought to keep at the proper distance, just like those who approach a fire to warm themselves. Ministers with understanding will not hold a king in little esteem because he happens to be young, because he happens to be a relation, of such and such a degree. They must always conduct themselves towards him as becomes the illustriousness of his position. Among ministers the highest quality is the capacity for understanding the wishes of the ruler without explicit direction. That minister who can understand the inner mind of his master with certitude is to be regarded as a god. A minister ought to weigh his words and use only such as are suitable to the assembly in which he speaks. In order fearlessly to speak in an assembly with success, a minister ought to cultivate the use of language by means of the proper sciences, viz., grammar and logic.

This brings us to the close of the section on ministers. In the ten chapters Tiruvaḷḷuvar deals with those that are worthy of being ministers to a government as a whole group. Although he lays down the qualifications and the duties of a minister in general terms, he indicates in the course of his treatment what classes were included among those that are called ministers. There is a special class of ambassadors, who stand distinctly out of the group. But among the general group other than those, we can find a detailed study of the socalled five groups constituting the ministry of Tamil monarchs, including in it not merely the actual counsellors but even those whose function it is to carry on the administration.

The next section deals with *Nāḍu,* what the Sanskritists call *Janapada,*[1] in general terms the country or territory that makes one of the important constituents of a state. The author of the Kuṛal starts with definnig Nāḍu as that which is capable of an abundance of production, and containing as its inhabitants men that are worthy and men that are possessed of growing wealth. By the plentifulness and value of its production it ought to be attractive, and by the absence of circumstances hindering production it ought to be capable of producing plenty. That is really good country which is capable of affording great advantages to its inhabitants, and at the same time maintain the income of the king undiminished. That is really good country which does not contain different communities of people (of opposing interests), internal enmities which are destructive to the country and the anarchical feudatories who are always a source of trouble to the king. That country is the best among countries, which is free from the evils of enemy occupation, and maintains its

[1]Ar. Śas. Bk. II. 1 & 2.

fruitfulness undiminished. The two sources of water (spring water and rain water), hills well set and perennial water courses coming from them, and well constructed fortresses, these constituents make a good country. That is a happy country which is free from diseases, is possessed of wealth, is capable of plenty, gives happiness to its inhabitants and is well provided for protection. These constitute elements that go to beautify a country. That is really good country which is fertile by nature; and that country which has to be made fertile by the work of man is nothing like so good. Even where territory is possessed of all these good features, it would be of no good to its inhabitants unless it be possessed of a worthy king. This, according to the Kuṛal, is what constitutes good territory and the territory that is really good by nature would not be of any good to the inhabitants unless it is equipped with a good government at the same time. So good government is something indispensable to the prosperity of the inhabitants of a country.

The next section deals with fortresses.[1] Fortresses are of value to those kings that aspire, with capacity, to do great deeds. It is equally indispensable to those who have not that capacity and want protection. Fortresses offering protection are of four kinds: (1) protection afforded by clear deep water; (2) protection afforded by extensive plains round about; (3) protection afforded by well-set hills surrounding the locality, and (4) protection offered by dense forests. Works bearing on fortresses declare height, width,

[1]Cf. *Ibid* Ch. 5.

strength and comparative rarity as the necessary qualities of a good fort. A good fortress must be capable of efficient defence by a small force on guard. At the same time, it must be vast enough to give protection to a large number of people. Similarly it ought to be very difficult of being taken by an enemy, and must contain all that is necessary for those that seek its protection. That is an efficient fortress, which is provided with all that may be needed by the occupants, and is defended by efficient guards who can assure safety to the inhabitants. Fortresses must be incapable of being taken either by siege or by assault or by mining. However well provided a fortress may be in all these particulars, it would be of no value unless those in occupation of it are capable of making proper use of it. The description of fortification given in general terms by Tiruvaḷḷuvar, is confirmed in full detail by a description which is given of the fortress of Madura in the Śilapadhikāram. The passage under reference in that classic gives an actual description of the fortress and enumerates the variety of the weapons both of offence and defence with which the fortress was provided.

The next section deals with the income of a state. The Kuṛaḷ begins with the statement that wealth is indispensable to a ruler. The author points out if only wealth could be acquired in the way that wealth should be acquired, by moral and legitimate means, it will give both happiness and subserve the ends of good morality. It will be noted that this particular kind of preeminence of the utility of wealth it is that gives the character to the so-called Artha. Śāstra, which deals only with wealth, as it were. Even where that preeminence is given to it, it is not done, it must be remembered, by negativing the other two, as has often been taken by some scholars. It was always intended to subserve the other ends as well. That is king's wealth for which there is no legitimate claimant. That is also king's wealth that is drawn from active trade and commerce. It is equally the king's wealth which is returned for the justice that the king administers. It will be noticed that there are three heads of revenue given here. The first is what may be regarded as unclaimed property. Both property left by those without claimants and property which had perhaps not been appropriated. The next one is the group which accrues by various customs and octroi sources of revenue. This is the revenue that is obtained by means of the commercial activity of the inhabitants. The third is the revenue that the king derives by the exercise of his authority, that is, the administration of justice. These are (have actually to be so regarded) over and above what is due to the king as his share, the recognised sixth of agricultural produce, etc., generally called by the Sanskritists *bhāga*,[1] his share of the general yield. A king ought, by all means in his power, to acquire wealth. There is nothing that destroys the enemy's power as efficiently as this. The section winds up with the following "acquired wealth as it increases in the legitimate process of growth, brings to the king the other two ends of existence, namely, moral life and legitimate happiness." Here again the Kuṛal treatment is quite general, not altogether without hints which would let us into the details which are expounded in the treatises relating to the Artha Śāstra.

[1] Ar. Śas. II. 24.

The next section has to do with the army. The army, divided into distinct arms, which is not afraid of defeat in course of action is counted the best among a king's possessions. The fortitude with which an army maintains itself against odds even in suffering defeat is possible only to the hereditary forces of a king. Here, of course, the reference is to the distinct section of the army, which is generally called *Mūlabala*, or the main forces of a state,[1] coming in hereditary succession therefore with a permanent interest in the kingdom. This description naturally implies the other kinds of an army which Tamil and Sanskrit literature know of. These are usually divided into the hereditary forces already referred to, mercenary forces that may be engaged for the time, levies made for emergencies from the country (*Nāṭṭupaḍai*), levies improvised from the inhabitants of the forests (*Kāṭṭupaḍai*), auxiliaries from allies and states neutral, and lastly enemy forces brought under subjection and made use of in war afterwards (*Pahaippaḍai*).[2] Of these the best is, of course, the first, and that is what is kept up in a state of efficiency and good feeling by the king. That is what the author wishes to draw attention to in the next following Kuṛaḷ. The army which is not easily destroyed in war, which shows itself impossible of corruption by an enemy, and that which has come down from generation to generation of the ruling family is the best among the forces of a king. This Kuṛal almost implies a reference to the famous poem[3] where a woman is made to say that her father stands a stone—that is the *vīragal* erected in honour of a warrior who fought and fell in

1Ar. Śas. Bk. VI. 1. 2*Ibid.* 3Puṛapporuḷ. Ch. VIII. 22.

the service of his sovereign—having fallen in battle; her husband died on the field of war, her brothers, fought at the front and fell, while her son occupying his place in the reserve behind, having been struck by an arrow, rushed against the enemy king and fell. That is an efficient army, which knows what modes of war are the most appropriate for the campaign in view, and marches forward to the attack in the face of an enemy charging. However efficient an army, and however firm the individuals composing it, it would be futile if it is not under good leaders. In regard to the bravery of individual soldiers, Tiruvaḷḷuvar has the following. When the army throws a javelin at him, the winking of the eye at the sight of it would be regarded as disgraceful as running away from the field. The warrior that is prepared to lay down his life on the field of battle, if it should go against him, is not counted less brave even where the king prevents him from going to battle. If it is given to a soldier to fall in battle to the regret of the king who maintained him, such a death is one that people ought to pray for and obtain.[1]

The author then passes on to allies and devotes as many as seventeen chapters to the subject. He divides the subject into two divisions describing what is good alliance in the first five, and what is not desirable in the next twelve. He begins by saying that a king could do nothing better than to secure a desirable alliance, because there is no more efficient protection to him than a good ally. He next lays down;—There is nothing in the field of battle, more hurtful than being alone with-

[1]Yāgñavalkya I. 324 and Mah. Bhar. Sānti. 97—25.

out an ally. The hand that salutes might hide a dangerous weapon. Even the tears of a secret enemy might hide in it something dangerous. Those who conduct themselves as dependable allies outwardly and harbour contemptible evil thoughts secretly, are best got rid of by oneself behaving similarly and putting an end to the friendship at the proper moment. Those that are extensively well read and capable of expounding their knowledge effectively to others, but are not themselves disciplined by that learning, they are, notwithstanding their learning, much worse than ignorant people. The friendship of an ignorant person is of great good as when their friendship terminates it brings no pain. The evil that those without knowledge can inflict upon themselves, is more even than what their enemies may have to inflict upon them. Those that are not capable of doing a thing even when directed, and are not able to do it properly by themselves, they constitute a disease to their friends all their days. Enmity is a disease which makes friendship impossible. Those whose knowledge extends to merely cherishing enmity cannot be held to understand the significance of the means for becoming victorious. Enmity produces all kinds of evil consequences, while friendship has good policy as its result. Where war is necessary, make an effort to avoid it as against those who are stronger. Adopt it as against those who are distinctly weaker. Accept the enmity of those vanquished in war, but never put yourself into enmity with those who are expert in the science of politics. Where a king has no allies, but has two enemies, the best course of action for him is to accept the better of the two enemies as an ally. Get rid of an enemy while yet in the incipient stages of enmity, because a thorny tree can be easily pulled out when it is young. If it is full grown, it will damage the hand that cuts. In regard to secret enmity, take every care to protect yourself against it. If neglected, it is likely to cut without your knowing it, like the knife of the potter. Having to get on with those not in agreement with you is like living in a bower harbouring a cobra. Not to be contemptuous of those who are capable of carrying out what they resolve upon is the best security among all that has to be secured for one's safety. Here the reference is in the first instance to those possessed of the three qualities that invariably bring success, *viz.*, efficient command (Sans. *prabhāva;* Tam. *perumai*), penetrating knowledge (Sans. *mantram;* Tamil *aṛivu*), capacity for effort, (Sans. *utsāham*; Tam. *muyarchi*).[1] Those possessed of these in ample measure ought not to be disregarded. Those of elevated circumstances in life should not be displeased. By their displeasure even great Indra, the king of kings, lost his kingship in the course of its full enjoyment.

The next five chapters of this section have to do with what the Arthaśāstra[2] writers call *Vyasanas.* Among them the most important, of course, is association with women. This is dealt with in two chapters; the first with what we might call legitimate and the next illegitimate; in other words to be henpecked is as much of an evil as to be led away by hireling women. Only the character of the dangerous consequences differs. The next is the vice of drink, which it is enjoined ought,

[1]Ar. Śas. Bk. VI. II. [2]Bk. VIII. 3.

under all circumstances, to be avoided. The next one is the vice of dice. The last is the chapter dealing with illness and its treatment. The illnesses to which human flesh is heir are divided into two classes; those which are the result of bad deeds in a previous birth and therefore incurable; the cure for such diseases being only the removal of the causes. But those illnesses that come of accident are curable, and the treatment of those are dealt with in this last chapter. With this Tiruvaḷḷuvar brings to a close his treatment of the limbs of soverignty, or the constituents that go to make up a state.

Next comes a section named miscellaneous, which consists of thirteen chapters. The first chapter deals with high birth, that is, birth in a family of standing, and what ought to be the characteristics of well born people. After defining what exactly is meant by high birth and the characteristic features that mark it, he proceeds to deal with the regard and esteem that one should cherish for the maintenance of the high standing. The next is that which constitutes greatness, that is, the doing of deeds difficult of performance, the avoidance of vanity or mean pride, complete control of the evil propensities of talking ill of others. The next chapter has reference to the maintenance of the dignity that is thus acquired, and how to persevere in it. The next deals with the conduct that such people usually adopt, and ought to adopt, in order to maintain themselves in that high position, which is their due. The next deals with wealth, particularly the wealth which is not applied for the legitimate enjoyment of him that earns it, and for giving to those that deserve it. To them that are not accustomed to giving to the deserving, nor used to enjoying it in legitimate ways, wealth is of no use even if it should be counted in a series of crores. That contains in a nutshell the idea of the whole section. The next section deals with shame, the feeling that makes people shrink from saying or doing things unworthy. The next one lays down instructions for raising the good family in which one may be born to a higher position. The efforts required to secure for it a higher position morally than what it actually possesses to start with. The following chapter relates to agriculture, which lays down the indispensable character and the ennobling virtue of agricultural work, as all good is possible only where living is possible, agriculture certainly comes in for the highest position in life. Then follows a section on poverty and what evils poverty is generally capable of producing. Then follows the section on begging. This is dealt with in two chapters. The first deals with the chapter, relating to cases where begging is not perhaps dishonourable, what is ordinarily understood by the term, mendicancy, which is held in high esteem rather than looked down upon. Notwithstanding this esteem, begging as begging is not held in high regard. It is generally looked down upon, and this feeling, and the other evil consequences that begging brings are dealt with in the next section. To the poverty that leads one to this kind of begging, death is preferrable. Then follows a chapter, the final one in this section, which treats of the vulgar, those given to low life and low living. Strangely enough, low people are compared to the Dēvas. But the comparison extends only to the similarity between the two in their being both alike not amenable to discipline. In the case of the Devas, they are a law unto themselves and are not subject to outside control, while in the case of the other, outside control is useless and self discipline is absent. The rest of the section draws attention to the features that go to constitute this vulgar crowd and by implication, Tiruvaḷḷuvar wants that these qualities should be avoided by those that do not wish to be regarded as vulgar men.

It will be seen from this abbreviated analysis of the section, the largest of the three in the Muppāl or Kuṛal, that, while the section on polity does follow the *Smritis* and the Arthaśāstra teaching generally, the dominant note in the treatment is the teaching of morality. While therefore giving details of caution, the Kuṛal proceeds both by way of command (*viḍhi*) and by way of prohibition (*nishēda*), to let its readers know what is commendable and therefore ought to be practised, and what is not commendable and therefore to be avoided. With this general moral purpose, dominating the whole, he still brings into his treatment, as far as is compatible from the point of view of literary propriety, as much of a detailed treatment of political life as it is possible to do. The Kuṛal polity therefore is not complete in itself. It requires to be supplemented, as in fact even the Arthaśāstra has to be supplemented, in certain particulars; but, being not so deliberately laid out for a detailed treatment of governance, the principles are given in general terms. When supplemented in the way it should be done, it gives a more or less complete, though general idea, of what political institutions were; at any rate, were intended to be.

DEVELOPMENT OF ADMINISTRATIVE INSTITUTIONS IN THE AGE OF THE PALLAVAS.

The Pallavas of the Inscriptions, who they were—Tiraiyans, their predecessors—Tiraiyan of Pavattiri Iḷam-Tiraiyan of Kanchi—These known as Toṇḍamāns, also Pallavas, alternatively—The Pallavas of the inscriptions were Pallavas of Kānchī—They ruled over Toṇḍamaṇḍalam and the territory north of it, up to the Krishna—Their early records, the Prakrit charters refer to the northern part of their territory generally—The glimpses of the administration from these charters—Same in character as the Āndhra Administration. How far are these in agreement with the Artha-śāstra and the Asokan organisation—Pallavas of the Sanskrit charters—Greater extent of their territory and influence. The Gangas and the Kadambas feudatory to them. The explanation of their dominant position. Glimpses of administration in the Sanskrit charters.

LECTURE III.

ADMINISTRATION IN THE AGE OF THE PALLAVAS.

The age of the Pallavas covers six centuries and like other chronological divisions is, more or less, an artificial division. It may be taken to cover the period from A.D. 300 to A.D. 900, the limits being only approximate in either case. These six centuries may be regarded as centuries in which the influence of the dynasty of the Pallavas of Kānchī was dominant in South India. Before proceeding to study the political institutions of this particular period, we ought to know who the Pallavas were and what influences are likely to have been introduced, if any at all, during the period of their dominance, in this department primarily, and perhaps incidentally in others. These Pallavas as they show themselves in the earliest of their records are Pallavas of Kānchī, that is, they were a dynasty of rulers who called themselves Pallavas, and who issued their charters, etc., constituting the inscriptional material that has come down to us from Kānchī, as the royal headquarters of that dynasty. They are therefore described as Pallavas of Kānchī and they were known throughout the period of history covered by their inscriptions by this designation. As far as the material accessible to us takes us at present, this dynasty of rulers seems to have come into the territory of Toṇḍamaṇḍalam of the Tamils, after the disappearance of the rule of the Āndhras in the Dakhan and the decline of the power of their successors, the Chūṭuṇāgas in the Karnāṭak and the Southern Mahratta country to the north-westward.

They seem to have advanced from the region known as the special province of the Sātavāhanas, and occupied the territory to which Kānchī gives the name, the Tamil division known as Tonḍamanḍalam among the Tamils, Tunḍīra or Tunḍākarashtra among the Sanskritists.

The term "Pallava" is one of evil import, according to the standard Tamil lexicons, which give to it as a meaning or synonym the term *kayavar,* to whom the Kuṛaḷ itself devotes a chapter, the last chapter of the 70 constituting the ***Poruḷ*** (***Artha***) section of the ***Kuṛaḷ***. The term, as it is applied in this class of authoritative works of Tamil, designates a class of people who must have been quite barbarian in character, and had not advanced much in culture and the other elements that constitute civilisation. That apparently is not the term as applied to this dominant dynasty of the Tamil land of the age of the Pallavas. The term Pallava, as applied to them, seems merely the Sanskrit word Pallava, meaning the tender twig of any plant or tree. The reason given for this use of the word is that the first man that had acquired this designation for himself was one who had to be recognised by the twig of a Tonḍai creeper (Byronia grandis). Hence the name Tonḍamān for him. Unfortunately for this derivation, however, the term Tonḍamanḍalam seems to be earlier and seems to have earlier use in Tamil literature; at any rate, the term Pallava as a synonym of Tonḍamān is not barred by this incompatability. As applied to this dynasty, therefore, the term is a translation of the word, and Tonḍamān the ruler over Tonḍamaṇḍalam irrespective of the family or the dynasty to which he belonged. Hence Toṇḍaiyar is the people, Toṇḍamaṇḍalam the land of the Toṇḍaiyar as a region inhabited by them; and Toṇḍamān or Toṇḍaiyarkōn is the chief or ruler among them: All of them alike stand translated by the term Pallava in Sanskrit, and, what perhaps adds to the confusion, is that the term is used in earlier Tamil literature as the synonym of Toṇḍamān, and even in a combination such as this, Toṇḍaip-Pallavan, which could only mean "the Pallava of the Toṇḍai twig", which perhaps indicates that the name Pallava originated as of application to this particular dynasty. Hence the dynastic name Pallava. It has therefore to be actually held as synonymous with the Toṇḍaiyar with this difference that in Tamil Toṇḍaiyar seems primarily intended to denote the inhabitants of the region, the dynasty deriving its name as being the ruler of those inhabitants by the very constitution of the word, Toṇḍaiyarkōn or Toṇḍamān. So far, therefore, it is clear that the name has had nothing whatever to do with the distant Pallavas or the Sanskrit Pahlava of the inscriptions and the Purāṇas, a dynasty of foreigners that settled in the distant north-west, where the Purāṇas speak of them, or in the region of Gujarat and Kathiawad and the north Konkon coast where the inscriptions refer to them. To affiliate the one with the other would require more historical evidence than has been produced, or for the matter of that than we can produce at present, and therefore it would be safer to leave the possibility of any connection between the two aside till we have a more clear indication.

Who were the inhabitants or rulers of Toṇḍamaṇḍalam before these Pallavas came into occupation of Kānchī? As far as we can trace, the name Toṇḍamaṇḍalam was the region, Toṇḍaiyar were the inhabitants. Hence it would be safer to regard the Toṇḍaiyar as a tribe of people with a totem in the Toṇḍai creeper, and consituting the earlier inhabitants of the locality. In the class of works known as the Śangam collections generally, two rulers come into view in this locality distinctly known by the term Tiraiyan. We have the name of a Tiraiyan in the Ahanānūṟu collection, whose territory comprised the territory round the hill of Tirupati, which was included in the Toṇḍamaṇḍalam, and who had his capital at a place called Pavattiri, Pavattiri that in later inscriptions is described as the Pavattiri in Kākandināḍu, which was swallowed up by the sea (*Kaḍalkoṇḍa Kākandināḍu*). What is more, this Tiraiyan of Pavattiri is described as possessed of Vēngaḍam as the hill par-excellence in his territory. With the *Nāḍu,* Toṇḍamaṇḍalam, capital Pavattiri and hill Vēngaḍam, this ruler would be ruler, if not of the whole of Toṇḍamaṇḍalam, at least of the northern part of it. The second name is that of a Tiraiyan associated with Kānchī, and known to this body of literature as Iḷam Tiraiyan of Kānchī. Iḷam Tiraiyan or younger Tiraiyan for this particular ruler involves *ipso facto* an elder Tiraiyan, who probably was the other Tiraiyan. This younger Tiraiyan's name is associated with Kānchī by contemporary writers, and literary tradition gets to regard him as a descendant of a Chola king by a Nāga princess. Nāga tribes were in occupation of at least a part of the territory included in the term Toṇḍamaṇḍalam, and a substantial part of the inhabitants of that territory seem to describe themselves as Nāgas even in later inscriptions; and the names of several Nāgas are found in inscriptions in Mahābalipuram even of a later date. Whatever be the value of the story, his descending from the Chola dynasty is acknowledged even in contemporary writings and a poem[1] composed in his honour, states in one place that he was called a Tiraiyan as having been brought first of all by the *Tirai* or *Kaḍal* (the waves or the sea used synonymously) referring, of course, to a part of the story, that when the mother sent him to the Chola monarch with the Toṇḍai creeper to distinguish him, the ship carrying him suffered shipwreck near the coast, and, while the baby was given up as lost by the merchant who had charge of him, the baby was lashed ashore and was discovered alive, and ultimately presented to the Chola ruler. In another context of the same poem, he is described as coming of the family of Rama of Ayodhya, and the passage may be interpreted as of the royal family of Ayodhya generally also. In later copper plate and other inscriptions which give long genealogies of the Chola family, a certain number of names of the dynasty of Ikshvakus is made to figure, among them the ruler Sibi, who cut off his flesh from his body and gave it to the hunter-bird to save a dove. The value of these traditions and contemporary references apart, Iḷam Tiraiyan of Kānchī was a Tiraiyan just as much as his predecessor of this name, and his association with the contemporary Chola family is stated in terms that admit of no doubt. He was a

1. Perumbāṇaṟṟuppaiḍai in the collection Pattupāṭṭu.

Chola prince, a prince-viceroy of Kānchī. It is in that capacity that all the poems that refer to him in Tamil actually describe him. All the Sangam poems that refer to Kanchi, and poems that are capable of being brought into association with them referring to Kānchī, do not make mention of the Pallavas, any of them, whom we find mentioned in, and whose succession can more or less be satisfactorily arranged on the basis of, the inscriptions, Prakrit, Sanskrit and Tamil. So the ruler Iḷam Tiraiyan has to be associated necessarily with the period to which these works relate, and must be regarded as a ruler anterior to the period of the inscriptions of the Pallavas of Kānchī. Any assertion to the contrary involves the responsibility of proof that the time to which this body of literature is ascribed was a time during which the actual Pallava that ruled at Kānchī was Toṇḍamān Iḷam Tiraiyan himself, or identifiable with him on satisfactory grounds. Such satisfactory evidence has not been forthcoming during the last quarter of a century and may not be forthcoming at all. The Pallavas of Kānchi, therefore, to whom inscriptions refer, have to be held as rulers of Kānchī undoubtedly, but rulers that came after the age of Iḷam Tiraiyan.

Among the inscriptions of the Pallavas so far made accessible to us, the oldest inscriptions are the so-called Prakrit inscriptions. These refer all of them to the territory north, or to the north-west of Toṇḍaman-ḍalam proper. The language in which these inscriptions are recorded is Prakrit, and the way that the dates are defined follow the system adopted by the

Āndhras in their inscriptions. This would naturally presume association with the Āndhras and contact with their territory, if not, the character of having been constituent parts of their territory so far as the localities to which these inscriptions refer are concerned. As a matter of fact, the more important of these inscriptions are all of them on the frontier of the Āndhra dominions, and certain parts, at any rate, must be held to have constituted a definite part of the Āndhra territory as such. Among the most important of these, the Maidavolu plates have reference to the territory quite close to the Krishna. The Hirahadagalli plates refer to the Bellary district probably, and the stone inscription of Khandanaga, of a time somewhat earlier than these, is on a rock near Adoni. These refer distinctly to the Sātāhani Āhāra and Sātāhani Raṭṭa, the Āhāra or the portion allotted to the Sātāvahana or Sātāhani Raṭṭa, a division belonging to the Sātavāhanas. In either case, it would mean the territory was the part of the country peculiarly associated with the Sātavāhanas. These inscriptions are not in the territory that is included in the Tamil division Toṇḍamaṇḍalam, but immediately to the north of it, just outside the territory coming within the definition of the term Toṇḍamaṇḍalam, in its widest extent. The Toṇḍamaṇḍalam frontier on the north could be taken only up to Gudur or the northern shores of the Pulikat Lake. A line drawn from there across into the interior would be bounded on the western side by the territory of the Bāṇas, and would not come very far from the Cuddapah District. But with the Pallavas of the inscriptions who issued their charters from Kānchī as their capital, their territory distinctly included a wider stretch on the north extending from the frontiers of the Bellary District, perhaps including a part of it, along the line of Tungabhadra down to the Krishna and thence to its mouth roughly. So from the beginning of Pallava rule, we find them associated with a wider stretch of territory. It was pointed out already that in early Tamil literature Vēngaḍam marked the northern boundary roughly; the frontier itself was described as the Vaḍuha frontier, and the territory on the other side of the frontier was territory where language changed, sometimes described specifically as Vaḍuha territory. Among those conquered by Karikāla,[1] we find the Aruvāḷar, the inhabitants of Aruvānāḍ and Aruvā Vaḍatalai, and on the farther north of them, the Vaḍavar which perhaps was only another form of the name Vaḍuhar. Therefore then, unlike the

[1]Paṭṭinappālai: ll. 272—92.

பெரும்பாழ் செய்து மமையான் மருங்கற
மலையகழ்க்குவனே கடறூர்க்குவனே
வான்வீழ்க்குவனே வளி மாற்றுவனெனத்
தான்முன்னிய துறை போகலிற்
பல்லொளியர் பணிபொடுங்கத்
தொல்லருவாளர் தொழில் கேட்ப
வடவர் வாடக் குடவர் கூம்பத்
தென்னவன்றிறல் கெடச்சீறி மன்னர்
மன்னெயில் கதுவு மதனுடை நோன்றாண்
மாத்தானை மறமொய்ம்பிற்
செங்கண்ணாற் செயிர்த்துநோக்கி
புன்பொதுவர் வழிபொன்ற
இருங்கோவேண் மருங்குசாயக்
காடுகொன்று நாடாக்கிக்
குளந்தொட்டு வளம் பெருக்கிப்
பிறங்குநிலை மாடத்துறந்தை போக்கிக்
கோயிலொடு குடிநிறீஇ
வாயிலொடு புழையமைத்து
ஞாயிறொறும் புதைநிறீஇப்
பொருவேமெனப் பெயர்கொடுத்
தொருவேமெனப் புறக்கொடாது
திருநிலைஇய பெருமன்னெயின்
மின்னொளியெறிப்பத் தம்மொளி மழுங்கி

Tondamans of Kānchī, the Pallavas of the charters ruled over an extent of territory, which, while it came to be known as Tondamandalam in an extended sense, constituted two distinct parts, the Tondamandalam proper belonging, as it were, to the Tamil country and a stretch of country outside the region of the Tamil country and described perhaps as peculiar to the fief of the Sātavāhanas, and therefore belonging to territory outside the limits of the Tamil land and Tondamandalam alike, and perhaps included, before this period, in the territory of the Andhras. The passing out of existence of the Āndhra power it is that brings the Pallavas to notice on this side of their frontier, as in fact it brings the Chutunagas into prominence on the south-western side of the Āndhra country proper. That being the character of the Pallava rulers of the south according to their earliest charters, and the prevalence of their authority over a region outside the strict frontiers of the Tamil land, such institutions as the charters indicate of a political character may be regarded as institutions belonging to a land outside the Tamil country proper. We shall proceed to a consideration of these and describe them as clearly as we can, before we make any effort to trace their influence upon such institutions as must have existed, purely of a Tamil character in the times before them, to estimate such influence as these may have exercised in modifying the character of the latter.

The most important of these inscriptions from our point of view are the Hirahadagalli plates conveying a grant of Pallava Śiva Skanda Varman. The grant is issued by Sivaskandavarma, Dharma-Maharajadhiraja Śiva Skandavarman, of the Bhāradvāja Gotra and of the Pallava family, who had celebrated *Agnishtoma, Vājapēya,* and *Aśvamēdha* sacrifices. The charter was issued from Kānchī. The following points deserve notice. The capital of the Mahārāja is Kānchī. He takes credit for having celebrated Brahmanical sacrifices. He gives himself the *gotra* Bhāradvāja, and describes himself as belonging to the dynasty of the Pallavas. He further gives himself the special title "*Dharma*" before the royal designation Mahārāja, a term affected by Asoka. This *Dharma* in the Asokan inscriptions has always been interpreted as involving Buddhism as the religion of the person who so described himself. It is hardly justified, as the maintenance of the *Dharma* was the first duty of all Indian rulers, Brahman, Jain or Buddhist, and *Dharma* has there its own particular application in political science, *dharma* that actually regulated life in society, and therefore based on the Hindu conception of society as such; or, to be more specific the Brahman conception of society as such which finds definition in the law books. We pass from that to the next section that is really what concerns us most. The charter conveys the grant of certain bits of land of a village already gifted away to a Brahman Golaśarman of the *Ātrēya gōtra,* to whom the Mahārāja Bappasāmi had already granted the free gift village *Chillarēka.* Bappasāmi here stands for the ruler whom we know only by this designation, which simply means the Lord Bappa, or My revered father (*Bappa*). In this case it merely refers to the father, and the term

"Mahārājādhirāja Bappa pāda anudhyāta" became a formula in later times, and inscriptions of the great Nandivarman contain this expression. The gift of a village and of lands lying adjacent to the village itself is a matter of concern to all those who are concerned in the government of the division in which the land lies. Naturally therefore we may expect some kind of a reference to these. As a matter of fact Indian charters when they convey these grants address the officers and the inhabitants of the localities concerned, and notify the gift as a public announcement with a view to informing the people and assuring to the donee the actual possession of the gift. So this charter begins by saying that the gift is addressed to all concerned in this *vishaya* or division. The officials concerned are successively *Rājakumāra, Sēnāpati, Rāshṭrika, Maḍabina, Dēśādhikṛita* and others; also *gama-gama-Bhojaka,* those in the enjoyment of the revenues of each grama, *Vallava,* those that are high in the affections of the king (confidential officers), *Govallava* (those who have the looking after of the management of the cows, perhaps domestic animals generally). Then follows the term *Amachcha* (Sans. Amātya or Tam. Amaichu) ministers; *Aranādhikate* (Araṇyādhikrita, superintendents of forest tracts), *Ghumike* (division commanders), Tūtike (Dūtakas or agents), Nēyike (leaders of platoons) and others such as, under our orders, travel through the territory as our officers. These have to note that we have "for increase of ourselves and of our family in respect of our good deeds, length of life, strength and fame as also victory and prosperity", added this as an additional gift to the free gift village of Chillarēka given by Mahārāja Bappasāmi "whose commands were unopposed and who made a free gift of many crores of gold coins and hundreds of thousands of cows and ploughs." The gift is given as a *parihāra*. This gift *parihāram* was rendered generally as meaning freedom from the incidence of the ordinary dues to Government upon the land. But *parihāra,* in a technical sense, is found in the Ārtha Śāstra which lays down *anugraha* and *parihāra,* as the two ways in which a gift may be given. Where gifts are made either by *anugraha* or by *parihāra,* the king should take care that they are so given as to make for the increase of the royal treasury. That is the literal translation of the passage where it occurs, and suitably to the context, Mahamahopadhyaya R. Shama Sastry translates it "the king shall bestow on cultivators only such favour and *remission* (*anugraha* and *parihāra*) as will tend to swell the treasury." When of course it is followed by gifts, these should not be made in a way to deplete the treasury. The idea seems to be generally that, where gifts have to be made, the gifts be made in a way not to prejudice the royal revenue but much rather in a way to promote it. While the general import of the position is quite clear, the actual application of the terms *anugraha* and *parihāra* cannot be said to be clear. Mahamahopadhyaya Gaṇapathi Sastrigal makes a distinction between the two. Pecuniary help that is given in order to improve the quality of that which is fit for yielding revenue is *anugraha,* possibly implying such advances in money, etc., which are made for purposes of improving cultivation; whereas *parihāra* is for bringing into condition that which is out of condition for yielding revenue. This would mean such considerations as may be shown for reclamation of that which has to be reclaimed. *Parihāra* therefore, in this sense, would mean not necessarily remissions of taxes, but such consideration as may be shown with a view to the improvement that is expected to be brought about by cultivators. It seems intended to apply to gifts, of which examples are not wanting in inscriptional literature, where various considerations are shown to individuals who in different degrees labour to bring uncultivated or uncultivable land into cultivation. In the particular grant under reference where agricultural land is given to a particular individual, the *parihāras* would mean perhaps such concessions of revenue as would enable the donee to go on prosperously with the gift made to him. In this case it probably was meant to release the land given from certain of the incidences of revenue and other miscellaneous demands that would fall upon ordinary lands. The term *parihāra* is used in the Maidavolu grant, which is actually addressed to the governor (Vāpaṭa, Sans. Vyāprita), the official agent at Dhannakaṭa (Dhānyakaṭaka). The *parihāras* are indicated as freedom from digging for salt, freedom from the control of the garrison of the division, freedom from the supply of bullocks in succession, freedom from the entrance of soldiers, and freedom from the supply of boiled rice, water pots, cots, dwellings, etc. The explanation given here of the *parihāras* is not exactly the gift of money or the remission of taxes, but seems to be much rather being excused from those demands, which, though not regular taxes, were still the customary demands of seigniorage dues, on the European analogy. The first term used is *aloṇakhādakam* that is freedom from others digging for salt. *araṭasamvināyikam* which seems to mean the necessity to render assistance to the Rashṭrīya (provincial) guards on occasions. Then the third is *aparamparābalīvardhakam,* the necessity to supply bullocks in relief for the use of travellers, official and other, which is one of the incidences of village life, and continues even now. The next one is *abhaṭapapēśam,* Sanskrit *abhaṭapravēśam,* which means the entry of *Bhaṭas* or royal servants. Taken along with what is laid down in the Hirahadagalli and other plates, it seems to imply the entry of officials sent by order of the king for various purposes, and seems to be intended for those commissioners of information deputed to look about and inform the headquarters as to what is taking place; and then the last which is rather dubious, *akuracholakavinasikhata-samvāsam,* which is freedom from the supply of boiled rice, water pots, cots and dwellings. Compared with what is contained in the Hirahadagalli plates, this actually seems to imply supply of food for the march, supply of water for the same purpose and things like that, although one part of the term is still quite obscure. For our present purpose this obscurity is not a great hindrance. The general sense is clear that the *parihāras* are the freedom from such duties and services to which ordinary lands were liable, and the possession of such lands subjected the owners to the duty of seeing to these supplies when called upon to do so. Apparently *Dēvadāya* and *Brhamadēya* lands were freed from these, which according to the general sense of the Arthaśāstra are inflictions upon the possession of land and their removal constitutes rather a relief than a gift.

What is more important to our purpose is really the different classes of officers referred to. The officers of a division are more or less described fully in the Hirahadagalli plates. The Maidavolu grant except mentioning just one of them, the official agent, does not appear to refer to any other. Perhaps a little closer attention is required in respect to these. Here are first the *Rājakumāra,* who probably, as in the days of Asoka, was the viceroy of the locality. Then follows the next one *Sēnāpati* or commander of the division. Then follows the *Rāshṭrika,* the civil governor of the district. Then comes in a word *Māḍabinu,* as it is written, and generally read *Māḍabinas* or *Manḍapikas* and interpreted differently. *Maḍubika* is taken to stand for *Maḍambaka,* and, on the authority of certain Jain works, which use the term, is regarded as a division. *Maḍamba* and *Maḍaba* seem to refer more or less to what is the modern word Manḍapa, which are centres for the collection of customs. In that sense it would mean the revenue officers whose function it is to collect the customs of the government. Then the smaller officials, *Dēśādhikritas,* the rulers over Dēśas or districts. Then follows another class, those in the enjoyment of single villages, that is people to whom villages have been given in various forms of assignment. Then follows the term *Vallava,* which is interpreted as herdsmen; but in the light of the term *govallabha,* which follows, it is not clear whether it should be so interpreted.

Another sense suggested is those that are in the particular confidence of the king, that is, those confidential officers of the king who are sent into these localities for the purpose of confidential information to the king. *Govallabhas* are those whose function it is to superintend herds of cows primarily, perhaps including other herds of cattle as well. Then the class called ministers or *Amachcha, Amātya,* and then the guards called here *arakhadhikata,* Sans. *āraksha* and *adhikrita,* officers whose function it is to protect the inhabitants. Then follows the word *Gumika* (Sans. *Gulmika*) referred to as captains. The word Gulma in Sanskrit seems generally to apply to a division of the army, a sort of complete army corps of the modern times. The term Gulma is used in the Ramayana in the sense of one of the seven parts in which an army is divided for the purpose of marching, and even for camping on the field of battle. *Tūtikas* and *Nēyikas* are not explained. *Nēyikas* may correspond exactly to Nāyakās commanders of platoons or small bodies of soldiers. Then follows the last division, the *saṁcharantaka* and *baḍamanusha.* They are both of them described as being sent out under the orders of the king (*amha pēsana payutte,* Sanskrit *asmat prēshana prayukta,* sent by explicit commands from us). Notwithstanding the fact that the significance of some of the terms is far from clear, this list of officers gives us a more or less correct general idea as to how exactly the government was organised, and, in respect of a grant such as that of a free gift of a village in a particular division, the whole class of officials that are concerned have necessarily to be notified. Even so, so much is clear that the whole hierarchy of officials mentioned are actually officers whose authority was a controlling authority, and not exactly what constituted the local administration. That seems the feature that is peculiar to these grants, which have relation to territory which is outside the Tamil land and, perhaps what is more, territory that had been under the government of Asoka and the Āndhras succeeding him. Even when the Pallavas succeeded to the government of these the administration still continued on the lines laid down by the predecessors of the Pallavas in the government of this tract. This is not just exactly what has been found to prevail in the Tamil country, which constituted one half of the Pallava territory. So far, at any rate, we have discovered nothing corresponding to it in the sources of information that are available.

We shall now have to consider, as far as it is possible for us to glean the information from sources accessible, what it was in the Tamil country proper. We have no information corresponding to this period in the Tamil country proper except what we have been able to put together from literary sources. Vague as the information is from these sources and perhaps not giving as much detail as some of these Prakrit charters, the general indications still seem to show that the organisation perhaps was not altogether dissimilar. We spoke of the officials, and the ministers and officials constituting a class of eighteen, and some of those[1] that are referred to in that large group would agree to some extent with some of those mentioned in this group of officers referred to categorically in these Prakrit charters. For the details regarding Tamil country under Pallava rule, we have to pass on to the Sanskrit charters, no Prakrit charters having been brought to notice relating to that part of the country in the particular period. But coming to the Sanskrit charters themselves, we seem to find the same kind of organisation, at least in the northern part of the Pallava territory. A charter of Kumāravishṇu describes him as a ***Dharma-Mahārāja*** of the Pallavas, reminding us, as it were of some of the edicts of Asoka. Taking the Chandalūr grant of Kumāravishṇu, the charter begins with the Karmākarāshṭra, in which was situated the Chandalūr ***grāma*** giving the larger division *rāshṭra,* and the unit ***grāma.*** The officials to whom reference is made in this do not pretend to be exhaustive; but, at the same time indicate the hierarchy of officials, mentioning, as they do, the *nyōgikas* and the *vallabhas,*[2] who are both of them employed in

[1]Śilappadhikāram 26 ll 37—42.

விரவுக்கொடி யடுக்கத்து நிரயத்தானையோ
டைம்பெருங் குழுவு மெண்பேராயமும்
வெம்பரியானை வேந்தற்கோங்கிய
கருமவினைஞருங் கணக்கியல் வினைஞருந்
தருமவினைஞருந் தந்திர வினைஞரு
மண்டிணிஞால மாள்வோன் வாழ்கெனப்

With the army with their flags held aloft in a line close to each other, the five great bodies and eight great groups, the administrative officers in the service of great kings, officers of the accounts, supervisors of the Dharma, and those engaged in other various items of executive work.

[2]Cf. *Samcharamtakas* and *Badamanushas* of the Prakrit charters.

exercising royal authority in relation to the *grāmas.* There is a broad classification between those that carried out orders, nyōgikas and those that are "in the affections of the king" meaning probably the officials in the confidence of the king. The reference in general terms to these two classes of officers connected with village administration indicates a continuance of the organisation, and the gift is made in the customary manner of free gifts to Brahmans exempting other free gifts to the Gods, with all the reliefs (*sarva-parihāra*) was made over by the way of the plough (*hala nyāyēna*). This last term *hala nyāyēna* seems to refer to the drawing of the plough round a village with a view to marking the boundary. So again in the period of the Sanskrit charters, which are later than that of the Prakrit, we get an insight into an organisation similar in character to the Prakrit charters extending even to detail.

In the Pikira grant[1] of Simhavarman, who belongs almost to the same generation as Kumāravishṇu of the Chandalur grant, we get a glimpse of perhaps the same organisation as in the former. The grant here was issued from the camp at *Mēnmātūra,* and refers to the grant of the village Pikira in the Muṇḍarāshṭra. The persons addressed are the *grāmyakas,* generally inhabitants of the *grāmas;* the *adhikritas,* officials placed over these, (*sarvādhyaksha*) officials exercising supervision or control. Then there follows the *vallavas,* that is, the confidential agents of the government, and the *śāsana sancharaṇas,* the same as the *saṁcharan-*

[1]Epi. Indica, Vol. VIII, page 161.

takas and *badamanushas* sent out under "our express commands" of the Hiragadagalli plates. These refer to the ordinary officials as detailed in the previous grants. These again refer to the northern districts only. The Ongoḍu grant, No. 1 is again a grant by Skandavarman perhaps coming in a previous generation to Kumāravishṇu and Simhavarman. This was issued from Tamrāpa the *Vijayasthāna*,[1] meaning nothing more than the victorious camp, and refers to the gift of Ongōḍu in Karmarāshtra. The charter is issued on the word of Skandavarman to the *adhikritas* and *āyuktakas*, that is, to those appointed to exercise authority and those who are sent out on commissions alike, and the gift is made in a kind of gift called *sātvikadāna*, and was made into a free gift to a Brahman excluding from it gifts to Gods and that which has to be excluded as uncultivated (*halavarja*) together with the eighteen kinds of reliefs, *ashṭā-daśavida parihāra*. What the eighteen *parihāras* are is not explained; but the general statement follows that the village must be free of all the *parihāras*. There again we seem to find the same kind of an organisation, and similar treatment of it in respect of the grant.

[1]*Sthāna* here, same as modern *Thāṇa*, stands for the central dominating town of the Artha-Śāstra, the *Sthānīya* set over 800 villages.

IV

DEVELOPMENT OF ADMINISTRATIVE INSTITUTIONS IN THE AGE OF THE GREAT PALLAVAS.

The Great Pallavas—The extent of their territory and the establishment of their ascendency. The earlier inscriptions of these. The light thrown upon the administration by the Vaikunṭhapperumāḷ inscriptions regarding the succession of Nandivarman Pallavamalla. How far in agreement with earlier notions of polity and practice. The Pandyan charters and the light they shed on administration in the Tamil country. Later inscriptions. Further development of the administration. Its composite character. Tamil local institutions and Asokan and Artha Śāstra Central Government.

LECTURE IV.

ADMINISTRATIVE INSTITUTIONS IN THE AGE OF THE GREAT PALLAVAS.

In regard to the Pallavas of the Sanskrit charters, their general position as a South Indian power has to be noted. While the mere find places of the Prakrit charters indicated an extent of territory to the north of Toṇḍamaṇḍalam proper over which the Pallavas exercised their authority, the Sanskrit charters seem to indicate a greater extent of territory over which the Pallava authority was acknowledged. During the period of the Sanskrit charters, the Pallava overlordship was acknowledged on one side by the Gangas according to their Penugoṇḍa plates where successive rulers were installed by representatives of the rulers of the Pallava dynasty as a suzerain power. The story relating to Mayūraśarman, and the way that the Kadambas rose to power as a ruling dynasty in South India seem again to indicate that the Pallava overlordship was more or less recognised by the Kadambas themselves, and this seems probable if the Nāga alliance between the Pallavas of the east and the Chuṭunāgas, the successors of the Āndhras in the south-west of their territory, should be considered historical. At any rate, the clear statement in the Sanskrit charters of the Pallavas that Vīrakūrcha became ruler of a kingdom as the result of a marriage with a Nāga princess would certainly warrant this assumption and this exactly was perhaps a title that placed the Kadambas, the successors of the Chuṭunāgas in this territory in a feudatory position to the Pallavas of Kānchī. Therefore the Pallavas of the Sanskrit charters exercised authority over a far greater extent of territory than perhaps those of the Prakrit charters, and their authority seems to have extended to take into it the whole of the Southern Mahratta country and the kingdom of Banavāsi or Vaijayanti, both of which were under the rule of the Āndhras, and after them of the Chūṭunāgas. If the Gangas were feudatory to the Pallavas, that would bring in the present-day state of Mysore within their territory, and the territory of the Bāṇas seems similarly to have been more or less under their influence. Thus the Pallavas stood the dominant northern power in the Tamil country proper, the territory to the south of them being divided among the three kings. We can therefore understand clearly the contact into which Kumāravishṇu II, comes with the Cholas, and at the end of this period, the Pallava power had extended to the river Kaveri, perhaps even to take into its territory Trichinopoly itself. The earliest achievement of the great Pallavas, whose authority begins in the last quarter of the sixth century with Simhavishṇu, is said to have been the conquest of the region of the Kaveri. His successor Mahēndravarman's inscriptions describe, in unmistakable terms, his authority over the region of the Kaveri. The period of the Sanskrit charters therefore is a period of the growth of Pallava power; and it is this growth of their power and the extent of territory, and the authority and influence they exercised over their neighbours, that paved the way for the achievements of the great Pallavas as a distinct dynasty, which began with Simhavarman, father of Simhavishṇu, and went on in succession through a number of generations till the dynasty came to an end. For a rough estimate of time, Simhavarman's dates would be somewhere about A.D. 575—580.

From what has been said of the inscriptions of this dynasty of the Pallavas, it would have become clear that these Pallavas exercised authority over a larger extent of territory, which was composed of a considerable part of the country beyond the limits of the Tamil land, and such details as we get of their administration, or details concerning the country beyond the borders of the Tamil land, are of a character not essentially different from that of the Sanskrit charters. Only here and there peers out a division, of which we get far more clear glimpses when we come to the rule of the great Pallavas and such of their inscriptions as are found in the Tamil country. For real light upon what actually the administrative details of the Tamil country were like, we have to go to the time of the great Pallavas, and it is only their inscriptions that throw full light. But even here, the charters that throw this light are charters not of the earliest members of the great dynasty of the Pallavas, but more or less of the later members, Paramesvaravarman I, or better, Nandivarman II, that is, from the middle of the seventh century A.D. From the charters of Nandivarman, we get an account of the details of the division of territory and the distribution even of the authority of government relating to the Tamil country. But before proceeding to consider these details, from the inscriptions, there is one incident of Pallava rule that has been brought to light recently which throws a considerable amount of light, indirect light though it be, on the principles and procedure in regard to the Pallava government. The incident is the historical incident of the succession to the throne of Nandivarman, Pallava Malla, who does not belong to the elder branch of the family of Simhavishṇu. Nandivarman used to be regarded as a usurper pure and simple. Considerable doubt had been cast upon this by the Pallava documents having been found to be contradictory in their statements in regard to his succession. The charters happen to be charters relating to the period of his reign or those of his successors. While some of them mention quietly that he succeeded Paramēśvara II, one of them goes the officious length of stating it that he was a son, or implying it, so that we are left in doubt as to the character of his succession. That doubt became somewhat enhanced, as, in his records generally, it is described that he had to fight against those who had taken part in favour of a Pallava prince Chitramāya. In the circumstances, the normal presumption was that Chitramaya probably was the legitimate successor trying to assert his claims with such support as he could get against the usurper Nandivarman Pallava Malla, and Nandivarman got the better of it after a serious and disastrous war. But luckily for history, the Vaikunṭhaperumāḷ temple in Conjeevaram, which seems to be a foundation of Nandivarman himself, contains on the walls of the *prākāra* a series of sculptures in stone divided into panels, each panel having a label, which describes what exactly the picture above was intended to describe. These sculptures have, in some cases, reference to things divine, but more generally human. The Epigraphical Department has succeeded in reading more or less satisfactorily a considerable number of these labels and given publicity to these in one of the later volumes of the South Indian Inscriptions, which were issued to the public without translations, etc., to save delay. Thirteen of these labels are read, and, excepting three or four which were considerbly damaged so as to make the meaning unintelligible, the rest of them could be read fully, and the few corruptions in the reading could be easily corrected. We are enabled to gain an idea of what actually took place. What took place throws some light upon the character of the government to some extent. It must be borne in mind that what is set down there in writing is a mere label, in each case intended to explain the picture above. With a picture before us to see, a label can of course afford to be very brief; and it is the picture that gives the idea, while the label is merely to indicate what the picture is intended to convey. Therefore the very brief statements that are made, though clear in themselves, are not meant to convey all the information. A considerable part of it has to be learnt from the picture itself. Each label is formed in this manner. "This is the place where such and such an incident took place," and the words are adjusted to suit this frame. The Pallava family came down in succession from Brahma. Paramēśvara Pōttarayan of this family went to Heaven. This is followed by the statement 'when the kingdom was thus upset, the ministers, the chief inhabitants of the Ghaṭika, Ghaṭika meaning the Brahman settlement, and the chief citizens called Mūlaprakriti met[1] and came to the conclusion that Hiraṇyavarma Mahārāja of the Pallava family (Kaṭavēśakula) was quite capable of bearing the responsibilities of ruling the kingdom, that he was of unsullied descent on both sides of his parentage, and that an embassy be sent to him to invite him to come to the throne'. The points to be noticed here are that the body of ministers were one group of people concerned. The chief inhabitants of the Brahman settlement was another group; and the Mūlaprakriti or the representatives of the citizens coming down in hereditary succession as the subjects of the Pallavas as the third group. These had to assemble and settle as to who should be the next ruler. While all the ministers may have assembled, it is impossible that all the inhabitants of the Ghaṭika could have assembled. All the learned Śrōtriya Brahmans of the Ghaṭika of the fame of Kānchī must have been too many for all of them to come together and be present. Whether this is so or no, there can be no doubt about the next item, the Mūlaprakriti, the hereditary subjects of the Pallavas, Prakriti, meaning here the general population, could not have been of such a number as could have come together even on an extraordinary occasion like this. They must have had some mode of bringing themselves together, so that the meeting may speak for the Brahman inhabitants and for the other inhabitants. That the population was so divided is likely as we find one of the Tamil groupings of the five great bodies contains the divisions, the Mahājana and the Brahmans,

[1]This corresponds to three out of the group of five: *Mahājanam*, *Pārpār*, Maruttar, Nimittar and *Amaichchar*.

Māśanam and the *Pārpār* constituting two of the five. Here the Mūlaprakriti stands for the Mahājana, the original and hereditary population of the country,[1] so that it is not the floating section of the population, or a new assembly somehow constituted, that is concerned here. It seems to be the old dominant division of the inhabitants and where they have to be consulted, they were probably consulted in the two divisions of the general population, and the Brahmans. The ministers are there as a body, and it was this body probably that took the steps to bring the people together, hold consultations, and do the needful to give effect to their resolutions. That is one point that comes out. The next is those people consult together, fix upon a possible successor, resolve upon a particular individual to be invited, and despatch a mission with authority to invite the individual chosen. They took care to see that the individual chosen belonged to the family of the Pallavas. His belonging to this family is at least a recommendation, if not altogether a guiding consideration. His capacity for bearing the responsibilities of royalty was the next point, and the next is that he was of unsullied descent on his father's as well as on his mother's side. Why should all this be done if there was a legitimate successor to Paramēśvaravarman who died? If we have to assume that there was a Pallava heir-apparent, though young, the description given to the territory that it had become *utsanna* by the death of the king would be inexplicable, or an interested lying statement. The Pallava whose name figures in the

[1] Cf. Aristotle's notion of citizenship.

war in which he had to be actually overcome by Nandivarman Pallava-malla may as well have been another collateral claimant rather than a regular heir-apparent. It would be very hard to characterise a specific statement of this description as a lie promulgated to cheat posterity unless we had evidence of the most direct character to the contrary. It can hardly be said that we have it. The embassy went to Hiraṇyavarma Mahārāja, and laid before him the proposition that they conveyed from the assembled inhabitants of Kānchī, and recommended his acceptance of the offer on the ground that his accession would shed lustre on the two families, meaning, in all probability, the family from which he descended in direct succession and the collateral family to which he was invited to become successor. That is the next picture. The third one is made to represent Hiraṇyavarman calling together the leading members of the Pallava family (Kulamallar), and putting the matter before them. He asked if any one of the leading members would be willing to accept the responsibility. All alike declined. Then he called together his four sons, viz., Śrīmalla, Raṇamalla, Sangrāmamalla, and Pallavamalla, and asked each one of them the same question. The first three declined on the ground that the responsibility was too heavy for them, while the last of them, Pallavamalla, otherwise Paramēśvara, the youngest among them gave a ready assent saying with alacrity "I shall go". The picture over the label shows the boy standing in an attitude of reverence and readiness to proceed. Hiraṇyavarman, who shrank from the responsibility himself now was a prey to mixed feelings. He is said to have suffered like one seriously hurt by an enemy's weapon, by the prospective pangs of separation from a promising son, who came forward with so much alacrity to shoulder a heavy responsibility, though it was not unmixed with the parental joy that the youngest of his sons gave promise of becoming really an ornament of the Kāṭaka family (family of the Pallavas). None the less, he protested that the responsibility was very great while his son was just a lad of twelve. He could not therefore let his son go. In this perplexity, Dharaṇikoṇḍa Pośar, who was the learned chief Āgamika said "this youth is designed to become emperor, having performed penance and pleased Mahāvishṇu". On hearing this Hiraṇyavarman stood consoled. The picture under which this label is, is intended to represent all this. Dharaṇikoṇḍa Pośar was apparently a Brahman and was an exponent of the *Āgamas,* that is, the procedure laid down for conducting workship in temples and matters relating thereto. Being in an analogous position to the priest (*Purohita*), naturally he tendered this advice.

The next is a picture where on the presentation by the ambassadors of what they had brought for presentation to the ruler-elect, Hiraṇyavarman presumably expressed surprise not being clear as to what exactly the things were. Dharaṇikoṇḍapośar explained to him that they were not elephant heads, but the crown and the head gear that his son, as the soverign elect, would have to wear, and Hiraṇyavarma Mahārāja is said to have felt greatly relieved. After this Hiraṇyavarman gave his assent and agreed to the departure of his son. It is rather surprising that Hiraṇyavarma Mahārāja, a comparatively old man, should feel surprised at the presentation of the ornaments. One would have expected he would have been present at previous coronations. It is not clear whether these were something different from the regalia ordinarily presented at coronation ceremonies. The fact that Dharaṇikondaposar pointed out that they were not the head of an elephant can lead to a presumption that the head gear was something like that of the Greek ruler Demetrios, whose head gear had an elephant trunk projecting in front, as exhibited on his coins. The peculiar kind of head gear referred to probably has reference to the custom of sending out a state elephant to find out a suitable successor, and, on such occasions, it was made to carry a garland in its trunk, which it threw round the neck of the individual chosen. The elephant sent out threw it usually round the neck of the individual, put him on his back and walked back, thus indicating the choice. It is not clear whether the ornaments conveyed by the embassy here had anything symbolical of this. The next picture has reference to the place where Pallavamalla gets down from his palanquin, falls prostrate at the feet of his father and his Brahman counsellor and companion, both of whom presented him with the weapons that he had to put on. The next one shows the prince as having arrived near Kanchi after a long journey, crossing hills, rivers and deep forests on the way. Pallavādhi Araiyar, on getting information of his arrival, went forward to meet him, and received him with great honour. He then took him upon the state elephant and going round the city followed by the Pallava army entered Kanchi. Having heard that the prince was within the city, the *sāmantas,* the great citizens, the chief inhabitants (*Mūlaprakriti*), and the *Kāṭaka Muttaraiyar*, all these came forward to meet him and took him into the palace. The panel above indicates this. The circle of ministers, the great *sāmantas,* the people constituting the two great *Ghaṇas,* the inhabitants of the *Ghaṭika,* all of them together annointed him with the title of Nandivarman. In the course of the ceremony, they placed to the south of him, *i.e.*, to the right of him the royal umbrella, the fly whisk, the great drum *Samudraghoṣa,* the great flag bearing the sword ensign (*Khaṭvanga*), the shield with the bull-mark. They proclaimed him with the royal sign-manual of authority (*Viḍēl Viḍuhu*), and thus annointed him to the kingdom. The following three sections are too far broken up to admit of an intelligible translation. But they hardly affect the general sense of the whole. They refer to matters that took place immediately after the coronation.

In this detailed recounting of the incidents attending Nandivarman's succession to the throne, the points that call for notice are the coming together of the main representatives of the people, whose function it seems to be normally to provide for the carrying on of the administration when, for one reason or another, the appointed ruler ceases to exist. We have noted the people that actually assembled and deliberated as to what arrangements should be made. Almost in a similar connection, the Śilapadhikāram[1] makes a reference to the great people concerned whose function it was to make the necessary arrangements in an extraordinary emergency.

[1] XXII—5—10.

The occasion is when as a result of the injustice done to Kaṇṇaki, both the Pandyan ruler and his queen died. This sudden death was not known; but the inner gates of the palace remained closed even after day-break. In this confusion there appeared in front of the palace, the "five great groups" priests, the great astrologer, the good people having charge of justice, those in charge of the accounts and those in charge of the Secretariat. These are the people who have to take upon themselves, as it seems there, to do the needful when an emergency like this occurred. They would apparently call in the assemblies of the people, the representative Brahmans, etc., and come to an acceptable conclusion before taking action, as is represented in the inscriptions regarding Pallavamalla. On another occasion when an important expedition had been ordered and the auspicious hour fixed in the evening, the royal umbrella, the sword, the big drum and such other insignia had to be carried out of the city as symbolical of beginning the expedition, the notabilities who assembled are mentioned again. These are mentioned generally as the five great bodies, the eight great groups, and then the body of learned Brahmans, those in charge of accounts, those whose function it was to look after justice and others that were engaged in the administrative offices of the state (*tandiravinaigñar*).[1] We may therefore presume generally that these were the men, or bodies of men, whose responsibility it was, as in charge of various important functions of the state, to consider well and ultimately adopt a course of action suitable to the occasion. Probably what took place on the death of

[1] XXVI—35—45.

Paramēśvaravarman II was not in its nature very different from what would have taken place in similar circumstances in the earlier period. In these matters people are usually conservative and are not likely to introduce violent changes rapidly. On the whole, the agreement seems to be far greater than the difference, and we may take it that the institutional arrangements continued the same as well as the procedure.

Coming to the actual character of the administration in the age of Nandivarman Pallava-Malla, he had a long reign of at least 65 years, it may have been longer. As the Vaikunṭhaperumāḷ inscriptions tell us he succeeded when he was twelve, and it would be nothing surprising even if his reign extended to seventy years. That would mean he would be a little over eighty when he died, an age not impossible in exceptional cases. It may not be the average or the normal, but does not seem impossible as an individual case. In spite of the long reign and of his great achievements, the number of records of his time that have come down to us is comparatively speaking few. They are still copper plate charters mainly; though stone inscriptions are just beginning to come into vogue. The larger ones with details are usually copper-plate charters as yet. One of them, coming from the heart of the Chola country, the Tanjore District, of the 58th year of this monarch, gives us details of the administration which brings it into more close proximity to what we have for a little more than a generation been accustomed to associate with the administration of the Cholas. This refers to the grant of the village Taṇḍantoṭṭam, just about three miles down Kumbhakonam, to a body of Brahmans, 213 of whom are mentioned, with 244 shares distributed among them. Excepting just a few which go to the particular officials concerned of the village, the larger part of them are shares allotted to the Brahmans, whose family and qualifications are detailed. The village is Taṇḍantoṭṭam in Naraiyūr Nāḍu on the south bank of the river, a sub-division of Chola Naḍu. This apparently involves that the sub-division Narayurnaḍu was itself divided into two parts, the Nāḍu on the southern bank of the river and the Nàḍu on the northern bank. This relates to the southern bank, and in the locality the river concerned Araśalār runs from east to the west. The land constituting the village consisted of unoccuped and uncultivated land. One plate seems to have gone here, and the details of how reclamation was intended to be carried out are gone. Of course we know these details from other inscriptions. Some of the details follow in the next following plate.

The first statement in the next plate following, which leaves the connection somewhat obscure prohibits doing certain things, and one of them specified is that they should not cut the sides and appropriate the land. What is implied seems to be that they should not form the land into fields and appropriate them, and the prohibition seems to apply to other inhabitants of the village, that part being included in the present gift. The statements that follow are not prohibitions but permissions. If the village is reclaimed, the first essential would be the source of irrigation. This was to be provided by constructing a head of water just above where the Kūttanūr[1] canal takes off from the river. The statement in the inscription therefore is that the head water of the new irrigation canal is to be just above the head of the existing canal. Then follows a series of reliefs, and they are all of them described as those which the king was entitled to take and enjoy. In the statement that follows, the Epigraphist's translation falls into another error. The Tamil expression is that the Brahmans of this village alone shall enjoy these and shall not be liable to pay any of these to the king as heretofore. The latter expression is mistranslated by setting down "shall be paid to the king". The Tamil word *iṛādu* means without paying, and the statement there is clearly that these shall not be paid to the king; and the Brahmans shall be entitled to receive them and enjoy them. They are

(1) *Śekku* (oil-mill) apparently duty that the owner of an oil mill had to pay for plying his trade;

(2) *Tari* (loom) a similar duty on looms;

(3) *Ulaviyakūli,* the corresponding term in the Kaśākuḍi plates is suggested by the Epigraphist as *Uḷḷiyakkūli* (digging well); *kūli* means of course wages, and the whole term would mean wages for well-digging. Possibly this means the charges for water supplied by means of artificial sources of irrigation made by the king on

[1]The Kūṛṛanvāy is translated by the Epigraphist as the main sluice. It is not clear how this meaning is arrived at. I believe in the locality, there is a channel, Kūttanūr Vāyakkāl, another irrigation channel.

royal lands, as in the Arthaśāstra; in other words, water rates for providing means of irrigation.

(4) *Kannālakkāṇam,* the cash to be paid on marriages.

(5) The next following is *Ūreṭṭu,* the significance of which is not clear.

(6) *Kusakkāṇam,* the cash (*kāṇam*) levied on potters.

(7) *Taṭṭukkāyam;* the Epigraphist points out that this is just in the place where in the Leyden grant, *Taṭṭār pāṭṭam* occurs, and suggests that it may be equivalent to that, in which case, it would mean a tax on goldsmiths. The term perhaps is breakable into *Taṭṭukku-Āyam,* meaning thereby *áyam* or due on hammering, which would justify its being taken as equivalent to *Taṭṭarpāṭṭam.*

(8) *Īḻamputchi.* Here the Epigraphist's note says that *pūtchi* is not found in the dictionaries, but suggests the probability that the term means a tax on toddy drawers. The word *pūtchi* is simple enough. *Īḻamputchi* would simply mean the profession of toddy drawing, and what it implies is a sort of profession tax on toddy drawing; *putchi,* according to the *niganṭhu* is body; also assumption, such as a profession, from the root *pūn,* wear.

(9) *Iḍaippūtchi,* similarly, it may be a tax on cattle rearing. The corresponding term for this in the Leyden grant is *Iḍaip-pāṭṭam.*

(10) The next term is *kūlam.* Kūlam simply means grain which is regarded as of eighteen kinds (*padineṇkūlam*), meaning all kinds of edible grain. Perhaps the selling of these grains in the market had to pay a duty.

(11) What follows is *Tarahu Pāṭṭam,* tax on brokerage.

(12) The next is *Tirumukhakkāṇam.* Kāṇam again here is cash or fee on Tirumukham, royal letter; probably a cash payment had to be made for bringing royal writ as a sort of postage or conveyance charge.

(13) *Uppu-ko-śeygai.* This breaks into *uppu,* plus *ko,* plus *śeygai,* salt plus king plus making. Probably what used to be paid to the king on the making of salt. In other grants the digging for salt is one of the *parihāras* from which relief is given. Apparently a fee had to be paid for digging salt.

(14) Then the *Nallā,* the good cow.

(15) Nalla-erudu, the good bull.

(16) Then follows *Vaṭṭi-Nāḻi,* which the Epigraphist translates as fee on baskets of grain brought to the market. The literal mean-

ing of it would be the *nāḻi* 1|8 of a grain measure paid on *vaṭṭil,* basket measure. Probably that is a fractional measure of grain that has to be paid by those who sold grain by dry measure, a basket or vessel of that shape.

(17) *Kāḍai Aḍaikkāy;* Arecanuts exposed for sale in shops; a tax on arecanuts on sale.

(18) *Pudā-Naḻi.* This term breaks into *pudā* or *pudām,* and *naḻi.* Again 1|8 of a measure of grain on something that is newly made. The Epigraphist points out that the corresponding term in the Vēlūrpāḷayam plates is Pudāri, and in the Leyden grant Pitānari. Of these two, in the Velūrpaḷayam plates, the term seems to be *pudanaṟi,* in which the *n* is dropped out; and the other seems again to be *i* mistaken for *a.* The term therefore would resolve into *Pudanāḻi.* That is the eighth of a measure on new made grain.

These make eighteen and end with "and others" so that the eighteen are perhaps not a strictly limited number. As a matter of fact, these count up to 22 in the Vēlūrpāḷayam plates. So while they seem to stand for what is gnerally spoken of as "*Aṣṭādaśaparihāras*", these *parihāras* do not seem to be limited to eighteen alone. What is to our present purpose is these were taxes or dues that the king was entitled to take from villagers as revenue over and above his share fixed by law and enjoyable by him. When the land was transferred as a *Brahmadēya* or *Dēvadāna,* the new owners or Brahmans of the village, or the authorities in management of temples, to whom the gift is made, became entitled to their collection and enjoyment.

One other small detail, which is of importance in this distribution of land is three shares of land are provided for *vāyttalai,* that is the head of the canal, and *uvaṅṛi,* such work as had to be made there and maintained in condition. This arrangement of the formation of a village, and its gift to a certain number of Brahmans is notified to the division concerned, according to the grant. Going back to another grant of the same ruler made in the 22nd year of his reign, viz., the Kaśākuḍi plates of Nandivarman, we find a few more interesting details, which are of value for our purposes. There the village is the village Koḍukoḷḷi, which is in the Ūṟṟukāṭṭu Nāḍu, in the Ūṟṟukāṭṭu Koṭṭam, and the grant is notified to the inhabitants of this division. This village was already in possession of others and was transformed into a *Dēvadāyam* at the request of Brahmādi Yuvarāja, the order being conveyed by Ghōra Śarman. The grant begins with the statement that the former owners were changed, and the cultivators were also changed, and made over to a particular Brahman, Śeṭṭi Ranga Sōmayāji of Pūni village belonging to the Bhāradvaja gotra and Chandōga Sūtra, on the principle of the common two *paṭṭi* division which means each share of the land was to contain two *paṭṭis* or two *nivarattanas,* a measure of the area of 40,000 square *hastas* (18 inches). Of course, a *hasta* is a measure of eighteen inches, or nearly an English foot and a half. The royal writ having conveyed this grant, the inhabitants of the Nāḍu or division accepted it, and as indicated by the *Viśavan* or the headman of the village, they walked round the boundary of the village by a turn to the right and marked the boundaries by means of stone and milk-bush (*kaḷḷi*) round it. A certain number of the *parihāras* are mentioned, but it is nothing like a complete list that was given in the previous grant. There is a general statement that what the king was accustomed to take from the village, the new owners were entitled to take. The village was to be irrigated by canals taken out from Śē-Āṟu, Veḥḥā and the tank Tirayanēri by means of regular canals as well as canals running out excess water on occasions of floods. They were to collect what was due for the purpose of cutting and keeping these canals in repairs. Those that attempt to utilise the water of these canals by baskets or by side bays for retaining water, or by short lifts would be liable to pay fines that the king was entitled to take from them. As in the grants generally, they were entitled to raise house of more floors than one, and houses with terraces built of burnt bricks and could cover the roof even with brick and mortor. As in the previous grant, it is also stated that all the *parihāras* which hitherto used to be enjoyed by the king were to be enjoyed by the new owners of the village. This grant (*paradatti*) was made with the assistance of *Nilaikkaḷattār,* the *Adhikāris* and *Vāyilkēṭpār*. *Nilaikkaḷattār* would mean the body of councillors and officers in immediate attendance upon the king; the *Adhikāris* were the executive and administrative officers concerned, and the *Vāyilkēṭpār,* the secretarial staff whose function it was to hear the verbal orders of the king and set them down in writing. For purposes of comparison may be set down here the *parihāras* as given in this grant. Over and above what is already recited from the other grant, we find here, Brahmana and Raja Kāṇam, that is cash that is payable for the Brahman and for the king. There is a new cash tax called *Śengoḍi Kāṇam.* 'Śengoḍi' is a creeper plant by means of which hedges are made. This probably means a fee that has to be paid for enclosing the lands. There is a *Kaṇṇeṭṭukunam,* a fee that has to be paid for supervision of some kind. There is a *Kadirkāṇam,* which probably would correspond to what is stated there as *Pudanaḷi.* Probably a similar one is what is mentioned here as *Arikoḷi,* that is taking the grain from out of the bundle of harvested paddy. There is a new due upon the selling of ghee and on *Puṭṭaham,* the meaning of which is not quite clear. There is another *Kāṇam* called *Paṭṭikai Kāṇam,* which seems to be one on cloth. What follows are some interesting privileges which are not mentioned in the other. Apart from freedom from payment of these, there was also to be freedom from *Nāyāḍis* (hunters), *Tūduvar* (messengers), *Kaṇikkaratti* (fortune tellers), and *Paṇṇu-Pāl-Eḍuppar,* probably dancing women, and fodder for horses.

Without going into further detail, we may point out that the total number of these *parihāras* count up to as many as 35 in this particular grant, taking the whole together, whereas in the other we counted only eighteen with a comprehensive "and others", so that it seems almost useless to try to fix the number where perhaps such fixture did not ordinarily obtain. These charters of Nandivarman, Pallava-Malla seem the charters issued actually at the royal headquarters. Such information as we get of the officials constituting the administration must necessarily have reference to the officials at the headquarters, and hence it is we find here the three classes of officials, *Nilaikkaḷam,* officials in immediate attendance, the *Adhikāris,* those whose function brings them into connection with the fiscal administration, and *Vāyilkēṭpār,* the Secretarial staff, whose function it is to submit papers and obtain verbal orders, to put them in writing, and, after the needful completion of official red-tape requirements, issue them finally. Notwithstanding the large number of details that we get regarding the localities concerned, we seem here not to get an insight into how exactly the rural administration was actually composed. That is because the copies of the grants available seem to be grants as they issued from the headquarters. In other grants, we shall come upon similar documents, but as received in the locality concerned and as recorded there. There we are likely to get the details that would give an insight into the actual constitution of the local administration. Before passing on to that, we shall have to consider what exactly the state of things was in the Tamil country away from contact with the north.

We may refer to the grants of contemporary Pandya rulers. They are not very many unfortunately, and the Vēḷvikuḍi grant of Neḍuṁśaḍaiyan published a few years ago, although known to us for more than a whole generation, gives us more details, which admit of comparison with what we find in the Pallava grants. There again an application for the grant is made by some interested party. In this case, it happens to be the person who was deprived of a grant which had been made to his ancestors and had been enjoyed by them for a number of generations before they were deprived of the benefit of it by an irruption of a new people or government which upset much that was in existence before. He carried his complaint in the usual fashion to headquarters by loudly complaining of the injustice which he was suffering from at the time. The king naturally summoned him immediately to his presence and enquired what the matter was that led to his making such a loud demonstration in front of the royal residence. A certain *Korkai Kiḻān*, Narchingan by name, a Brahman, represented that he was subjected to the injustice that the village Vēḷvikuḍi which belonged to his ancestors as a free gift, he had been deprived of owing to the act of the Kalabhras that were in occupation of the territory. On hearing his account, the king told him immediately "Establish your former claim by proof"—and take possession of what, by hereditary claim, is yours" (*nāṭṭā-ṉin-paḻamaiyādalkāṭṭi nī koḷga*). He then and there adduced proof to the satisfaction of the monarch and obtained from him the gift. The Pandya gifted the village by pouring of water to this *Narchingan* to be enjoyed by him on the terms, on which his own ancestors had given the village to the ancestors of the donee. So the *Āgñapti* or the officer, whose function it was to see that the order was carried out was the minister Māran-Kāri. Then follows how *Narchingan* divided the village thus acquired between him and his agnatic relations, as also one or two others to whom he was bound to allot a certain number of shares. Here again we have only the order as issued at the headquarters and the provision made for enforcing the order. Who received it and how the order was actually carried out is not given, and hence we are not let into the actual form of the rural administration. But the one side of it is clear, and there is such a closeness in point of similarity between the Pallava charters and the Pandya that we would be justified in assuming that there was a common system that obtained all over the Tamil country, whether it be in the land of the northern Pallava, or in the southern Pandya.

When, however, we pass on to the later inscriptions even of the Pallavas we seem to get an insight into the other side which was wanting. Taking the Vēlūrpāḷayam plates for instance, we find that it is as much a grant by a Nandivarman, not the Pallava-Malla, but his grandson. It refers to the grant of the village of Tirukkāṭṭupaḷḷi in Nāyaru Nāḍu of Puḷar Kōṭṭam, made in the sixth year of Vijaya-Nandi Varman. The request for the grant was made by a Chola Mahārāja while the *Vigñapti* of the grant was a certain Namban of Irāyūr. The grant was made to the temple of Yagñēśvara built by a learned Brahman Yagña Bhaṭṭa. The grant there is said to have been made as a *Nāṭṭu Nīngal,* which means that 'land granted was removed from the registrar of tax paying lands of the district or Nāḍu'. There is the other expression which is that the land is granted as *Uḷ-Puravu. Puravu* is an expression which has not been so far understood; but it seems to be a term which means a revenue unit of land, the unit consisting in not the land being of a single, piece, or in a single locality. It may be actually composed of a number of units in scattered areas. The unity consists in this that these are all grouped together as one property and assessed as such. In the tax register, it would figure as one item bearing a certain amount of revenue. The best way to translate it would be of course revenue-unit. Therefore *uḷ-puravu* would simply mean the revenue-unit, which was a matter of concern to the village itself, not as constituting part of the Nāḍu, and liable to pay the revenue at headquarters. Otherwise the grant is made exactly as the other grants are, and the same expression is used that it was made a *paradatti,* a grant to another. But there is one little detail here that the record was actually received by the authorities at the other end at the village; and something like an endorsement that the *panchavar* of Tirukkāṭṭupaḷḷi take note of the *paradatti,* the alienation of the land. The expression *panchavar* would mean the five who had the administrative control of the village. We often come upon expressions like this in later inscriptions very frequently, and the fact of this term occurring in these Pallava inscriptions would indicate that perhaps in regard to rural administration the features that we know of from among the Chola inscriptions very frequently were also the features of Pallava rural administration.

We have only to take ourselves to a generation or two later even of the Pallavas for us to see that rural administration had attained almost to the same condition as under the Cholas. There are a number of inscriptions relating to that famous village of Uttaramallūr, Uttaramēru-Chaturvēdi-Mangalam of the Chingleput District, of which we shall have to say more later on. The inscriptions most of them refer to the period of Kō-Vijaya-Kampavarman and Kō-Vijaya-Nripatunga Varman. The village is already described as a unit by itself (*tarkūṟṟam*), and belonged to the Kāliyūr Kōṭṭam. It mentions already the Sabha and the Ghaṇattār, and the Sabha gives the order and the *Madyasta* reduces it to writing.[1] Another inscription[2] relates to a grant by a lady to a Vishṇu temple, and, in regard to this *Dēvadāna,* the Mahāsabha makes the endorsement that they had received, from Vaikhānasa Śrīdharabhaṭṭa's son Damodara Bhaṭṭan, all the gold that was required to compensate for all royal dues, and made the land tax free, and made it over to the temple as a *Dēvadāna.* The document was written by Āchārya Śrī Purusha under the orders of the Sabha. Another[3] grant refers to a similar gift, but in this case, it is a gift of land for performing worship in the temple for which the land was given to the *Archaka* (the priest). Grant No. 290 has reference to a general arrangement that the Sabha made. There is no reference to any higher authority, except the reference to the ninth year of Kō-Vijaya Kampavaṟman. It refers to a number of house-sites which were reserved for the purposes of the Sabha. They were purchased for the full price from the owners, and were to be kept for the use of the Sabha exclusively, and no one ought to sell or alienate these house sites. If they did so, they would be liable to the

[1] S. I. I. Vol. VI, 285.
[2] *Ibid* No. 287.
[3] S. I. I. Vol. VI, No. 288.

punishment that is awarded to those who erred in the discharge of the duties attaching to the administration of the village. This is what is called the *Vyavasthā* of the Sabha, which means a settlement or order made by the Sabha. Another one[1] of the fifteenth year of this very Kampavarman refers to the *āḷum ghaṇaṭṭar, ghaṇa* or the group which administered the affairs of the village. It refers to the gift by a lady of land forming the pin-money given to her by her parents. She made it over for the expenses of the daily worship of the temple. The Sabha accepted the gift and agreed to see to it that the temple services, for which the land was given, were regularly conducted. Another one[2] of the same year refers to a large grant of ten thousand pieces of gold, which the Sabha received similarly for the purposes of keeping the irrigation tank Vairamēga Taṭāga in good repairs for irrigation. This refers to the reign of Danti-Vikrama, and refers to the Sabha of Uttaramallūr, the settlement of lands among the villagers, and is of particular interest as it refers to a previous distribution of land, of which a certain number of pieces or parcels remained uncultivated, and a certain number turned out to be in the hands of people who could not pay the dues on the land. The Sabha took over the lands from those that could not cultivate it, and arranged for its cultivation from out of the funds already in deposit for the purposes of repairs, etc., to the Vairamēga tank. The land was to be held in the interest of the tank, and, if those from whom it was taken for default should come again to claim it before three

[1] *Ibid* South Indian Inscriptions VI, No. 314.
[2] *Ibid* 325.

years expired, the lands may be given back to them taking from them what was due in cash. In case the land was not recovered for three years, it would become the permanent property of the Vairamēga Taṭāka and its management. If anybody transgressed or damaged this arrangement, his land would be appropriated and will be made the property of the Vairamēga Tank. Here there is no reference to any higher authority, nor of any officer who had to take notice of it. The whole arrangement, far-reaching as it is, is made under the authority of the Sabha itself. No. 346 of the time of Nṛpatunga refers to the receipt of a certain amount of money for the maintenance of a perpetual lamp by the great people of the management (*Vāriyam*). No. 347 relates to a private grant for the performance of worship in the temple of Mahā-Vishṇu. The village assembly declare "they have accepted from the person making the gift the amount of gold that was necessary for releasing the land from all royal incidences upon it and undertakes the responsibility of its not being subjected in the future to any of these incidences". This was declared by the assembled Sabha of the village, and was put in writing by the Uttaramērūr Perum Tachchan, that is the stone mason of the village. If anybody destroyed this Dharma, the Sabha undertakes to pay 25 *kaḷanju* of gold. No. 348 is of interest as mentioning the great people constituting the *Ēri-vāriyam,* the supervision of tanks. This body had to invest a certain sum and from the interest accruing, keep the tanks in condition. This is just enough to indicate that already rural localities were placed under an administrative system, of which full information becomes available under the Cholas. Enough of it is available in the last period of Pallava rule to indicate that the system which is found in full working order under the Cholas was not altogether the invention of the Cholas, and perhaps was a system that had developed gradually and reached its full development under the Cholas. We may close this part of the subject with the general position that while the central administration seems in essence to be administration which has very considerable analogy to the administration of the headquarters, as in the Artha-Śāstra generally, we see there is a considerable development in rural administration, for which perhaps it would be difficult to find analogies in the Artha Śāstra. We may describe the government under Pallava rule as being composed of a central government very much like that projected in the Arthasastra, and a local government of a more indigenous character, which had attained to a high degree of development.

A—17

LECTURE V.

RURAL ADMINISTRATION UNDER THE CHOLA EMPIRE.

As was stated in the concluding part of the last lecture, we emerge from out of the period of Pallava rule with a more or less fully developed local administration providing for all the requirements for the satisfactory government of rural localities. for which we have had but indirect hints in inscriptional literature almost down to the time of the great Pallava, Nandivarman, Pallava-Malla. With the grandson of this great Pallava and his successors, we seem to be already provided with abundant material for forming a correct idea of local administration as it obtained in the Tamil country. While undoubtedly local administration is seen at its best under Chola rule, we seem to find it in as fully developed a condition almost, under these later Pallavas. From what we see of the organisation for local administration under the Pallavas themselves, we may feel clear that these institutions must have had a ong anterior vogue reaching back to distant beginnings, and it is impossible to believe that the institutions constituting the local administration could have sprung into existence Athena-like in her full panoply of dress and accountrement.

The material that we have for a study of these local institutions is principally inscriptions. These are in such number so far published that it would be difficult to control the material, if all of them should be taken at once into consideration. It would be just as well to confine ourselves to a few chosen localities with a view to projecting a picture—a fairly complete picture—of what actually the rural institutions were by means of which the administration was carried on in localities away from headquarters. Fortunately we are provided with some few of such localities where the institutions show themselves in more or less complete development, and, at the same time, the information that is available, from the inscriptions collected from the locality, is also in sufficient detail to give us adequate material for a fairly full picture.

I

Administration in Uttaramallūr.—

One such locality is the village named Uttaramallūr, now in the Madhurāntakam Taluq of the Chingleput District. It was known in those days as Uttaramēru-chaturvēdimangalam, a Brahman village, but still a large enough village, possessed of all the features of a fairly full sized town with the adjuncts of temples, wards, dependent villages, tanks, roads, etc., in fact all the appurtenances of a really typical town, the government of which would at once give an idea of how a complicated rural locality was actually administered. Uttaramerūr, in her best days, was a village with twelve dependent hamlets, and divided into thirty wards for the purpose of efficient government. The government was, as the nearly two hundred inscriptions in the locality give us to understand, in the hands of a powerful assembly, or the Mahāsabha, composed of all the male inhabitants of the village, even including the young men and the old men, who were generally excluded from holding administrative offices of the locality. They had the complete control of the administration and did everything that had to be done by way of administration; in other words administrative work in the village had to be done under their direction, and, on the instructions laid down by them generally. What they had really to administer can be understood by a general recital of the things that they took notice of. They are indicated as being owners of all unoccupied lands in behalf of the town, and had power to dispose of these unoccupied and unappropriated lands as they pleased for various purposes that may arise from time to time. It is they who made provision for the laying out of the land and bringing them under agriculture, dividing them into large plots and into smaller fields, providing them with facilities for irrigation, and seeing to it that they were also provided with suitable approaches, both for people and cattle to move about, and for conveyance to carry produce from the fields and carry to the fields what may be required for the purpose of cultivation. They provided for irrigation channels, and had even to manage large irrigation tanks from which water was drawn for the purpose of irrigating the whole area comprised within the control of the village. In almost everything that they did, they acted independently of any reference to the head-quarters, either on their own initiative, or on their attention being drawn by the subordinate bodies which worked under them. Even where royal officers appeared on the scene actually, and the members of the royal family themselves had to make, say, gifts to temples, they had to adopt the same procedure of passing through this great assembly for the acquisition of lands and arranging for their gift. Even in the disposal of the gifts in the various ways in which donors wanted they should be made, they had to meet with the approval of this assembly, and in fact it is this assembly that laid down the details of how even these gifts should be disposed of from persons other than themselves. The administration therefore, we may say, was completely in the hands of this Mahāsabha, which sometimes described itself as *Perumkuṛi Mahāsabhai,* which could be translated, 'the Mahāsabha with the great seal'; in other words, the Mahāsabha or great assembly as thus constituted was the highest authority in the locality.

For purposes of administration, this Sabha either from among themselves, or otherwise created, a certain number of smaller bodies. These bodies were in charge of various of the departments of administration in general, and conducted them as a subordinate administrative authority under the direction of this general assembly. Of these, from the Uttaramērūr inscriptions themselves, and from just a few others which mention them, we get as many as eight or ten committees, and from the nature of those which are actually mentioned as such, we can infer that the number could be multiplied indefinitely as the purposes for which the machinery was wanted actually increased. A small list ought to suffice to indicate the character of these committees and how they were actually called into existence. The Committees mentioned are:—

Samvatsara Vāriyam, the committee for administration, for the year;

Tōṭṭa Vāriyam, the committee that looked after gardens;

Ēri Vāriyam, the committee that looked after irrigation tanks;

Kaḻani Vāriyam, the committee that looked after the cultivable fields.

Pancha Vāra Vāriyam, formed of representatives of various bodies. It seems to be a committee and looked after the affairs of the village generally through the year.

Kaṇakku Vārigam, the accounts committee;

Kalingu Vāriyam, the committee that looked after sluices;

and *Taḍivaḻi Vāriyam,* the committee that looked after roads, etc.

In another record we get a new *Kuḍumbu Vāriyam;* that means the committee that looked after the cultivating inhabitants of the village; and then there is a division here of those that looked after the cultivable fields in general, and those who looked after the fields on the northern side of the river. Then there are the Brahmans, who constituted a separate unit by themselves and managed their own affairs more or less in a general sort of a way, and had a distinct place in the general assembly. The division of the committee of cultivable fields into two, gives us clearly to understand that, if the work of a single committee proved too heavy, the assembly did not shrink from creating several committees to manage one and the same department. Much more therefore could be inferred than that; as new departments called for special attention, they could create committees for each new department, so that the number of committees that are created would depend upon the complicated interests of the locality. There may be villages and village unions with two or three committees; while on the contrary there may be villages and village unions with a very large number of committees. As a matter of fact, these administrative village units, which are called *Kūṟṟams,* constituted a certain number of villages thrown together and forming something like a union in modern times. That seems to be the general order. At the same time, there appears to have been a pretty large number of townships, which were large enough to stand by themselves. They constitute divisions by themselves, and are usually described as *taṟ-kūṟṟam* in inscriptions. This Uttaramērūr was a *taṟ-kūṟṟam*; other instances, such as Takkolam, Ukkal, Mahābalipuram, and a number of other villages could be cited as constituting divisions by themselves. It may be remembered here that the smallest division of agricultural villages known to the Arthasastra is the union of ten dominated by a fortified place called *Sangrahaṇa* which is a centre with villages grouped round it.

We mentioned already that practically all the inhabitants of the village even including those that were particularly young and those that were very old, formed part of the general assembly, while, in the constitution of the committees, they were usually excluded. The election procedure is clearly on record in connection with this particular locality. The procedure seems to have been the usual procedure, but in this case, it had been collected together, put in a formal document and, to some extent, revised and brought up to date in two inscriptions issued by the Chola Emperor, Parāntaka in the 12th and 14th year, of his reign respectively. Naturally a document of the later year is an improvement on the previous one. But then it does not appear to have been imposed upon the inhabitants of the locality by fiat of royal authority. When the document was received, the general assembly met to discuss the document, and it is when they approved of it that it became the rule of the locality. That it was actually carried out is in evidence in inscriptions of the following year where they had to make arrangements for the election of a gold committee. In the carrying out of these the general assembly seems to have felt bound to carry out the circular merely in spirit, and not exactly to the letter of the details of this general circular. For the general committees, the usual practice was that the general assembly met and put down on slips of writing material the names of individuals in each ward who were eligible for holding office as members of the committees concerned. All these names were bundled up with a covering docket for each particular ward. In a general election, the assembly came together in the usual meeting place, wherever possible a big temple hall. The priests were all of them in their places. The senior most priest took charge of the bundle and brought in a pot. He turned it upside down to show that it contained nothing, and having done this, he untied the bundle, and put into the empty pot all the tickets in the presence of the assembly standing in the middle of it, so that everybody may see what he was doing. A young boy was chosen from the assembly, and he was asked to take out one ticket at a time which the chief priest received, read out the name to himself and passed it on to the Madhyasta, who read it out to the assembly. Thus thirty members were elected of whom the number for the general management was taken out by the choice of those who had already been members of a committee and had acquired some administrative experience by being on one or other of these smaller committees. In regard to the other committees, they made the choice on the basis of the qualifications required for the work. This part of the work therefore was done 'by verbal expressions of opinion' as the documents say; that means by common consent after discussion having regard to the particular details of the qualifications called for. This was the general way that committees were constituted. We have the actual details of a gold committee, where it is laid down that the general assembly came together in this particular fashion and chose from the residents of the village those who *were tax-paying inhabitants of the village.* That means the proletariat were excluded, and by divisions of the various wards, they chose a certain number for each, four for one, three for another and two each for two other wards, and thus was constituted the gold committee. In a committee like this, the wards that already supplied men for the previous year were excluded, and the names of other men that were chosen were put on the ticket. They were to be men competent, to the best of knowledge of the writer, and should have had knowledge of gold estimating. The circular then lays down as a general rule that those alone were to be entitled to a place on the assembly, or on the committees who, as a necessary preliminary, were generally educated and were of good character. They must be either owners of a quarter of veli of land, about an acre and a half, or must be learned in one Veda and capable of expounding thoroughly one of the Sastras. It was already pointed out that those that held the office in the previous year were to be excluded. But here is a general qualification that those that held office during the last three years were to be excluded from the particular committees. Those who had houses built on sites of their own were eligible for offices. So also one possessed of 1|8 of a veli of land, and at the same time was possessed of an amount of learning just inferior to the qualifications of learning otherwise imposed, was also eligible. Then there is a schedule of disqualifications. They were not to be eligible for the next year who defaulted in the work in the previous year. Not merely that, all their relations of the first degree were to be excluded from the privilege of holding office. Those that had shown themselves to be incompetent, those that had been addicted to the ordinary vices, such as drink, theft, etc., were to be excluded altogether. Those who were generally foolhardy or otherwise guilty of acts of rashness were to be avoided. Those that committed prohibited acts were regarded as sinners and were to be kept out for life, even though they should expiate for the sin in accordance with the prescriptions of the Śāstras. For a village like Uttaramērūr consisting of twelve hamlets and thirty wards, one was chosen for each ward, thus making thirty. From out of these, two committees of twelve and one of six were constituted. If more committees had to be appointed, this could be done by electing another shift of thirty. They probably repeated the elections and thus constituted all the committees that they wanted. The circular of Parāntaka states that the object of the ruler in issuing the circular was merely to make the administration more efficient by keeping out the wicked ones from the governing bodies of villages. There is some little of an indication who the wicked ones were, and it would be possible to guess whom they had in mind.

In the Toṇḍamaṇḍalam to which Uttaramērūr belonged, the next higher division to the Kūṟṟam was the Koṭṭam, and the still larger division was the Maṇḍalam or the province. So the divisions would be, the divisions, the districts and the provinces. Similarly in the Chola country, the divisions were the Maṇḍala, the Nāḍu or Vaḷanāḍu and the Kūṟṟam or the sub-division. Throughout the empire either these divisions themselves, or divisions of a similar character, obtained. There were something like six of these Maṇḍalams, sometimes making up to as many as eight. In certain places, at any rate, the largest division is also called Nāḍu. But then it is not difficult to distinguish the use of the word in that sense from the ordinary sense of a district.

It was already pointed out that, in regard to the character of the administration, the revenue administration was entirely in the hands of the assembly. They exercised also comparatively large powers in the ordinary criminal administration and even in respect of hineous offences. It was they that had to decide as to the guilt, although punishment in the case of heavy offences were fixed according to law by the king. The police work, the work of protection against theft and robbery, was also provided for by the assembly by means of a committee, whose function seems to have been to look after the roads and provide for protection. There was the village official Veṭṭi, a man in charge of the highway and in certain inscriptions, we are given the term Mukhaveṭṭi, an official at the head-quarters, as if to indicate, he was the chief of those who were in charge of road protection, a sort of an Inspector-General of Police. The lands were very carefully divided, classified according to quality in a comparatively large number of classes. We have mention, in these records, of seven or eight according to quality. But otherwise lands were laid out in plots, and in Uttaramērūr, the plots seem to have been divided by general roads on one side and oblong bunds running at right angles all to one side of the road on the other, constituting *Pāḍahams* of 240 *kuḻis* each normally. Those large fields of that extent, and each large plot was numbered arithmetically into so many *Pāḍahams,* and the plots were usually named from the small irrigation canal from which it drew water. As many as twenty of these irrigation canals are mentioned in this particular locality. Whatever was the condition of the lands at the original distribution, whenever land was required for certain purposes, it had to be picked up from various of these divisions and put together to constitute one parcel of the required quantity. This single parcel was called by the technical term *Puravu,* and there was a department of accounts at the headquarters which had charge of the *Puravu-vari,* that is the tax due upon the land on the basis of this unit, or *Puravu,* consisting of bits of land scattered over various localities, but still constituting one individual property paying a certain quantity of the tax. The division of the land was carried to a point of nicety, lands being calculated to the minute point of 1|52,428,800,000 of a *vēli* of land, which would work out to something like 1|50,000 of a square inch. In the *Puravu* register was entered whatever was due from the land according to the original arrangement. This is what is known as *Kāṇikkaḍan* (that which was due on ownership or possession); sometimes, on cultivation and at the time of taking revenue, which the village authorities did, differences were discoverable owing to variations in estimating, measurements, etc. Sometimes more was due, sometimes less. The taxes were taken accordingly on actual yield, and therefore there is an entry *Iṛaikaṭṭinadu*; there is, the tax actually paid.

In Uttaramērūr, there was a big tank, viz., the Vairamēgha Taṭāka, which was the source of the supply of water for purposes of irrigation. We mentioned already that there were as many as twenty irrigation channels, which carried its water to the fields. The tank had to be kept in repairs. A certain number of boats even were maintained for taking out the silt and throwing it upon the tank bund. They had provision for keeping a margin of land all round, a comparatively narrow margin, free from cultivation and debarred from being enclosed by any private owner. For the maintenance of this margin of land and for the repairs of boats, provision was made from time to time by the assembly itself, or by individuals so minded, and these were made over to the tank committee, whose function it was to keep the tank in repairs.

Similarly there was a roads committee, whose function it was to keep charge of the roads and look after them. There is an interesting record where a road going near the tank became water-logged and so miry that it was not fit for any class of human beings to make use of and even useless for cattle. It required an elaborate process to make the road of uniform width and bring it back into condition. This was done efficiently, according to the record, by the great men in charge of the roads from funds placed at their disposal. Other committees similarly are mentioned also.

There were gifts for education as well; and, what was really admirable about them, they came from ladies for the purpose of education. There is a record of a fairly generous grant by a lady for the purpose of a Vedic school, in which the Vedas and the sciences accessory thereto, were to be taught to a high degree of proficiency. The land that was given by the lady was divided into a number of *Bhaṭṭavrittis,* lands for the maintenance of *Bhaṭṭas* or learned Brahmans, and this was to be given to those who came out with a very good record of performance at this school. There is even record of a provision for one that was expert in administering antidotes against poison. A provision is made for this man to exercise his skill for the benefit of the public. But then the land provision that is made to him is limited strictly to last his own lifetime, as is generally the case where provision for special expertness is made.

Thus we see that, with a Mahāsabha at the head composed practically of all the male inhabitants of the village, the administration was provided for by means of a number of committees according to need, and the administration was carried on to the minutest detail. Men and women alike, the well-to-do and not so well-to do, all of them seem to have borne their responsibility cheerfully and contributed towards the success of the administration, which, it must be remembered was not always uniformly successful and was not free altogether from the incidents of an unsatisfactory character, such as misfeasance and imperfect performance of duties, calling for punishment and rectification. But from what appears in these records, it seems to have been, on the whole very successful.

Before closing this portion of the subject, we must mention that although the village was a Brahman village, provision is made for temples to various deities other than Brahmanical on almost the same scale as provision for the temples for Brahman-worship. Temples for Sapta Mātrikas, not altogether un-Brahmanical, are mentioned. In addition to these, a temple to Jēshṭādēvi, the goddess of poverty and misfortune, temples to Pidāriyār, the *Grama-Dēvata* (Village Deity), and even a temple to the *White One, Madurai-vīran,* as he is popularly called, answering to Bacchus of the Greeks. Provisions were alike made for these and the same Sabha, through special committees, managed these properties as well.

Rural Administration in Uttaramērūr :—

The character of rural administration in the period extending from almost the beginning of the ninth century to the fourteenth, and perhaps even later, is most conveniently studied by a careful choice of one or two, or if need be, just a few localities where the administrative details are available in the fullest measure. The inscriptions available for this period are so many and the details lie scattered so widely that anything like an exhaustive sorting of it would be a matter, which would prove to be too much for control to suit the ordinary limitations of space. The sorting has to be done of course, but it need hardly form part of what is actually written about the administration itself. For convenience of treatment, therefore, we may take a choice. The village Uttaramērūr, in the Madhurāntakam Taluq now, offers the best illustration by the completeness of the institutions that we are able to see at work in it, from the number of inscriptions from the locality that have come to our notice and have been made available. The village happened to be a Brahman village (*agrahāra*) containing a number of temples and otherwise laid out and organised completely. It shows the administration in full detail; perhaps it shows it at its best. Not to prejudice the position, however, by chosing that which offers perhaps the best, we might compare it with other localities of a different character so far as administrative details regarding these may be available. Even granting that it shows rural administration in its best, it cannot be regarded as a disadvantage to have a view of the picture of rural administration at its best. We shall, therefore, proceed in the first instance to exhibit the administration of the village Uttaramallūr.

The earliest inscriptions refer to the reign of Vijaya-Kampavarman and go down to the eighth year, and the latest inscriptions go on pretty late under the rule of the Cholas. Uttaramallūr was called Uttaramēru-chaturvēdi-mangalam, *Uttaramēru* is the Sanskrit sacerdotal name of the village, and *Chaturvēdi-mangalam* means that it was a Brahman village. It was a village inhabited primarily by Vedic scholars, reciters of the four Vedas. In the Tamil country, however, it is a name generally given to a village of the Brahman-caste primarily; the gift is made to those who are expert in the *Chaturvēda,* or the Veda in its four sections. This is what is called a *taṛkūṟṟam,* constituting a division or sub-division by itself. In the Tamil country this constitutes a unit of rural administration. Ordinarily villages are grouped together into unions and such unions took into them as many, perhaps, as a dozen villages; or say eight on an average, at any rate. But more important and perhaps villages with larger population constituted divisions by themselves, e.g., Mamallapuram, Takkolam, etc., in the same province. In this very same locality in addition to Uttaramērūr, Ukkal constituted a sub-division by itself. By the mere fact of this distinction, these have to be taken as villages of importance, and of a size far larger than the average of villages, and of sufficient importance to be treated as separate units. In connection with this, we may consider a division recommended in the Arthaśāstra. Villages were to consist of no less than a hundred families and not more than five hundred of agricultural people of the Śūdra caste. It may comprise a boundary of about one *krośa,* about a mile and a half, or 2250 yards according to Dr. Shama Sastri. They should be so placed that they can protect each other. Boundaries are to be denoted by natural features, or otherwise marked, as indicated in these inscriptions themselves, as was noticed already, by planting stones or milk-bush. But these villages were to be grouped together in divisions dominated by something like a fortress. The smallest division is a division of ten villages with a fort called Sangrahaṇa at the head of it. Groups of two hundred villages were placed under the control of a fortified centre called Kharvāṭika, and a larger centre for four hundred villages is called Droṇamukha; and a still larger centre commanding eight hundred villages is called Sthānīya, corresponding to the Ṭhāna of modern times. The unit of village division for purposes of rural administration may be regarded more or less as ten, as the ten of the smallest division of the Arthaśāstra. But that does not debar bigger villages being placed in a division by themselves. So Uttaramērūr constituted a sub-division by itself of a Koṭṭam, or a larger division called Kāliyūr Koṭṭam. In the Pallava inscriptions no higher division is generally mentioned. But when we come to the Chola inscriptions, there is another division to which reference is made. The next higher division is also given. Usually in this locality, it would be Jayamkoṇḍacholamaṇḍalam, a Chola title given to the locality, or its original ancient name, Toṇḍamaṇḍalam. It is the Cholas that are traditionally credited with having brought Toṇḍamaṇḍalam into civilised administration, and in doing so, they are said to have taken the whole territory, and divided it suitably, placing villages lying in the open country, under the protection and government of twenty-four fortified places in the centre of groups of villages dependent thereon, possibly corresponding to the largest division of the Arthaśāstra, the Sthānīya being placed in the midst of eight hundred villages. But the point of view here seems to have been that being somewhat of an unsettled country, even rural localities required a common place where the herds of cattle that constituted a substantial part of their wealth may be driven in for protection and for defence against being captured and carried away by enemies. Once provision is made for this, it would become a centre dominating the rest of the region and then would develope the other adjuncts to make the town a fortified centre. Kōṭṭam therefore as the name of a larger division remained the peculiar feature of the Toṇḍamaṇḍalam country. The corresponding division in the Chola, and the Pāndya countries, and to some extent, even in the Chera country was, in the Chola days, the Vaḷanāḍu. The first part of the word is an attribute, a sort of complimentary fertile. The real division is merely Nāḍu. Nāḍu will correspond to the Kōṭṭam of the Toṇḍamaṇḍalam country. The division within the Nāḍu is of course the Kūṟṟam in the Chola country, as it happens to be in fact even in regard to Toṇḍamaṇḍalam. The main divisions were large enough to be regarded as provinces, and usually were, before their reduction to the condition of provinces administered under the Chola Empire, more or less independent kingdoms. In regard to Uttaramēruchaturvēdimangalam therefore we see that it is a unit division constituting part of the higher division called Kōṭṭam here, and being in the province of a still larger Toṇḍamaṇḍalam. This village had a considerable Brahman population being an *Agrahāra,* but not without the other adjuncts of village life, such as a corresponding number of other people, discharging each his own respective duty in the village economy. It was large enough to be divided into a number of *Chēris* or wards, of which for this Uttaramērūr, we could count about as many as thirty mentioned. The village government had to be carried on on the one side ward by ward, and on the other, as we shall see department by department. The village also had the other adjuncts of village life. If it was laid out in wards, it must have had roads, streets and lanes, and could well be divided into easily distinguishable divisions. The agricultural land must have been laid out and divided into plots and understandable divisions for various purposes of a revenue division, revenue collection and for other incidences of fiscal administration. We do find references to numbers of roads, streets and even lanes, and the divisions of the land itself are marked off clearly. This comes out where they have to buy a certain quantity of land for a new purpose. Much of the land would be occupied and whenever they wanted to make a new acquisition for a new service, they would have had to make up the requisite quantity of land by parcels of it taken from various localities of unoccupied land. In this way we get an idea of the divisions of the land. Lands here seem to be divided along side of roads of varying breadth, and naturally, of course, of length. But there was an effort to make the roads of uniform width and for keeping them in condition. Along side of the roads on either side, lands were divided into very extensive plots called *Pāḍaham* in Tamil, and each one of the larger divisions, which seem to have been made on the basis of the channel, the smaller channel that actually brought the water for the irrigation of the fields, called *Kaṇṇāṛu,* were divided into a number of *Pāḍahams,* and these water channels were numbered, 1, 2, 3, etc., so that when a gift of land has to be made, bits of land are taken from a number of these larger divisions, and constituted into one revenue unit of the required size.

In respect of Uttaramēruchaturvēdimangalam a number of these smaller irrigation channels (*Kaṇṇāṛu*), as many as 20, figure in the records, and the divisions of land along the *Kaṇṇāṛu* into *Pādahams* also get numbered; so that parcels of land are taken out from each one of these divisions of the fields, from each one of the divisions named after the channels and constituted into one revenue paying unit, usually called *Puravu.* There was the further division of land into classes, first, second, third, etc.

The whole administration of the division was in the hands of a particular general body called Sabha or Mahāsabha, sometimes even Mahāsabha 'of the great seal' (*Peruṁkuṛi Mahāsabhai*) according to occasions. This Sabha was the body that was responsible for the whole administration. They met and made their dispositions either of detailed gifts of land, or of distribution of houses and house sites in the villages, or of acquisition of property for the general purposes of the village, of alienating property by sale or otherwise, and making general arrangements other than those, in various ways. The procedure adopted was: the assembly came together and met in a particular locality usually set apart for that purpose, made the necessary enquiries, deliberated upon the best course of action to meet the case, and adopted certain resolutions; and these were set down in writing by the *Madhyasta* or the common village official, whose function it was to record these resolutions as secretary of the assembly. In its deliberative capacity, therefore, and in the exercise of the general managing power, the Sabha operated in this fashion.

On the side of administration, on the executive side, however, the Sabha seems to have worked through committees of a comparatively small number, easily manageable and capable of doing everything that was required either individually or in small groups. The ordinary number seems to be five. Hence the name *Panchāyat* (Sans. for five), occurring before the names of various committees, not necessarily meaning that the committees were all of them necessarily and strictly five, the more usual number seems to have been six. Sometimes these smaller divisions go by the name *Ghaṇam,* which seems to be a somewhat smaller assembly than the large governing assembly of the whole division. We come upon an expression *Āḷuṁ Ghaṇattār,* which seems to imply the small group that carried on the administration as against the larger group, the Mahāsabha, which was the ultimate authority in all matters. Other assemblies are also spoken of, the Māhēśvaras where Śiva temples are concerned, and Mahāvaishṇavas or Vaishṇavas merely where Vishṇu temples are concerned, and communities of that kind. It was the function of the Mahāsabha to set free revenue-paying lands of the village into free-gift lands. This was done usually by taking over possession of the land given, and along with it the capitalised value in money for the annual revenue from the land due to the government. The resolution generally took the form that, having taken the sum of money from an individual named, "we have made the land tax-free, and we hold ourselves responsible for all the incidences of revenue due upon the land ourselves and see that the land is kept tax-free". This is in case where an individual purchased the land himself for its full price and made it over to the village assembly.[1] There is another way of setting free revenue-paying lands. This is described as in the manner customary in the village (*pūrvāchāra*). Then they proceeded to describe what land it was that happened to be thus dealt with. No. 286 is a record by this Mahāsabha, where land which was paying no royal dues, is concerned. The land belonged to a lady, the wife of the Brahman, Guṇḍakramavittan, and belonged to the Madhusūdanachēri of the village. This was purchased by the villagers next adjoining for a price. They also purchased from another individual belonging to Padmanābachēri of the village one square. Both these pieces were put together, and were made over to the temple for daily worship and other requirements of the temple service. The Sabha records that they made this land tax-free by accepting the *pūrvāchāra* from the inhabi-

[1]See South Indian Inscriptions, Vol. VI. 285.

tants of Tiṭṭāttūr, the village that made the gift. The next record[1] has reference to one who describes himself Aḍiyarangamangaḷattūr Araiyāṇḍai—He describes himself as *Pramāṇiyan*, whatever the term was intended to signify. It perhaps means a man who states the truth for the occassion, as a mild substitute for administering an oath. It refers to a gift to Mahāvishṇu in the Manṭapa in Vāmanachēri, another division of the village. The land required for the gift was 960 *kuḻis* made up of four bits of land:—

(1) land to the west of the Paramēśvaravadi the roadway named Paramēśvara, 2 *Pāḍahams* from the first square, from the first section under the ninth *Kaṇṇāṟu;*

(2) One *pāḍaham* of 240 *kuḻis* purchased from Śiva Dāmōdara Chaturvēdi and others of Nāraṇachēri;

(3) another bit of land 1 *pāḍaham* of 240 *kuḻis* in the same square bought from Vāmanachēri Kēśavakramavittan.

The total of these four pieces of land form four *pāḍahams* constituting 960 *kuḻis* and was made over to Vāmanachēri Dāmōdarabhaṭṭa for the various purposes of worship in the temple. In return for this gift, he was bound to conduct daily worship, see to the repairs of the image of the god, etc. The gift was made with pouring of water as usual, and was constituted to be a gift to pass down to the generations following the donee. Probably there is a misreading in the first part of the inscription. The Araiyāṇḍai Pramāṇi ought to

[1]*Ibid* 287.

read Brahmani, and would mean that the wife of the Adiyaranga-mangaḷattūr Araiyāṇḍai made the gift actually. But the Sabha put on record the gift of the Brahmani, and what was more, they took from Dāmōdara Bhaṭṭa the temple priest, the capitalised value for the annual dues upon the land in full, and made it tax free land. This was the resolution of the Mahāsabha, and under their orders the mason, Śrī Purusha Āśāri put it in writing. The next one refers to a gift to the temple of Mahā Vishṇu from out of land which remained unappropriated, and was regarded as property of the village itself as a whole, and therefore at the disposal of the governing body of the village. This is given as an *Archanābhōgam* (for services and worship) to the same individual. The Sabhā puts on record that they made it tax-free land and gave it over to the *Bhaṭṭa* concerned. It also declares it was open to the *Bhaṭṭa* to cultivate it as a flower garden, or a fruit garden, and derive whatever revenue he could from out of it. The next inscription contains the name of another road Avani Nārāyaṇavadi, and relates to a gift in the *pūrvachāra.* It also mentions an irrigation canal from the Tank called Sarasvati Vāykal.

The next one, 290, is of importance. It is a settlement of a general character made by the assembly of the village. It refers to the fourth street from the west of the village and the southern part of it, where there were some shops, to which a pathway led; and the house sites concerned were on the southern side of the street called Mādāṇi Mangalam. These four house sites were almost at the east end of the street in the southern row. That was changed by exchanging, selling, acquiring and otherwise adjusting, and a plot of land of almost about that size was reserved for the purpose of the Sabha by purchase after the payment of its full price. Nobody was to dispose of the land by sale, gift or otherwise. If any one "should transgress these arrangements and sell it, or otherwise alienate it, he will be held to the same penalty as one that failed in his official duty." The next one No. 291, is of very considerable importance. It is a record of the 15th year of Parāntaka I, and refers to a certain number of gifts to two temples, the temple of Tirupulivanam and the temple of the *Tulābhāra* (Tulābhārattaḷi). Apparently the arrangement had fallen into desuetude and the Sabha had to make renewed arrangements for carrying it on. Here the property given for the performance and conduct of services, etc., in these temples is decribed as *Kuḍi Bhūmi* lands, under or in possession of cultivators. The Sabha sold these lands, and from the price realised, they made arrangements for not merely the same services as before, but offered twice the services; and to assure themselves that the services would be conducted without fail as before, they placed the money under the control of the great ones constituting the annual management (*Samvatsara Vāriya Perumakkaḷ*), who were to record the document on stone. The latter Sabha accepted this responsibility and others of a similar import from three other individuals, and obviously undertook to carry out the instructions of the Sabha. Unfortunately the closing part is gone, and we cannot be sure what exactly was done.

The next following is one of very great interest and has reference to the maintenance of the roads of the village. This document has reference again to the time of the same Parāntaka, but is dated in the 16th year of his reign. The Mahāsabha here makes the statement that the Paramēśvaravadi at the southern end of the town had been overrun by water, and had been absorbed with waste land and grown slushy. It thus became unfit for the use of any of the castes and communities about the locality. In order to rectify this, which was three rods broad, they acquired by purchase and by various other ways bits of land constituting various properties of different individuals, and ultimately made the road two rods broad throughout its whole length. The funds for the purpose were funds at the disposal of one who is described as *Ūrmēl Ninṛa Tiruvaḍikaḷ*. That means a person whose function it was to superintend the town in certain departments of its administration. The money for the acquisition of the bits of land was placed with the committee for garden supervision, who were to make the necessary acquisition and provide for the other expenses to make the road. The orders were issud by the Mahāsabha. The details of the acquisition of land from various parties are given in full and these *Tiruvaḍikaḷ* supervised the carrying out of the details and when the road was thus made completely, the lands devoted to its maintenance were made tax-free after taking the equivalent thereof, and the maintenance of the road was placed under the charge of the garden supervision committee. This was put in writing under the orders of the great ones of the Sabha by the *Madhyasta, Śivadāsa,* who describes himself as the Alankāra Priyan of the 12,000. The next record has reference to the burning of a lamp. This was placed under the supervision of the *Samvatsaravāriyar*.

The next one, No. 294, is of interest. This town had the advantage of a big irrigation tank called Vairamēghataṭaka. Probably it came into existence three generations before the ruler in whose reign the document was issued. This refers to the gift of one *pāḍaham* of 240 *kuḻis,* which was made in free-gift by one Agnikramavitta Somayāji from out of property that descended from his father. He belonged to the group (*Ghaṇa*) that administered the village (*Āḷunghaṇam*). This property was made over for the purpose of annual repairs of the *taṭāka,* and the repairs by cutting down and removing the silt had to be done annually under the supervision of the committee for tanks. The next one is an interesting document relating to how these committees and other functionaries were usually elected. We shall deal with that in the next section (Refer to 295 Ibid).

No. 297 relates to the reign of Parāntaka and of his fifteenth year. The Mahāsabha is said there to have met in the big Manṭapa and put on record the making of a piece of land tax-free. The land was to be made over to the Vishṇu temple and was given by a Śāttan Maṇināgan, son of Vēśālipāḍi Araiyan, who is described 'as our son', whatever that meant. The land was sold by Govindachēri another ward of the town, and the Sabha took from this Maṇināgan the capitalised value of the revenue dues and made it tax free. The Committee declared that "they will not demand from the cultivators of this land Veṭṭi (free labour), Amanji, again services that had to be rendered without remuneration and Iṛai, tax due. It is followed by the usual statement that those that hindered the perpetuation of this would become sinners, and such would be punished by the Dharmāsanam by a fine of 25 *kaḷanju* of gold. This was the resolution of the Mahāsabha and the *Madhyasta*, Śivadāsa put it in writing.

No. 312 relates to an educational provision in return for which the recipient was to be primarily resident in the village and teach. No. 314 refers to a grant made by Tāyichāni, who was the junior wife of a Brahman Agnichitta Sarvakratu who belonged to the *Āḷunghaṇattār* for the purpose of the daily worship of the temple. No. 317 is the usual grant of land made tax-free by the Mahāsabha, which was put on record on stone. Failure to carry it out, or obstruction to the carrying out of it, was to be taken notice of by the *Śraddhāmantar* (by those whose interest it is to keep watch over these), and a fine of twenty-five pieces of gold was to be imposed either through the judicial body or otherwise. No. 322 is a very interesting document from the point of view of education. A *Bhaṭṭavritti* provision was made by a lady Śannaichāni. Certain families were to have the joint supervision of this charitable gift along with the Mahāsabha. The actual interesting part of it is the very high qualifications that are insisted on for those to whom the *Bhaṭṭavrittis* are to be given. The general qualifications insisted on seem to be a thorough knowledge of one Veda and a complete knowledge of one of the sciences constituting the Vēdānga, which the receipient of the Vritti ought to be able efficiently to expound (*vakkāṇittal*). This work of teaching or expounding was to take place in a

Manṭapa built on the tank bund by this Brahman lady Śannaichāni, who is given the title Uttaramēru Nangai (the daughter or lady of Uttaramēru). These were to teach the coures lasting for three years at the end of which the candidates were to be examined. Those that came out efficiently successful were probably to receive these *Bhaṭṭavrittis.* Unfortunately the document is not quite full, but what is left is interesting enough to give us a general idea. The next one, 323 is of the usual tax-free land being granted by the Mahā-Sabha. The property was made over to a somebody who was to feed twenty Brahmans every day in the temple. This charity was to be carried out by those whose function it was to manage the temple. The next one, No. 324 is a grant to the Uvachchar, a class of Non-Brahmans, whose function it is to play a conch and recite Tamil verses of the Tēvāram and other similar works. The interesting part of it is that this is a grant of the time of Krishna III of the Rāshtrakūṭas, and is dated in his reign. A certain number of taxes are mentioned as usual, indicating the continuance of the administration even when we pass to the rule of another foreign dynasty.

The next is a very interesting document, which records that a thousand pieces of gold were made over by an individual for the purpose of the Vairamēgha Taṭāka, the irrigation tank Vairamēgha, to which was added another similar grant of two hundred, and they were appropriated for the purpose of maintaining the tank. The next one, No. 337, refers to a number of gifts of goats and sheep for the purpose of perpetual lamps in the temple. These were taken possession of by the management of Śrīgovindachēri of Uttaramēru-chaturvēdimangalam. Similarly Vāmanachēri also gets mentioned in these inscriptions, and the document is ordered to be indited by the *Āḷunghaṇattār* generally. This seems to indicate that each ward had its own management, and where a general grant was concerned, they all of them together took note of whatever was made of general interest. The next No. 341 refers to the maintenance of a perpetual lamp, but the funds for this were given to the committee in charge of tanks. No. 342 is an interesting grant for the Sapta Matrikas (the seven mothers) in the town, for which lands had to be purchased and the Sabha sold the land. No. 344 refers to the settlement made by the Sabha. The settle ment referred to is at the request of the cultivating in habitants of the village praying that the lands may be made *Sāmantu* as it is called. It is to distribute land in possession to the various individuals of the village, and that is a function which fell upon the Mahā-Sabha of the village. The interesting part is this. Certain lands that were given in possession had not been cultivated, and certain other lands, for one reason or another, had failed to pay the dues to the village. These lands were taken over by the whole community of the town after paying the dues, and whatever was not paid by the others were paid from the funds of the Vairamēga Taṭāka, holding the land as the property of the Tank Committee. The arrangement was—it seems to be quite a general arrangement—that the land was to be held in hypothecation by the Committee for three years during which it was open to the original owners to pay the debt and recover the land. If they failed to redeem it in the course of three years the land would become the permanent property of the Tank Committee. What must be noted here is the interesting word *Sāmantu,* and *Sāmanta* therefore would mean primarily a land owner. The next one, No. 345, mentions that the *sabaiyār* assembled in the big manṭapa of the village, and in these general *Sabhā* meetings all could assemble including the *bāla* (young) and *vriddha* (old people). These two classes are generally excluded where executive or administrative offices are concerned. The meeting was for the purpose of making some general arrangement in regard to the village. No. 350 is one of the time of Kulottunga Chola III, and is of interest as indicating that the arrangement for the government of the town continued just exactly what it was at the commencement of the period; and what is more, the record here actually makes reference to previous gifts and brings them up to being followed even where they had fallen into desuetude. It refers to provision made for burning perpetual lamps in the fourteenth year of Raja Mārttāṇḍa Aparājita Vikrama, probably the last Pallava prince that we know of. This grant was made by Aparājita on the day of an eclipse of the sun. Then another gift for a similar purpose of the days of Kannāradēva's eighteenth year, that is, the eighteenth year of Krishna III, the Rāshṭrakūṭa. Another item refers to the thirteenth year of Parāntaka I. Another one of the fourteenth year of the same reign. All these refer to the maintenance of eight perpetual lamps. Those that had undertaken to maintain these eight lamps by the acceptance of the provision made for them found it impossible to continue to do so; after some time a certain change in the arrangement was made with the agreement of the Māhēśvaras or the Brahman elders of the temple and the citizens of the town, and, instead of maintaining these lamps, certain festivals on certain fixed days in the year had to be conducted, when these perpetual lamps were to be maintained also. This new arrangement was ordered by the Mahā-Sabha and was put in writing by the *Madhyasta*.

The next one is of the time of Vikramachola and is dated in his fifteenth year. This refers to a document having reference to a sale of land in payment of debts due to the temple of Tiru-Ēkambamuḍayar in the locality. They borrowed certain sums of money for certain services which they discovered they could not find the means to carry out from year to year, and this accumulated to 230 and a half gold pieces. With this responsibility for the accounts, when the Māhēsvaras of the temple demanded the payment, the community that borrowed pleaded inability, and sold certain lands belonging to them in lieu thereof. The Mahā-Sabha placed on record this transaction, transferred the ownership of this land from the previous owners to the temple, and in the usual fashion, transformed it into tax free land after the usual consideration. This was to be entered into the book of records of the town. That was also to be entered into the tax register. The resolution was made by the Sabha as usual, and was recorded by the *Madhyasta*.

No. 363 is an interesting grant which relates to 73 *kaḻanju* of gold for maintaining a second boat for the purposes of the Vairamēgha Taṭāka. The object of maintaining this boat is the excavating or taking out of the silt, and throwing it out on the bank. The man in charge of the boat was maintained, and his daily duty seems to have been to remove the silt, as it accumulates and throw it on the bank. No. 355 is of interest as making provision for one to conduct daily worship. The person who was to conduct the worship it is insisted on should know the Vēda in the *pārayaṇa* form, apparently meaning that he should be in a position to recite it, chanting it as is customary. He must be a Brahman of character and unmarried. No. 359 refers to a deposit of 20 *kaḻanjus* of gold. This revenue was derived by the sale of the manure in all the various wards of the town. The money thus collected was set apart by the Sabha for the repairs to the Vairamēgha Taṭāka. This was to be credited to the tank funds, which the committee of the tank was to apply from time to time for the purposes of keeping the tank in repairs. No. 360 refers to the acceptance of 20 gold pieces from an individual for the purpose of maintaining a water shed in front of the *Pramāṇi Manṭapa*, probably the pavilion in which the courts were held, and it was a charitable provision for water supply. No. 361 refers again to the reign of Kulottunga III. This is provision by the Sabha for the *Grāmadēvata* goddesses (Piḍārimār), and refers to the grant of ten *vēlis* of land. This gift was put on record in the temple of the white one, probably again the *Grāmadēvata Madirāvīran.* The order of this gift was received from the headquarters which the local governor Chēdi Rājadēva transmitted. The *Perumkuṛi* Mahā Sabhai of the town carried out the order by marking out the land and registering the gift in the proper form. No. 362 refers to the reign of Kannāradēva, and details the arrangement that had been come to by the *Perumkuṛi* Mahā Sabha, which had assembled in the great hall of the place. The assembly was held by day and refers to the fines that the Sabha imposed and collected. The Sabha resolved that the great men of the administration of the village should collect these fines and pay it to the Sabha. If these were not paid within the time, they were to bring it to the notice of the Sabha, and get the defaulters further punished till payment was made. This was to apply even with regard to the members of the Sabha who were fined, the members of the committee of the Sabha who had been fined, and all those people of the Sabha including the Madhyasta and those holding positions in the administration of the village. The fines imposed on all these must be collected by the administration committee, default thereof being brought to the notice of the Sabha. What was insisted on was that these fines should be collected within the year, failure in which would make the administrative committee liable to a fine. This refers to a certain grant made to the temple, and a certain other grant made for the maintenance of the tank. They are both of them rolled together into one from the interest of both of which the committee of the tank should make provision for keeping the tank in condition. In consideration of this charity the individual donor was excused the dues upon certain lands. No. 370 refers to a deed of sale of land, the lands having been sold to three Brahman brothers as a *Bhaṭṭa-sāmantu,* that is under Brahman ownership apparently.

A certain narrow piece of land all round the tank was taken over and reserved as a desirable margin for the tank, and that was not to be enclosed or otherwise obstructed, and such as do it are put under a liability to pay a fine. No. 371 is an arrangement made by the Sabha for feeding a thousand Brahmans on occasions of certain festivals. No. 374 again refers to the 18th year of Kannāradēva, Krishna III, and refers to a grant made by Śiriya Nangai Chāni, the wife of Iḷaya Chandravēḷa Bhaṭṭa. The grant seems to have been made for a perpetual lamp on her death-bed.

The Principle of Election and Procedure.—

The procedure adopted at the elections of these important committees for the government of rural units, villages or groups of villages, is on record in a practical form in the instructions laid down for electing the gold committee of the Uttaramēru-chaturvēdimangalam. It is the Sabha that promulgated the rules in the 15th year of Parāntaka I. The document declares that it was an arrangement made by the Sabha for the constitution of the committee whose function it was to test and certify to the standard of quality and weight of the gold that circulated in their town. The electorate consisted of those in the village who were neither too young nor too old; these were to set down, from among the inhabitants of the village who paid revenue on lands cultivated by them, the names of those who, in their opinion, were good estimators of gold. When the tickets had been collected, the inhabitants of the main streets assembled, and, these tickets had been put into the pot as prescribed, they were to elect by drawing lots, four representatives for their chēri (ward). In the same manner they should elect two for Sēnaichēri, three for Śankarapāḍi; these should be estimators of gold impartially for all people alike. They shall not use a big stone for estimating quality; but shall give their estimate otherwise. The gold that was collected daily in lac from the small rubbing stone, they must make over, without reserving any bit, to the great men supervising the tanks. Every three months they were to present themselves before the committee for the year, and declare before them solemnly that they would not make false estimates, and that, if they should do so, they may suffer from hunger. Thus "we arranged for constituting a committee for the assay of gold in our village. We, the Sabha of Uttaramēru-chaturvēdimangalam"—A part is here gone and what is left over seems to imply that the fee for doing this work was to have been seven and a half *manjāḍi* of gold per month. This was put in record[1] by the Madhyasta, Śivadāsa. This shows the actual working of the election rules and the safeguards provided against misfeasance. The procedure indicated here for the specific purpose of a special committee seems to have been generally adopted, and even incorporated in a general circular of which we have records in the inscriptions in Uttaramallūr. They incorporate the election rules, and what follows is an analytical summary of these.

II

General prevalence of these institutions through the Tamil country.—

This account taken from records of only one locality, viz., the Brahman settlement or township of

[1] South Indian Inscriptions Vol. VI, No. 295. (A.D. No. 12 of 1898).

Uttaramēruchaturvēdimangalam may be liable to the suspicion whether that was not a mere exception rather than the rule. If it is the only place where the evidence was available perhaps the suspicion would be fairly just. But while the information from Uttaramallūr may be full, because of the large number of records preserved in the place, we have a pretty large number of places, from which fragments of these records have come down to us, which give details here and there of the same character, though not in the same degree of fulness and variety. The absence of records, in this case, at any rate, would not warrant the conclusion that the institutions of which these are records never existed. Such remnants as have come down to us from various localities, imperfect in their nature—made perhaps more imperfect still by the ravages of time—still make it clear that the character of rural administration was generally what it is described to be from the records at Uttaramallur. In 1899 when Mr. Venkayya published an account of the election rules from the two records of Parāntaka I, to which allusion had already been made, he found that as many as 190 centres gave indication, by the inscriptions collected from them, of the same character of rural administration. The records since published and the inscriptions since collected by the epigraphists ought certainly to have added to the information that he had at the time, and choosing just a few from salient localities, we can easily show the general prevalence of institutions of the kind over the whole of the Chola dominions, which during the greater part of Chola rule was more or less synonymous with the Tamil country as a whole.

There is one other point in regard to the character of these, which ought also to be noticed. The largest number of inscriptions are records of gifts to temples, and, preserved more or less in temples only, so that one may be tempted to state it that these were institutions peculiar to a class of villages, concerned with gifts to temples or to Brahmans only, and not villages otherwise normally inhabited by people other than the Brahmans. Even here the examination of the large number of records published show that it was not so, however complete may be the records in respect of these particular villages. It was not merely the privilege of the Brahmans to have had these self-governing rural institutions; but the privilege seems to have been fairly widespread, though in all communal matters each community settled its own affairs, and members of the other communities did not interfere except by invitation in the great majority of cases. The position of the officials of government also was almost the same. To take but a few instances, No. 90 of Volume III of the South Indian Inscriptions refers to the temple of Tirumeygñānam where the market fees were sold by the assembly of Nālūr belonging to ŚēṟṟurKūṟṟam to the temple at Tirumeygñānam. The inscription is undated but is ascribed by the epigraphist to Āditya I, the second ruler of the Chola dynasty. The part of the record which is interesting is this "from those who bring from outside villages and sell such articles as paddy, rice, etc., which are sold by measuring shall be received *one naḻi* for each *kāśu* (realised), and for other articles placed on the ground and sold (*one*) *nāḻi* shall be received on each heap (*kūval*). For articles sold by weight one *palam* shall be received on each weighment (*niṟai*).[1] For each basket of betel leaf shall be received one *paṟṟu*,[2] and two arecanuts from each basket (of them). There is also rather an imperfect statement that something was received on each *vaṭṭi*, but what this is is not clear. The right to collect these market dues was sold to the temple for 25 *kāśu* by the great men of the *Perumkuṟi* including the great men, the Bhaṭṭas of the village. No. 96 of the same Volume refers to the village Tiruchenduṟai, where one of the daughters-in-law of king Parāntaka I raised a temple and gave, for the daily expenses, sixty *kaḻanju* of gold of the *Tuḷaippon*. This is a gold coin which probably received a punch mark. Possibly the punching was made by the gold estimators as a mark of its having been authoritatively estimated. This was received by the *Paruḍaiyār* of Īśānamangalam, of which Tiruchendurai was a suburb. The *Paruḍai* here is the Sanskrit *Parishad*, and perhaps corresponds to the Mahā Sabha. They put the amount out at interest, and from the income of 60 *kalams* of paddy, they carried out what was intended. The next one, No. 99, of the same volume is of interest as referring to the village Tiruppāṟkaḍal in the North Arcot District where a general of the Chola king made a grant in honour of

[1]The Epigraphist supplies the information that the term *Niṟai* equalled 100 palams according to Winslow's dictionary. Even apart from Winslow, one *niṟai* or its synonym *iḍai* in Tamil means usually unit weight. Even now by the country steel-yard with which they weigh, ordinary bazaar people sell by one or two or three or a number of *tūkku* or *iḍai* (meaning a vis and a quarter). It would therefore be very much better to interpret the passage as one palam on each unit measure of weight, which may be a vis and a quarter ⅟. In the Tanjore district, that is usually called *Tūkku*, which means exactly the same thing as *Niṟai* or *Iḍai*. A *Tūkku* is a vis and a quarter. It is *iḍai* elsewhere. But the unit measure may vary from place to place.

[2]This seems rather a false grammatisation for *Pattu* (ten).

warriors that fought and fell in battle. The general was Śennippērararaiyan of Araiśūr, and the battle is said to have been fought at Vēḷūr between his king Parāntaka I, and the allied Pandya and Ceylon kings. The village is here described as belonging to Kaverippākkam, otherwise Avaninārāyaṇa Chaturvēdi-Mangalam. It is called popularly Kaverippākkam as a rule, though actually it is Kāvidippākkam, the village of the account officers or officials. The people that assembled are said to have been composed of the management for the year and that of the Kuḍumbu or ward, the committee for the gardens, the committee for the fields, the committee for the northern fields and the Bhaṭṭas, and others constituting the great Sabha. Under their orders the committee for tanks issued the document. They received 120 pieces of gold for the purpose of investing it as capital for the keeper of the boat in the great tank in their village. From out of the interest, four Brahmans, learned in the Vedas, were to be fed in the feeding house constructed by him in the village Kharapura on the banks of the Palar. The committee for tanks took the responsibility upon themselves of carrying out this charity. No. 106 refers to an agreement between the Sabha of Narasinga Mangalam near Ānaimalai close to Madura, and an officer of the Chola king, Aruṇidi Kaliyan of Marudūr. It refers to a certain annual amount of 18 *kāśu* of Ceylon which the temple had to pay to the Sabha every year. This together with a certain amount of cash paid by the temple authorities to the Sabha was made use of for certain purposes of the temple. They made over all the liabilities therefor to the officer Kaliyan who had to take upon himself to discharge all the liabilities due under this head, in return for the possession of the tank called Kaliyanēri, which he was to keep in repairs not only, but was also allowed to raise the bund or lengthen it as it seemed necessary. He purchased two *vēlis* of land under this tank, and from out of the 300 kalams of paddy, which was the income therefrom as landlord, he set apart one half for the needs of the temple requirements for feeding five Veda-Brahmans, and made certain other provisions also for the annual requirements of the temple. In accordance with this agreement entered into with him, the Sabha of the place and the supervisor of the temple management made themselves responsible for seeing to it that this was done every year without fail from the particular day mentioned. Failure to do so made both the Sabha and the *Śrī Kāryam* (manager) alike liable to a fine of two gold pieces a day. The concluding sentence includes in this responsibility the Vaishṇavas whose business it was to supervise the servants of the temple. The point to notice here in this record is the irrigation tank of the village given over by the village assembly to individual management for particular purposes under the control of the temple management. No. 112 refers to the assembly of Tirupālatturai, otherwise Uttamaśīli-Chaturvēdi-Mangalam. This refers to a *mā* and odd of land made tax free on receipt of the capitalised value of ten *kāśu.*

No. 156 is of importance as it refers to a pretty large number of committees. This comes from the place, Tiruppārkaḍal, already referred to above, and was under the control of the assembly of Kāvidipakkam, (which has become Kaveripakkam since then as in this case), otherwise known as Avani (Amani) Nārāyaṇa Chadurvēdi-Mangalam. The committees actually mentioned are the Samvatsaravāriyam (the committee for the annual management), Tōṭṭa vāriyam (garden committee), Ēri vāriyam (tank committee), Kaḻani vāriyam (fields committee), Panchavāra vāriyam (the committee of five (?) for daily management), Kaṇakku vāriyam (the accounts committee), Kalingu vāriyam (sluices committee), Taḍivaḻi vāriyam (perhaps roads committee measured by the *taḍi* or rod). Besides these, the assembly included the general body of Bhaṭṭas or learned Brahmans of the village. Two other individuals are mentioned as being among them and associated with the issue of this document. The first of these is Pallavan Brahmādarāyan, the governor of the place, probably the headman of the village, and Kangāṇi Arumbankiḻān. Kangāṇi would simply mean one that supervises, and what exactly he supervised here is not stated. The arrangement that they came to refers to lands belonging to the temple having been damaged by floods and made uncultivable. This state of affairs was brought to the notice of the Sabha. The Sabha ordered that, in lieu of this, an equal quantity of land in what lay as the common property of the village may be measured and handed over to the temple by "the assembly for the fields" for the year. The order of the assembly was accordingly carried out by the committee. It is stated that land which paid no tax to the village on the northern side of the northern irrigation channel (Vaḍa-Vāykāl) was given. The document was written by an accountant under the committee for the management of the fields by name Gangadhara Māilaṭṭi of Maṇimangalam, and other officials of the village also signed the document.

No. 157 comes from Uttaramallūr itself, and refers to a declaration of land as tax free on the usual conditions. No. 158 is of particular interest as referring to a certain number of roads not heard of elsewhere, such as Avani Nārāyaṇa Vadi, Vairamēgha Vadi, Viḍēl Viḍuhu Vadi, etc. No. 159 is of interest as it refers to the assembly having made tax-free lands belonging to Durgā Bhaṭṭāraki on receiving *pūrvāchūra* accruing from the interest due to the temple from documents executed in favour of the goddess and in favour of the Sabha. There is mention here of the irrigation channel Śrīdēvi by name, the streets Pallava Nāraṇavadi, and Mārpiḍugu Vadi, new names. No. 160 again is making lands tax free on the usual terms to a new temple of Ḳurukshētradēva, rather an unusual name, perhaps standing for Krishṇa. No. 161 is of interest. It makes provision by the Perunguṛi Sabha of Uttaramallūr for those who taught Vyākaraṇa by commenting on it. The land thus disposed of was made over by a Vāsudēva Bhaṭṭa Somayāgi of Bhadramangalam. Among the boundaries are mentioned Subramanya Nārāśam, the lane named Subramanya. There is also mention of the land being of the third class, and another bit as belonging to the first class (*talai taram*). There is a reference to a Vyākaraṇa Manṭapa in Tiruvorriyūr, which the epigraphists take to mean a grant made over for expounding the science of grammar in a Manṭapa called Vyākaraṇa Manṭapa. This is a record of Chola Kulottunga III, (No. 202 for 1912 Epig. Coll.). This seems there to a stand for the provision for the conduct of a festival in the temple in accordance with the tradition that Pāṇini received the science of grammar from Śivā, and the Vyākaraṇa Manṭapa is a hall in which this festival was celebrated of Siva making the gift of grammar to Pāṇini. Provision was also made for teaching grammar in the hall throughout the year. The provision that is made here is merely for the actual teaching of the science of grammar.

No. 162 is the usual gift to a temple of village lands which were long uncultivated and not paying tax. There is a reference to a temple to Tirumāl-irunjōlai Perumāḷ This is the Vishṇu god at Tirumālirunjōlai near Madura. No. 177 is of particular interest. It was a gift by the Sabha of Uttaramallūr for the maintenance of a physician, who was expert in the removal of poison. This is called *Vishahara Bhogam,* and was given to the man as a tax free land. It was to be enjoyed by those that were expert in the removal of poison and by no other, which means it was not to be a hereditary gift. The next one, No. 180, comes from the village Tiruvaḍandai in the Chingleput District and refers to a gift of land by a resident of Talai-Śayanapuram or Taiyūr, other names for Mahābalipuram. No. 181 comes from Tiruvalidāyam, otherwise called Pāḍi, which refers to a sale of 1350 *kuḷi* of village land (*manjikkam*) by the assembly of *Kuraṭṭūr* alias Parāntaka Chaturvēdi-Mangalam. The interesting detail in this document is that the unit of measure was a rod of sixteen spans. No. 186 refers to a present of fifteen *kaḻanju* of gold to the Vishṇu god at Tiruvaḍandai by two residents of Talaśayanapuram or Taiyūr already referred to. The assembly of the village as usual received the money and agreed to pay the annual interest. But the document is attested by the *Sabhaiyōm* (members of the Sabha) as also the inhabitants of the village. No. 188 is of interest as it refers to a gift of land as *Taṇṇipaṭṭi* by the residents of Kāṭṭūr to the *ambalam* constructed by Paṭṭaiyanār, who is described as the chief superintendent of the *Perumdaram*. *Taṇṇipaṭṭi* would mean a piece of land for the supply of water. Here it seems to mean provision for the supply of water to the assembled people in the common hall of the village (*ambalam*). The donor is described as *Perumdarat-tukku-mēl-Nāyagam* (the presiding chief or president of the great ones).

No. 190 is of interest, as it comes from the village Takkolam, a division by itself in Maṇaiyir Kōṭṭam. It refers to the gift of 92 *kaḻanju* of gold provided for the sacred offerings to the god. This was put out at interest and fetched 92 *kādi* of paddy a year. This was to be measured by the grain measure of the *Pancha-vāriyam*, the authorized measure current at the time. No. 191 is of interest. It is a provision by the Maha Sabha to the Śelli Amman temple by the assembly of Vēḷachēri, making provision for the daily offerings of the Sapta-Mātṛs. The land is made over, as usual, by the village Sabha, after having made it tax free. It was taken over by the Brahmans in charge of the temple, Mātṛ-Śivas, who made themselves responsible for the daily offerings. No. 193 again belongs to Uttaramallūr. It is of interest as being the gift of the queen of Pārthivēndrādhipati-Varman. She set up an image in the temple of Tiruvayōdhyai, and the assembly made it tax free after obtaining *pūrvāchāram* from her. No. 195 is of interest, as it is provision for two perpetual lamps in the temple of Veḷḷai Mūrti Perumān. This name would mean Balarāma, or the village god Madirai-Vīran-here it seems to indicate the former by the style of the name. This is again provision that was made by the queen by the grant of 192 sheep. The Veḷḷāḷas of Paṇṇaichēri received 96 of these and the merchants of the middle bazaar, the other 96, and between them they promised to maintain the lamps without fail. No. 198 is of interest as it refers to a gift in connection with Śrīgōvinḍappāḍi in the Vaḷanāḍu belonging to the Dāmar Kōṭṭam. Provision was made for feeding a Brahman in the Vishṇu temple daily. The donor is described as a person whose name was Kaṇṇan, described as *Kannamoga Vāraṇappēraraiyan*. He is stated to have been a man, who got on the elephant immediately behind the Perumāḷ, that is, the king, and is otherwise described as "one of the elephant corps, *Ānai Āaḷ Kaṇṇan.*

No. 200 belongs to the town of Kumbhakonam and refers to the sale by the *"Mūlapaṛaḍai Perumākkaḷ"*, or the great men of the original assembly. It refers to the sale of 2 *vēli* of land out of the 24 *vēli* they possessed as *abhishēka dakshiṇai,* the fee for bathing the god Tirunāgēsvara Svāmin in the village Mērkāvēri in the Innambar Nāḍu. This was purchased by one Śiṟṟingamuḍayān Koil Mailai alias Parāntaka Mūvēnda Vēlān, and made it into a *Bhaṭṭavṛtti* for one who was to teach Prabhākara. This is a school of Mīmāṁsa, which, at one time, seems to have had considerable popularity. Prabhakāra was a contemporary of Kumarila Bhaṭṭa and is regarded as among his pupils, sometimes also as a follow student. It is interesting that a grant for the teaching of this Śāstra should be made by a Vēḷān so early as the third year of Parakēsari Varman. This same official who is described here as auditor or supervisor of the state work, made provision in the temple at Tiruviḍaimarudūr for the dramatic performance called *Āriyakūttu* to be performed every year in the asterism Pūśam in the month of Thai, a date which would usually fall in the January or February of every year. This officer, along with the Sabha of Tiraimūr, the citizens of Tiruviḍaimarudūr, also the management of the temple of the locality, all of them assembled in the theatre hall and made the grant to one Kīrtti Maṛaikkāḍan alias Tiruvēḷai Araichchākkai. Śākkai is a class known as Śākyas, the Chākkyar in Malabar even now, who were a people born of a Brahman by a woman of a lower class, whose function it was to exhibit dramas on the stage. Here was a provision made for the enacting of a drama on the occasion of the greatest annual festival of the temple through the chief of the troupe. No. 203 relates to an enquiry conducted by this very same official into the affairs of the temple. After enquiry he found it necessary to enhance the scale of offerings, and made provision for them from the unpaid balance of paddy from the assembly of Tiraimūr, a *devadāna* village. He found on enquiry that 256 *kalams* of paddy were due from this Sabha by the measure *Panchavāram*.

The details of additional information gathered above from volume III, Part III, of the South Indian Inscriptions, containing miscellaneous inscriptions copied from various localities in the Tamil districts, go only to confirm the details of rural administration which we are able to glean from a study of the inscriptions in a single locality like Uttaramallur. It adds also to the knowledge acquired from these latter by giving us the names of a few more committees and details in regard to the exercise of the power vested in the committees. We learn from these that there was practically nothing connected with the village units, which generally does not come within the competence of the general committee of the village; and while resolutions in regard to the action to be taken were always arrived at in the assembly as a whole, the carrying of the resolutions into effect was usually entrusted to the particular committees concerned, whose special duty was actually to carry out the resolutions of the general committee. While therefore the general position is quite clear as to the relation between the general committee and the departmental committees, we perhaps have to look a little farther afield before we can state it with confidence that that was the general state of administration in the Tamil country as a whole. It is hardly necessary for us to study other localities in the fullest detail for doing this. It would be quite enough for our purpose if we collect from some salient localities such details as are available to make sure that the system of administration of rural localities that obtained was the same all over. Some of the details are such as cannot by themselves exist unless it be as part and parcel of the whole system adumbrated above. Such details we do get from various localities, and we shall take, for example, two or three to gain an idea of the whole.

The village, Tirumalavāḍi, not far from Tanjore but actually in the Trichinopoly District, gives some interesting details, which, apart from their own interest, supply also the information required in regard to the general character of rural administration that we are looking for. We may take that locality as typical of the Chola country proper. No. 635 of Volume V of the South Indian Inscriptions refers to the reign of Rājādhirāja, where there is an interesting reference to the Chāḷukyas of Kalyāṇi. The Chāḷukyas are described as descended of the families of Vēḷ, petty governors of subordinate governments. The record is that of the Perumkuṛi-Mahā-Sabha of the village Gaṇḍārāditya Chaturvēdi Maṅgalam, belonging to Poygai Nāḍu in the division Rājēndra Śinga Vaḷa Nāḍu. They had assembled in full, without shortage, and ordered the assignment of the revenues of certain villages for as long as the sun and the moon last, and, in accordance with this resolution, they issued the order *niyōgam koḍuttōm*). A number of high officials signed this, and the official endorsement takes the form 'under the orders of all these great ones, the *madhyastan,* Tiru Aranga Nārāyaṇan of "the thousand two hundred" wrote it.' No. 634 contains a detail of some interest that a certain amount of land is made over to a man, who was to supply water daily for the bathing of the idol. But the land is said to have been given to him for his maintenance and for his *veṭṭi*. *Veṭṭi* ordinarily is, what is called in Sanskrit, *Vishṭi,* and means such services as people have to render gratuitously, when called upon to do so for certain fixed purposes. It is very probable that this man, whose general function it was to carry water from the river for the purpose of bathing the idol, had perhaps to render certain other services also without separate payment for it. No. 637 refers to a gift by a Brahman lady, the wife of one who enjoyed the title Uttamachola Brahma-Mārāyar. His proper name is obliterated in the inscription. The whole title contains two terms, of which the first is the title of the Chola ruler for the time being, or it may possibly be one of his predecessors. Brahma-Mārāyar is a title of distinction conferred upon Brahmans. We have the authority of the Tolkāppiyam that persons who rendered distinguished services could be given titles *Mārāyan* ordinarily, from the Sanskrit form *Mahārāja*. That could be conferred almost upon anybody. We have the term Śākkai-Mārayan[1] occurring in an inscription of Rājēndra, the Gangaikonḍa Chōla. That means the Mahārāja among actors, as the Śākkayar were a people who formed dramatic troupes, and performed before audiences of all kinds. The title was conferred upon the chief among them. So here the Brahma-Mārāyar is an indication that the holder of the title was a Brahman. His wife shared the honour, and she is called *Mārāśiyār*, Sans. *Mahārāgñi*. No. 638 refers to a grant to the temple in the 20th year, probably of the same king. The grant was made by the Chola-Kula-Sundari, daughter of Rāman, who is also called here Mahārājiyār, as the wife of a Brāhman Nārāyaṇakṛamavittan, who is also called Madhurāntaka Brahma-Mārāyan. She made provi-

[1]Ep. Rep. 1915, p. 98 Sic. 22. No. 64 of 1914 at Kāmarasavalli.

sion in the temple for certain articles, such as stand-mirrors and so on. The temple management (*deva-karmins*) accepted the grant, and agreed that, from out of the cash that was given and the revenue that was assigned, they would keep the tank Śembiyan Mādēvi Pērēri in order, and 'will not show it in the register' otherwise.

No. 641 contains the important detail in regard to the character of the revenue incidences upon villages generally, a point which has been very much animadverted upon and discussed. Rājādhirāja is declared in this inscription, as also in several others, to have conducted a prosperous administration from what he received as tributes from subordinate kings, a number of whom are actually mentioned. His other important source of revenue is mentioned as the sixth share of the land under his rule. This is quite in agreement with what we find in one of the Kuṛals where the royal revenues are three general items; that which comes to the king for lack of owners; that which comes to him by means of tolls and customs; and that which comes to them by way of fines upon subjects and tributes imposed upon enemies. This here refers only to one of the three, as in fact the Kuṛal excludes the sixth share as being more or less fundamentally a part of what was due to the king. No. 978 of the same year gives almost the same details. No. 641 gives, in great detail, the specification of another grant of land by the Perumkuri Mahā Sabha, which had assembled in the Śrīgaṇḍarādittachēri, and made the settlement that they should pay the dues on the land under this particular class of revenue assessment (*ittaram*). One interesting detail is that they released the land under reference from the payment of small taxes and from the free services usual. No. 642 is of interest. It disposes of a piece of land, which, not having an owner, was made over to the God of Tirumalavāḍi by the Brahman owner of the village, Kalayamangalam, to which the land belonged. Apparently the land was in an uncultivable condition and had to be reclaimed for purposes of cultivation. It was so reclaimed by investing temple funds for the purpose, and came to be known as land reclaimed by *Nandikēśvara-mayakku.* The local unit of measure was the rod of twelve feet, which would be the same as the rod of sixteen spans. The charges of reclamation are placed under the supervision of the Mahēśvaras of the temple, and the officer in charge of the temple affairs. On an average of four men to a *kuḻi* to bring it into condition, it took the labour of 12,096 men, and they were paid at the rate of one *kuṛuṇi* per man, and the actual quantity of paddy distributed was 1008 *kalams.* This was made over to the temple after releasing the liability for small dues on the land when it was lying unreclaimed. The net total of paddy that accrued from this land to the temple was 255 *kalams.* Those that were engaged in the cultivation of this land of the village were to be free from the small taxes, from the bigger taxes, and other such incidences to which ordinary lands were liable. Of course, a number of people concerned signed in token of their knowledge. No. 644 is of interest, as it gives the detail that the actual demand on the land for ownership was at the rate of 100 *kalams* of paddy per *veḷi*; a figure arrived at by calculation by me about 25 years ago.

No. 651 refers to the renovation of a temple in Tirumalavāḍi. The interesting reference there is that when the temple *vimāna* had been constructed, an order was issued, that the old inscriptions, copied out in a book, should be cut out carefully as far as may be in their original places. This order was issued by the Danḍanāyaka Nārākkan Raman Arumoḷi alias Uttama-chōla Brahma Mārāyan. This officer addressed the communication to the *Śrīkāryam* of the temple, and to another distinguished man of the village, who seems to have been an ambassador, possibly a resident of the village, to the Brahmans having the management of the temple at Tirumalavāḍi, to the Sabhā of Ganḍarāditya Chaturvedi Mangalam, and to the Sabha of Perumbuliyūr. The order was carried out, and the inscriptions properly indited under the direct supervision of a certain Paṇaiyan, the superintendent of the cultivable lands of Kaḷattūr for the *Śrīkāryam,* and another one Pichchan, who received a communication from the above-mentioned officer. There were a number of others present also who were witnesses to what took place, as also representatives in behalf of the *Sabhā* addressed on the matter. One of these is described as Bhaṭṭālaka, who was the Madhyasta keeping the accounts of the temple, for Araiyan Madhurāntakan, the Perum-Kāvidi (the High Superintendent of Accounts). In the presence, and with the approval, of these, the inscriptions were re-written in accordance with the book. The next one, No. 652 refers to the same transaction, but really to the previous part of the transaction as it relates to the order, and the actual carrying out of the order, to copy down the inscriptions in a book before putting the work of repairs in hand, and goes into the details almost similar to the details given in the previous one.

No. 662 gives some interesting details not hitherto taken note of. It was a general order by the emperor Kulottunga, issued in the fifth year, that 360 Śiva temples in the Chola Manḍala be granted each one *vēli* of land. This grant is a grant of a *vēli* made to the Śiva temple at Tiruvālanturai, now called Anbil on the northern bank of the Kaveri. This village belonged to the Uttunga Vaḷa Nāḍu, otherwise Kuṉṟakūṟṟam, and the land was actually given from the village called Karuṇākara Nallūṟ, the lands of which are included in the register under the head Kanḍarāditta Chaturvēdi Mangalam belonging to Poygai Nāḍu, a division of Bhuvana Muḻudaiya Vaḷa Nāḍu. The land is described as being entered in the account of lands of the village kept by the accountant of the village Śengamala Udayān. It was composed of a number of bits taken from various plots, which are again described as adjoining particular roads and being irrigated from particular channels, altogether similar in detail to what we find in Uttaramallūr. But one detail which we have not come across in the Uttaramallūr inscriptions is of the highest importance. The revenue that was due from these separate bits of land are divided into two classes in this record. One of them is described as the revenue as it was actually paid (Iraikaṭṭina paḍi); and the other class is the old rate of assessment (paḻa iṟai). There also occur the expressions Nichayitta Nilam (lands actually measured) and *Nichaiyāda Nilam* paying *paḻa irai*, that is, land not confirmed in regard to its measurement by actual measure, and paying the old dues accordingly, as in the old register. These details together indicate that lands were surveyed and entered into the register of holdings kept for the purpose. These measured lands and the registers were verified from time to time by re-measurement and calculation of dues based on these measurements as well. These were entered in the register of holdings under each *puravu*, or a number of plots constituting single holdings of land paying the revenue. Two departments are mentioned in this connection as also the chief officer concerned therewith. The first is *Puravu-vari Śri Karaṇam,* that is, the chief accounts officer, whose function was to maintain the register of holdings with the revenue due on each holding. In addition to the Śri Karaṇam or the officer, there is a Mukhaveṭṭi, or headman of this particular department. There is another department of accounts, whose function is described to be, in the next following record No. 663, the division of royal dues upon the land (*Vari kūṟu śeyvār*). In respect of these grants, the lands were taken on the basis of this register, verified and certified to be correct by the departments concerned, and then the necessary reliefs were given and arrangements made by the Sabha, and the lands were gifted over ultimately and so placed in the register. These two documents therefore give an insight into the details of the actual accounts of revenue administration.

The next is No. 670, which is of interest as making provision for burning a perpetual lamp for men, who fell in an affray on the frontier. No. 671 contains the important detail that a certain officer issued an order for a grant of land. While a certain other officer named was examining the accounts when the princess, the wife of Vikramaśoḷa Iḷango Vēḷār, made to the god at Anbil a grant of a certain quantity of silver for making a vessel for the temple service. No. 673 is an inscription of the time of Vikramachola, of the sixth year. Here the point of interest is that a village is described as having belonged to Kanḍarāditya Chaturvedi Mangalam, but at the time had been taken away from it and recorded as a separate unit by itself; and the name of the village is given as Vāṇavidyadhara Nallūr, apparently in the name of the officer who describes himself as Vaṇakkō Araiyan.

In this group therefore of inscriptions taken from Tirumalavāḍi in the heart of the Chola country, we find the organisation of the administration for rural loca lities almost the same in all its details. Passing on to a place like Mannārguḍi, which, like the previous places, was a Brahman centre and a unit by itself, we find one or two details of considerable importance not met with elsewhere. Several details mentioned in the other records from the places that we have considered occur in all their fulness of detail. No. 47 is of a Pandyan king, Vīra Pānḍya, of his nineteenth year, and refers to a meeting in the hall, Bhuvanēka Vīran, in a place called Śariyakkoṭṭai. It refers to a grant by a community, as distinct from the village as a whole, and they describe themselves as coming from "the four quarters and the eighteen divisions". We shall come to that in some little detail in one or two later grants from Ālangudi. No. 48 is of importance, as it refers to a general settlement made at a meeting, where a number of assemblies gathered together for a general purpose. The meeting assembled in the temple of Rājarājēśvara in the 22nd year of Rājādhirājā. Mannargudi is described as a *Taniyūr,* a unit by itself, belonging to Śuttamalli Vaḷa Nāḍu, and the people that assembled were the Maha Sabha of Tirugñāna Sambandar Chaturvedi Mangalam in Pāmaṇi Kūṟṟam, and the Sabhas of Gangaikondachola pēr Iḷamai Nāḍu, Rājarājēśvara pēr Iḷamai Nāḍu, Nālāyira pēr Iḷamai Nāḍu, Āḷapirandan pēr Ilamai Nāḍu, Gangaikondachola pēr Iḷamai Nāḍu. These assemblies all of them jointly met and came to certain agreements as to how to deal with free services to be demanded of villagers and what services could be legitimately demanded of these. They prohibited destraints of person or property in certain cases, and forbade certain other irregularities, which apparently prevailed at the time in an unauthorised fashion. They also fixed the revenue upon lands due to the Sabha, and bound themselves not to take any more, unless it be with the authority of the Maha Sabha. Those that would speak or act otherwise, were held liable to the usual fine. Being a general decision of the Maha Sabha, this was ordered to be inscribed in the local Śiva temple as well as in the Vishṇu temple. No. 50 is of great importance. A complaint was made to the same Maha Sabha that in a particular village—it may be villages as the name is worn out in the record—the dues were collected irregularly, perhaps more than once, and a complaint in that behalf was made by the people, who stated that, in those circumstances, it would be impossible for them to live where they were and cultivate the lands. On the basis of this, all the Sabhas mentioned in the previous record assembled. They laid down again what exactly was due from these villages, what could be taken and what ought not to be taken. It is laid down in considerable detail and is attested by a number of people of importance, and the same punishment is prescribed as in the previous document. No. 54 refers to an assembly which looked after the affairs of the village. No. 57 refers to a new assembly. This is a document of the 48th year of Kulottunga. The assembly had come together under a great mango tree in the courtyard of the temple of Śrī Kulōttunga Viṇṇakar. The assembly is here described as *Dharmiyudhi Peruṁkuri Ghoshṭi.* They had assembled in full and without absentees, and came to an agreement in regard to the regulations concerning lands and the incidences of revenue due. They agreed to pay 30,000 kāśu as revenue upon an area of land consisting of forests, cultivated country, towns, and lands in possession of the Kaḷḷar. This was distributed among a certain number of people for purposes of cultivation and rules promulgated for regulating the relations between the Sabha and those that held the land under them. No. 58 is a complaint in almost about the same terms, as the one previously referred to (No. 50), and the settlement made almost in the same terms. No. 59 relates to arrangements for the holding of certain lands made over for services to the temple and the regulations that were made by the temple authorities to those that actually cultivated the land.

Nos. 439 and 440 of Volume VI of the South Indian Inscriptions relate to the agreement, which is called the agreement of the *Śamayam* by the artizan classes of the village of Ālanguḍi. These people describe themselves as Rathakāra of the four divisions and six occupations, and give themselves out as a prosperous community standing on its own footing in society. The document refers to an agreement that they came to in the year Śaka 1186. The Śaka year is unusual in these inscriptions. These came together to discuss certain matters relating to their *Samayam,* and assembled in full and without a vacancy. The record actually refers to a grant of land as usual to the god in the temple at Ālangudi, and how the income from the land was to be applied. The next one, No. 440, refers to a grant to the temple, which was made in the third year of Vijaya Rājēndradēva, who died on the back of the elephant after taking Kalyāṇapuram and Kolhāpuram, that is, Rājādhirāja I. In lieu of certain monies that they had taken, both gold and silver, amounting to 1011 *kaḻanjus* of gold, and 464 *palams* of silver, they gave instead land which had been made over in lieu of interest on this amount in the days of Rājarājadēva. They had got into confusion in course of time along with a certain number of other grants made for similar purposes. They were all brought back into account and provision was made for the carrying out of the original ideas of the various donors in the reign of this Rājarāja, Rāja Mahēndra, Kulōttunga I, by the Maha Sabha. The lands were measured out by the rod of sixteen feet and on the basis of 108 such *kuḻis* making one *mā.* This was measured out by the rod in use in the place. This document shows clearly that the accounts and grants were preserved not only in the accounts books, but even in inscriptions from which they could always find out what was actually due and bring about a rectification when things got into confusion for one reason or another.

We have given enough detail in the above pages to carry home to the mind of the reader to what extent of detail, the administrative arrangements went, and how carefully these were recorded notwithstanding the fact that practically all of them have apparently been destroyed and are not forthcoming for our use. These detached bits that we get from here, there, and everywhere, all over the Tamil country give enough detail for us to form a general idea as to how exactly the general administration was organised, and how it was actually carried on in all its detail, and what checks and balances were provided for for the efficient carrying on of the administration. Even the failures, the malfeasance, and the actual short-comings of the administration come into view, so that, the picture that may be drawn in imagination may be regarded as full and complete, even to the minutest detail. We shall proceed now to consider the other correlative matters relating to the other side of the administration.

III

Elections: their principles and procedure:—

We have seen that the supreme governing body of every local unit was the general assembly. This assembly worked through a number of committees in regard to practical administration. The general committee as well as the special committees were chosen by a form of election by the people at large. The actual exercise of the franchise depended upon two principles, (1) the possession of property, and (2) educational qualifications of a comparatively high order. The general assembly seems to have consisted practically of all the inhabitants of the village unit possessed of sufficient intelligence to understand and transact business. It is in respect of the appointment of committees in particular that rules are specifically laid down, and these rules have come down to us in two documents preserved again at Uttaramallūr. The documents are orders issued by Parāntaka in the 12th and 14th years respectively, and lay down the rules for the election of these various committees which carried on the administration. As the epigraphist pionts out, the inscriptions do not bring into existence these committees, but rather fix up the long existing previous practice, and give to practice and customary regulations upon which the practice depended, the fixity and character of law. Certain defects had shown themselves apparently in the course of the working, and these rules were devised to remedy these possible evils. The rules were promulgated not in the name of the king, but on the authority of the assembly for the election every year of committees for annual supervision, for garden supervision, and tank supervision particularly. Almost practically the same rules seem to have applied to other committees as well, as we have already pointed out in respect of the election of a gold committee. It is laid down for Uttaramallūr that the town be divided into thirty wards, as in fact it was, and, as a general principle, those that lived in each ward were to assemble and choose men for these committees by putting the names of worthy individuals on tickets which were collected together and put into a pot, from which were drawn tickets for one member for each ward. This process of election is what is called *Kuḍavōlai.*

Qualifications for membership.—

The following were entitled to have their names put upon the pot-tickets:—

(1) They must be of an age above 35 and below 70;

(2) Those who were owners of a quarter *vēli* of tax paying land, a *vēli* being equal to 6 & 2|3 acres;

(3) Those who had a house built upon their own site;

(4) In case, however, of those not having this landed property, those that were possessed of learning of a certain degree were entitled to vote, viz., (1) those who knew the *Mantrabrahmana.* One must know it himself and be able to teach it to others; (2) those who possessed only 1|8 *vēli* of land and therefore not entitled to vote, would become eligible if these had learned one Veda and one of the four Bhashyas, and were capable of imparting their knowledge to others. This last seems intended to cover those cases where the property owned was not enough to entitle them to be elected, and those whose qualifications in point of learning similarly was not enough to entitle them by itself either. A combination of the two is therefore made.

Among those possessing the foregoing qualifications it is only the following that were entitled to election:—

(1) Only those who were well conversant with business and who conducted themselves generally according to sacred rules of conduct (*āśāraṃuḍaiyra*);

(2) Only those were entitled who had acquired their wealth by honest means, *artha-śauśam;* whose minds were pure *ānma śauśam;* and who had not already served on any of these committees during the three years preceding.

The following classes of people were disqualified:—

(1) Those who had been members of one of these committees and had not submitted their accounts. Their relations specified as under were also debarred from holding places on these committees:—

(1) The sons of the younger and elder sisters of their mothers;

(2) Sons of paternal aunts and maternal uncles;

(3) Brothers of their mothers;

(4) Brothers of their fathers;

(5) Their own brothers;

(6) Their father-in-law;

(7) The brothers of their wives;

(8) Husbands of their sisters;

(9) The sons of their sisters;

(10) The sons-in-law who have married the daughters of disqualified persons;

(11) Their fathers;

(12) Their sons.

It will be seen from the above that neglect to do one's duty during one's period of office was visited with a very severe punishment. It not only debars the individual, guilty of neglect of public duty, from holding office again; but it disqualifies likewise all relations of the first degree who are likely to come under their influence in one way or another. Then follows a number of other disqualifications which spring from ill conduct on the part of the individual. Among these are specified those against whom are recorded illicit intercourse, or the first four of the five great sins, viz., killing of a Brahman, drinking of intoxicating liquors, theft, committing adultery with the wife of a spiritual teacher and associating with those guilty of these crimes. Even in this case, the various relations of the first degree, as in the previous case, were also disqualified from holding office. The next important class of men who were similarly disqualified were those thrown out of caste for association with low people. But these can regain the privilege by performing the expiatory ceremonies laid down in law. (1) Those who were fool-hardy were also excluded. Those who were guilty of stealing, or plundering the property of others; those who have taken forbidden food, even if they should have performed expiatory ceremonies; those who have committed certain sins, even though they should have performed expiatory ceremonies. The details of the sins are here gone in the original. (2) Those who had been village pests even after they had become pure by performing spiritual ceremonies. (3) Those who have been guilty of illicit intercourse and had become pure by performing expiatory ceremonies. All these classes of people specified above were debarred during their life from the right to have their names put on the ticket. Thus they were not entitled to hold a place on any one of these committees.

Procedure.—In regard to the method of election, the procedure followed is somewhat as follows: the tickets for each ward were collected separately, and were tied up in a bundle with a covering docket specifying the number of tickets and other details necessary; and similarly the tickets for the thirty wards were first collected. These were taken to a general assembly convened for the purpose. This assembly was to be a full meeting, which included the young and the old as well. The meeting was held in the village hall, either the hall of a temple or some other place specially set apart for the purpose. Among the assembled, the priests of the temple took their seats in the middle, and one of them the seniormost, the eldest among them, had to stand up in the middle lifting an empty pot, holding it upside down to show that it contained nothing. Then a young boy was made to hand in one of the packets docketed and tied up as stated before. The priest was to untie the packet and put all the tickets into the pot. The pot was to be well shaken and then the young boy was asked to draw tickets from the pot to the number required. As each ticket was drawn it was handed over to the arbitrator who had to receive it on the open palm of his hand. He then read the name written on the ticket. This ticket was to be read by each one of the priests present so as to be assured that he read the correct name. Then the name was put down as accepted; perhaps it is to be taken that the name was open to a challenge and the acceptance was probably conditional upon there being no challenge. In this manner, one from each ward was chosen making up the total of the elected 30.

From out of the thirty, the committees were constituted. Of the main committees, the committee for annual supervision, the committee for garden supervision and the committee for the tank supervision, those that had already served on the latter two committees, those that were advanced in age, and those possessed of considerable learning, were chosen to constitute the committee of annual supervision. That is for this committee of annual supervision, those chosen should be experienced, should be possessed of a high degree of learning and should be men of mature age. Twelve were thus chosen from out of the thirty for this committee of annual supervision. Of the eighteen left over, twelve were to be chosen for the garden supervision committee, the remaining six constituting the tank supervision. But these two committees were to be elected by *an oral expression of opinion.* This perhaps implies that the men fit for doing the particular work were chosen, and this was apparently done by one of those present recommending the individual and the others accepting it. The great men thus chosen for these committees "shall hold office for full 360 days and then retire." Any member of the committee was liable to immediate removal on being found guilty of any offence. When these committees retired and new committees have to be appointed, the committee for the supervision of justice had the right to call for a meeting through the arbitrator, the *Madhyasta* of the village, and the process of election was exactly as described above. For the committee named *Panchavāra Vāriyam,* and that for the supervision of gold, names were put on tickets as in the other case and names drawn as before, and from out of thirty names thus drawn, six were chosen for the gold supervision. From out of this thirty, twelve were selected presumably by another drawing of the lot and six out of these twelve formed the committee for gold supervision and the remaining six constituted the committee for *Panchāvāra Vāriyam*. In regard to these committees when they were appointed for the following year, the wards which had representatives in the previous year were to be excluded, and the appointments were made by an oral expression of opinion. Those that were excluded from appointment to these committees are described as those who had ridden on asses and who had committed forgery, which seems to imply those that were guilty of disgraceful acts.

Accounts.—The accounts of the village were to be kept by arbitrators. They must be men who had earned their wealth by honest means. One that was writing accounts during one year was not to be appointed to the next year unless he had rendered accounts satisfactorily for the previous year, to the great men of the larger committee of accounts, and whose accounts have been accepted by them as having been honestly rendered. The accountant who wrote the accounts for the year ought to submit the accounts himself, and other accountants ought not to be brought to close his accounts. These were to be the arrangements for election as permanent rules from the year of issue onwards.

It was already pointed out that the documents laying down procedure are documents issued respectively in the 12th and 14th years of Parāntaka I, that is, A.D. 918 and 920 respectively. How exactly this intervention of the king was called for is not explained to us in either of the documents under reference; but the documents under reference state it that these documents were issued by the village assembly while the local or provincial governor, who produced the documents as authority, was not merely present but actually presided over the assembly when these were promulgated in order that the evil-minded ones may be destroyed and the good may prosper. We may infer from this explicit statement that there were those who were inclined to disturb the orderly progress of the administration, that the assembly of the town itself was not able to get them efficiently under control, notwithstanding the fact that they were able to impose heavy fines, and presumably collect them also by processes of destraint; and therefore royal intervention was called for. There is however nothing on record that the intervention was actually called for, or application made in this behalf. The intervention here seems to have been undertaken *suo moto* by the monarch who proceeded to commission the local governor to get a set of rules framed, put them before the assembly of the village, and get for them the approval of the assembly, and then bring them into operation. The rules therefore are promulgated in the name of the Sabha itself, although they were drafted and forwarded from the headquarters. The fact however which has not been clearly brought out in Mr. Venkayya's translation is this; that in the first case, Tattanūr Mūvēnda Vēḷān being not merely present, as Mr. Venkayya's translation itself puts it, "but convening the committee" as it is put under interrogation; the word convening under interrogation raises a doubt in regard to the correctness of the translation. The expression used 'Mūvēnda Vēḷān *irundu vāriyam āha.*' This personage was present without a doubt, as the first term *irundu* implies. But he was not merely there but he became *vāriyam*. The word *vāriyam* has been misunderstood not merely by Mr. Venkayya, but also by both Hultzech and Keilhorn.[1] I think it was Keilhorn that was primarily responsible for the mistaken sense of the term *vāriyam*. He gave it a wrong turn in his edition of some of the Eastern Chaḷukya records in the Epigraphia Indica, Volume V, page 138, where he gives it as his opinion that it is the same as the *vāra* or *vāri*, and means a committee, as the term occurs in the *Pancha vāra vāriyam*. The word *vāriyam* occurs in the documents under discussion in the terms *Eri vāriyam*, *Tōṭṭa variyam*, etc. The word *variyam* seems to be there nothing more than the Tamil word the most familiar instance for the use of which is in *vāśi vāriyan*, the equivalent of the Sanskrit *aśva damanaka* the man who is expert in controlling and bringing horses into discipline. Therefore *vāriyam* would usually mean control, one that controls the assembly; but here the governor was made the *vāriyam*, the controller, when the assembly met in regard to this particular business. Therefore it is clear that *vāriyam* means the act or the business of controlling and looking over a particular department, or work, or business. It is hardly necessary for us that the word should be of Tamil origin. The form of it looks Sanskrit, and probably it is a Sanskrit word. The word *vāri* in the Sanskrit has the significance of that which controlls or puts under restraint elephants. That apart there need be no doubt about the meaning of the

[1]See page 135, A. S. R. 1904-05.

word *vāriyam* in the various forms in which it occurs in these expressions in the inscriptions. In regard to *Panchavāra variyam,* the actual doubt is not in the *vāriyam,* but in the significance of the term *Panchavāra.* Unfortunately for us, the *Panchavāra vāriyam* is a committee of six and not of five, and therefore the *Pancha* has nothing whatever to do with five. *Vāra variyam* could be made to mean the control of something from day to day, and if the committee were composed of five people, we can say the five that controlled, say the accounts, from day to day. But the committee being six that meaning of five is difficult to accept. It therefore was a committee, whose function was the control and supervision of a particular department, unless we could presume that it was a committee of five to begin with, and for some reason had been changed to a committee of six, while retaining the name as in the case of the term *Panchāyat* in modern use, which more often than not consists of people other than five in number. One man could be a *Panchāyat,* ten could be; the whole inhabitants of a street might act as a *Panchāyat* for drawing up a *māhzar.* The *Panchāyat* there has got the significance of *Madhyasta,* and lost its original significance of number. So the *Panchavāra vāriyam* committee could be a committee which supervised the administration, probably the accounts from day to day. In actual fact it seems to have been a committee composed of the heads of five bodies or five groups originally. That apart, that this Tattanūr Mūvēnda vēḷān was present and became *vāriyam* means therefore that he was present in the assembly and conducted the proceedings of the assembly. That term occurs almost in the identical position in the two inscriptions and in the two cases, the royal officer presided over the assembly, which promulgated the royal order in the name of the assembly itself. Such action seems to have been called for by irregularities which showed themselves in the course of administration; but whether this was brought to the notice of the headquarters by the assembly and intervention was sought by them as the responsible local authority, or whether the headquarters intervened on their own motion is not made quite clear. Either way, royal intervention was legitimate, and was brought about whenever it was necessary.

The next point of importance that arises out of the two documents is what indeed was the necessity when the order had been promulgated in the year 918 that it should be revised and another order issued in the year 920 hardly two years later. Nothing is stated as to the necessity that called for the revision in the later document itself; but the actual difference between the one and the other may possibly lead to an inference. The only essential differences are that the earlier document puts the age limits as between 30 and 60 whereas the later document would make them respectively 35 and 70. This may be regarded as a minor difference, though important from the point of view of inclusion of the really mature people. The other one is that in the earlier document the combination of qualifications of property and learning is not set down. Possibly that is a change that was necessitated by the actual character of the community for which the rules were made at the time. The community was essentially a Brahman community, where perhaps the possession of even so much as a quarter *vēli* of land was not usual, while the possession of learning to the degree demanded may not have been quite so general either; while the possession of a smaller amount of landed property may be more usual in combination with learning, which may not reach up to the degree laid down in the rules. So this change may be attributed to the need of the locality peculiarly. The rest of the changes that are made are not changes in substance at all. It is more or less changes of form to make the position clear. But there is one whole group of those to be kept out which are included in the second document, of which there had been no mention in the first. These have reference more or less to those who had been guilty of sinful acts. While the first document lays down nothing about them, the second document seems to exclude them rigorously. It does not prohibit explicitly those who have been on the committees once. On the whole therefore the general character of the changes introduced seem to subserve the questions of practical convenience, and do not seem to affect the character. Therefore perhaps the inference may safely be made that when the rules were brought into force these minor defects showed themselves one way or another, and they were rectified in the later document, which became the law for all time afterwards. It is doubtful whether the fact that the provincial governor in the first happened to be other than a Brahman (a fact not open to doubt in itself), and in the latter case a Brahman, is of any importance. It may be merely due to the accidents of the administration, and may be quite an ordinary incident of administrative changes, and may not go quite so far as perhaps

Mr. Venkayya's reference to it, in the introduction to these in the Archaeological Survey Report, would go. The explanation probably is that, when the document was returned to the headquarters, perhaps it underwent a careful scrutiny by the record office, and such possible defects as were noticeable were rectified, and the revised document issued more perfect in the matter of drafting, and more complete as an instrument to base action upon.

There are just a few details, which give us clear indication that this was the character of the revision. The first of these documents is content merely with stating that the near relations (*aṇiya bandukkaḷ*)[1] of those that held office previously, during the three years immediately preceding that for which the elections are being held, should be excluded. Naturally the question would arise who are the near relations. The second document gives a precise and elaborate definition of what is to be understood by this term. Almost the same kind of exclusion is under reference in a slightly different connection,[2] which again seems to call for a definition as to what classes of people were exactly meant. It therefore seems clear that the revision was brought about merely to make matters more clear, and has had nothing to do with the actual character of the community to which the individual governor belonged.

IV

Rural Assemblies:—Administration of Justice:—

We shall now proceed to consider what powers village assemblies exercised in the matter of the admi-

1 Line 5, A Text.

2 Line 9 of the same inscription.

nistration of justice. Here again the general assembly of the village was apparently the body whose function it was to administer justice. It is equally clear that even here the general assembly exercised its function through a committee, a committee of justice. This committee seems to have been regarded as a committee of the highest importance and influence. Apart from the mere administration of justice, this was the committee to which was entrusted the summoning of the assemblies for purposes of election, and perhaps smaller powers of general administration. There was a place usually set apart which went by the name *Dharmāsana,* a permanently appointed hall of justice as it were, where this committee could assemble and carry on their work from day to day as a body whose work was continuous and more regular than that of any other committee. We have a few instances scattered through the inscriptions of what sort of cases came before this committee. Our information naturally is limited here; it must be remembered, the inscriptions being mostly those found in temples, unless the cases had something to do with one or other of these temples, there is no reason why these inscriptions should refer to them at all. Therefore the kind of information that we get in this particular department would be comparatively speaking narrowly limited, which would, at the very best, give us an inadequate idea of the extent of the judicial power that this committee exercised if we went by these instances alone. But luckily some of these instances are so typical that it would not be difficult to imagine the general character of the matters that would have come before them, and the manner in which they were disposed of by this committee. The first class of cases that meets our eye happened to be criminal cases, in which the people accused were charged with bringing about death. The normal punishment for causing death seems to have been the death of the culprit.[1] The punishment of death, however was not awarded in all cases. Three instances are noted in the epigraphist's report for 1900, section 26. Nos. 64 and 77 of 1900, both of them refer to the reign of Kulōttunga-choladēva, perhaps the first Kulōttunga. The first of these two has reference to the shooting of a villager by another individual of the same village by mistake. The governor of the district and the people probably of the village assembly met together, and decided that the culprit in this instance should not be made to pay the extreme penalty as death was caused by a careless and negligent act of his, and not brought about with a deliberate motive. He was punished, however by being asked to maintain a perpetual lamp in the local temple of Tūṇāndār at Siyamangalam. But then it was not left to his pleasure to maintain the lamp, in giving effect to the said decision, by such arrangements as he himself might choose to make. The maintenance of the lamp had to be assured, and he was asked to deposit the capital amount necessary for the maintenance of the perpetual lamp. At the time it was assessed that, for the maintenance of a perpetual lamp, it would be necessary to provide the temple with sixteen cows from the ghee product of which the lamp could be maintained. The punishment had two objects in view apparently, the one that the guilty man ought to be punished adequately

1 Epi. Karnātaka Vol. IV, Hg. 18.

by being mulcted in a substantial sum as deterrent of crime; and such sum as he was mulcted of may be so applied as to bring him some merit and thus prove a means of expiation for the sin of killing even by a careless act. The assessment of sixteen cows for the maintenance of the perpetual lamp, or as in other cases 48 sheep, seems to have been accepted as a general standard. The other instance under reference here took place in Tiruvottiyūr, a northern suburb of Madras. Here it was a case of an accident at hunting. The culprit missed his aim and instead of shooting the animal shot a man dead. The people of the district assembled immediately (and there is no mention of the governor of the division) and decided that the culprit should make over sixteen cows as in the previous case to the Tiruvottiyūr temple. Although the two places are in the same district, they are a considerable way from each other, and it could not perhaps be that the judgment in the one case was necessarily on the precedent of the other. It looks as though that was the general idea prevalent at the time. There is another record referring to the ninth year of Kulottunga and concerning the village Tirupulivanam also in the Chingleput District. In this case the culprit provided fifteen cows for the maintenance of the perpetual lamp for the merit of the person who was killed by mistake.[1] No reference is however made in the record either to the governor or even to the people of the district. Probably it was taken so much as a matter of course that the writer of the document did not consider it necessary to mention the assembly. In this department again perhaps the

[1] No. 44 of 1898.

assembly exercised as much power as in the department of general administration to which elaborate reference has been made in the pages above.

There is another interesting case where death was not due to accident exactly. A merchant of Jambai in the South Arcot District had a concubine, a native of Nāvalūr (Tiruveṇṇainallūr) in the South Arcot District. Another man attempted to commit an outrage on her by night. The merchant managed however to stab the criminal and death resulted. In this case again, the punishment was the making of a provision for a perpetual lamp in the Śiva temple of the locality.[1] But there is an interesting detail here in the provision that it was made not by himself alone but by himself and a relative of the deceased. The inscription is dated actually in the year A.D. 1012-13 and is of the time of Rājarāja I. There are seven other instances of death brought on by negligent acts, and they relate to the period of the Cholas from the 10th to the 13th centuries. The first one of date A.D. 1054[2] has reference to a case of a village officer demanding taxes from a woman who declared that she was not liable to be taxed. The officer however insisted on the claim being satisfied, and seems to have brought about her going through an ordeal. The woman took poison and died. It is not clear whether the taking of the poison was the ordeal. In this case, there was a meeting of the people "from the four quarters, eighteen districts, and the various countries" which means a general assembly of all the people when

1 No. 67 of 1906.
2 No. 80 of 1906.

grave issues were awaiting decision. The officer whose compulsion brought about death was held liable for death, and was made to pay 32 *kāśu* (about four times the value of the usual 16 cows) for burning a perpetual lamp in the local temple. The next two instances have reference to the reign of Kulottunga, but the points calling for notice are no more than that a Śūdra in the course of hunting is said to have missed his aim and shot a Veḷḷāḷa dead. Agriculturists from the "79 districts" assembled together and declared the Śūdra guilty. He was ordered to present sixty-four cows to burn two perpetual lamps in this case.[1] That the heaviness of the fine was perhaps due to the distinction in caste between the two is noticeable. The other instance[2] from Grāmam refers to a similar accidental death. The next one is of the reign of Vikramachoḷa, A.D. 1118—1135 and refers to a case in which a husband pushed his wife, and brought on her death by so doing. In this case "1500 men of the four quarters" are supposed to have assembled, and declared the husband guilty of causing the death of his wife. The punishment was as usual the providing of the perpetual lamp.[3] The next instance has reference to the same reign where three men happened to be comparing their skill in arms; one of them stabbed to death, another in the friendly contest. With the consent of the relatives of the deceased, provision was made for burning a perpetual lamp, the guilty person making over 32 cows for the purpose to the temple. The

1 No. 67 of 1906.

2 No. 88 of 1906.

3 No. 91 of 1906.

next one is a case in which a woman threw a stick at her daughter, which however, struck another girl, who died twenty days after the hurt. Here again the punishment was the maintenance of the perpetual lamp. The husband of the woman provided 32 cows. The last case in this list has reference to hunting a boar by night. The man missed his aim and killed a human being instead. He had to make over 32 cows for the maintenance of the lamp for the merit of the deceased. These constitute a group of crimes, and the fixing of the guilt was the function either the assembly of the village, or the community to which a man belonged, or of the people at large. The punishment was punishment which was regulated by law or precedent, and the punishment awarded in these cases seems to have been regulated more or less by the spirit of the law; and once it was awarded in a particular case, it seems to have been generally understood and similar awards were made in all such cases. No royal officer or the king himself intervened, much less took it upon himself to pass judgment as to the guilt. This was done by the peers of the man or woman concerned, and punishment was fixed according to law or established precedent. In case of doubt, however, the matter appears to have been referred to the king. But in such a case, the reference was not for the purpose of adjudging a man guilty. That was done by the people. The reference was merely to make the actual award of punishment.

One record coming from Uttipākkam[1] provides a case of some considerable importance. This refers to a grant made under unusual circum-

1 No. 315 of 1909.

stances, to the Śiva temple in the locality by the residents of the Brahman villages (Agara-Brahmadēśa), the agricultural villages (*Vēḷānūr*), and towns of 2,000 *vēlipaṟṟu*. That means it refers to a division consisting of two thousand vēlis of cultivated land, equivalent to about 13 thousand acres. The case has reference to five Brahman brothers, whose names are mentioned and a certain number of Vēḷḷāḷa Śūdras. The Brahmans are named Ālkondavilli, Pāmbaṇaiyān, Malaivāykkōn, Varadan and Śelvan, and some Vēḷḷāḷa Śūdras. They are said to have given up the legitimate duties of their castes and had taken to the profession of the lower classes. which is explained as follows: 'They wore weapons dangerous to human life, murdered Brahmans, cut off their ears, insulted Brahman ladies, committed robbery, destroyed cattle and sold them "to the great distress and dismay of the other members of the district". The matter was reported to the royal officers, Vikramaśoḷadēva and Tirumalai Tandār and others who were in charge of the country. They "collected the offenders together, beat them, fined them, pulled down their houses and kept them under surveillence(?)." This did not effect any improvement in their character, and they apparently persisted in their misdeeds. The people preferred their complaint again, and brought their misdeeds to the notice of Prince Pottapi Araiyar, who at the time happened to be in charge of the country. This prince ordered the chief Vaḷḷuvanāḍu Āḷvān Irungōḷar and a band of Malayāḷa soldiers to arrest these people and bring them to distress. The criminals however managed to escape to the hills after a fight in which they managed to kill a few of the soldiers, successfully wounding several others, and even robbing the rest of their weapons; in other words, the force that was sent was apparently inadequate and they fared very badly at the hands of the dacoits. They however managed to secure the persons of the two of these, Āṭkoṇḍavilli and Pāmbaṇaiyān and locked them up in the prison house. Sometime after when they were being removed along with some other prisoners, and taken to the king who was in camp at *Kaṇṇāttūr,* the three other Brahman brothers of these two attacked the guard in charge, in the forest near the northern hamlet of Uttippākkam, and with the assistance of a number of others actually killed the guard and liberated the prisoners. All of them escaped capture. The king therefore issued strict orders, on hearing of this, to recapture these criminals wherever they should be, and punish them in accordance with the rules applicable to the lower classes, which involved not only personal punishment to them, but the following in addition. Their hereditary property was to be sold to the temple and charitable institutions. From the money realised, the fine imposed upon them may be recovered first, and the balance left over, if any, should be presented to the temples above referred to as a permanent charity in the name of the criminals. The order was accordingly carried out by the people ultimately. This happened about the middle of the thirteenth century and gives an idea of the way in which people were brought to justice even where those involved were criminals of a very unusual character. What is to be noted in regard to this particular case is that when the apprehending of the criminals became too much for the village assembly and its officers, the local officers first, then the king himself last of all was compelled to intervene with his greater resources. The forces of governors and the royal forces came to their aid, and where in the case of a body of desperate people like these dacoits, even these forces proved inadequate; the co-operation of the people achieved what was impossible of achievement for the mere royal forces alone. In the matter of punishment, the punishment seems to have had prevention of crime and the putting of the criminals beyond possibility of repeating the mischief as the objects to be attained. But their ultimate welfare in the life beyond was not lost sight of, and one important factor that went into the award of the punishment was that something was done for the welfare of the souls of the culprits.

APPENDIX TO LECTURE V

Extract from the Archæological Survey of India.—
Annual Report, 1904—5; pp. 131—145.

[*Published*
with the permission of the Government of India,
conveyed in their Order No. A.-637,
dated 17*th October,* 1930,
in the Department of Industries and Labour.]

TWO INSCRIPTIONS AT UTTARAMALLŪR.

Uttaramallūr is a village 10½ miles north-west of the Madhurāntakam station on the Chingleput-Villupuram section of the South Indian Railway. There are seven temples in the village, all of which bear inscriptions. Of these, the Vaikuntha Perumāḷ temple is the most important, as it is full of ancient epigraphs belonging to the Pallava, Ganga-Pallava, and Chola dynasties.[1] The name of the village in all these earlier records is *Uttaramēru-chaturvēdimangalam,* i.e., the Brahmaṇa settlement called after the 'northern Mēru.' As the similar name Prabhumēru is used for a Western Ganga king,[2] Uttaramēru may be taken to be the surname of some ancient Pallava or Ganga-Pallava king

[1]See the Government Epigraphist's *Annual Report* for 1897-98, pp. 18 to 21.

[2]Epigraphica Indica, vol. III, p. 75.

who founded the village. But the analogy of Dakshiṇa-mēru, which was the name in ancient times of the Śiva temple at Chidambaram[1] in the South Arcot District would lead us to suspect this derivation of the name of the village. The mythical mountain Mēru is supposed to be of gold, and the Śiva temple at Chidambaram probably got the name 'Southern Mēru' after its gilding either by the Chola Parāntaka I the king in whose reign the two subjoined inscriptions were engraved, or by the anterior (Pallava) king, Hiraṇyavarman.[3] None of the temples at Uttaramallūr is gilded at present, and neither is there any tradition about any of them having been gilded in ancient times. Beside in other similar compounds (ending in *chaturvēdimangalam*), denoting names of villages, the first member is almost invariably either the name or surname of a king or chief. Consequently it may be concluded that the village of Uttaramallūr was called Uttaramēru-*chaturvēdimangalam* after a king whose name or surname was Uttaramēru. We have at present no evidence to ascertain either the name of the king who bore this title, or the dynasty to which he belonged.

Of the 71 inscriptions (Nos. 1 to 41 and 61 to 90) copied in 1898 in the Vaikuntha Perumāḷ temple at Uttaramallūr, the subjoined two have been selected for publication here as they throw some light on village administration in Southern India in the tenth century

1 The most important shrine in the Rājarājēśvara temple at Tanjore was called Dakṣinamēru-Viṭanka probably after the temple at Chidambaram, see also the Tamil *Tiruviśaippa* p. 107, verse 4, where Mēru-viḍangan, occurs as the name of the God at Chidambaram.

2 South. Ind. Insc., Vol. II, p. 379.

3 See the Tamil *Kōyirpurānam*, p. 245, verse 17.

A.D. They are engraved on the west wall of the temple close to one another. The second occupies a space of about 23 feet by 4¼, and the first 1 foot 10 inches by 9⅓ feet. The last three lines of the latter extend to a length of 26 feet 8 inches. The writing is well executed, and the size of the letters is, on an average, 1 inch. The characters are Tamil and Grantha of the regular type of the period to which the inscriptions have to be assigned.[1] Two forms of lingual *n* and dental *n* are used—one which is comparatively older, and the other in which the loops are fully developed.[2] In A, the former is used more generally than in B. The distinction between medial *ā* and *r*, which is not found in later Tamil inscriptions, is observed in a large majority of cases. The *ā* is a short vertical stroke, while *r*, which is similar, occupies the full height of the line. But this distinction is not so carefully observed in B—particularly in the second half of it. Very often the secondary *ā* is a curve added to the right side of the consonant to which it belongs, *e.g.*, *ā* of *vāriya* in l. 2 of A; of *uḍaiyar āy* in l. 5 of A; of *iḍuvad āgavum* in l. 9 of A and of *vēḷān* in l. 12 of A. Double *k* is sometimes written as a group. As in other Tamil inscriptions, secondary *ī* and *ū* (combined with the consonants *m*, *l*,

1 A number of inscriptions of Parāntaka I have already been published. Four in the Tamil alphabet have been edited with photo-lithographs. Of these one is on copper-plates (South Ind. Inscs., Vol. II, pp. 375—90), while the other three are stone inscriptions (*ibid* Vol. III, pp. 18 to 20; Ep. Ind. vol. III, p. 280 f. and plate facing p. 284; and Vol. VII, p. 141, and E and F on plate facing 9. 144). One in the Vatteluttu alphabet has also been edited from Suchindram in South Travancore (*ibid.* Vol. V, p. 43). The endorsement on the plates of Nandivarman (*Ind. Ant.*, Vol. VIII, plates facing p. 168) belongs also to his reign, while that of the inscription of Nandivarman Pallavamalla (*ibid* plates facing p. 274) purport to belong to his reign, though the alphabet is perhaps slightly later.

2 Compare South Ind. Insc. Vol. III, p. 90.

ḍ, l and *r*) are, as a rule, not distinguished from *i* and *u*. But I have inserted the length wherever it is required in order not to swell the footnotes unnecessarily.

As regards orthography, the hard dental *t* is used for the soft *d* in *chaṁtra, dēvēntra* (l. of 11 of A and l. 16 of B) and similar words, as in other Tamil inscriptions, while the hard *k* takes the place of the soft *g* in °*maṁkala*° (l. 18 of B). The palatal sibilant is used for the hard palatal in *śauśa* (for *śaucha*) (ll. 5 of A; 4 and 15 of B) and *śaridai* (for *charitai*) (l. 16 of B). Both the letter *m* and the nasal into which it is altered on account of *sandhi* are retained in *vāriyaṁnjeyginṛa* (l. 9 of A), *pādagaṁnśeydu* and *prāyaśchittaṁncheydu* (l. 8 of B) and *përiluṁndōṭṭa* (l. 11 of B). The nasalisation of the dental *t* before *m* in the middle of a word occurs in *ānmā*° (l. 4 of B) and the palatalisation of the dental *d* in *vijyā* (l. 11 of B).

The language is Tamil prose intermixed with a number of Sanskrit words written in Grantha. A few Tamil words are also written in Grantha. The following peculiarities of the language require to be noted. The termination *ār* or *ān* is used in a number of cases where *ar* or *an* would be enough in modern Tamil, *e.g.*, *panniruvārum* (l. 7 of A), *panniruvārilum* and *aruvār* (l. 10 of A), *māmān* (l. 5 of B) and *Aruvār* (l. 14 of B). *Mēlpāṭṭār* (l. 4 of A), *Pārāntakadēvan* (l. 1 of B), *mākkaḷaiyum* (l. 5 of B), *paradrāvyam* (l. 7 of B) and *māhāsabhai* (ll. 9 and 10 of B) are evidently mistakes for *mẹlpaṭṭār, Parāntakadēvan, makkaḷaiyum, paradravyam* and *mahāsabhai*. The Sanskrit word *ājña* occurs in its transitional form *āñai,* (ll. 1 and 12 of A; l. 17 of B), which is anterior to its assimilation in Tamil in the form *āṇai,* while *viddha* (ll. 10 and 12 of B) occurs as a *tadbhava* of *vṛddha.* Forms like *ilāttār,* (l. 5 of A and l. 4 of B), *allāttār* and *ariyāttān* (l. 6 of A), *perāttār* (l. 6 of B) are found in Malayalam, while their modern representatives in Tamil are *ilādār, allādār, ariyādān* and *peṛādār.* Forms like *iḍuvidu* (l. 3 of B), *koḷvidu* (l. 12 of B), *koḷuvidu* (l. 4 of B) and *āvidu* (ll. 7 and 10 of A), though not uncommon in the language of inscriptions, do not occur in the literary dialect of Tamil.[1] The addition of *y* after an *i, e* or *ai* at the end of a word is allowed even in literary Tamil, and this is found in a large number of cases, *e.g., kuḍumbilārēy* (l. 3 of A), *iruppānaiy* (l. 4 of A), *vaḻiyēy* (l. 6 of A), *minbēy* (l. 7 of A), *manḍagattilēy* and *naḍuvēy* (l. 10 of B), and *kuḍavōlaiy* (l. 13 of B). Cases of its insertion in the middle of a word are not quite so common. But they occur in the following words:—*ōduviytt-aṛiy-vān* (l. 3 of B), *aṛiyvān* (l. 4 of B), and *anaiyvar* (ll. 8 and 9 of B). Y is elided and the preceding vowel lengthened in *śēda* (l. 2 of B) and *śēdu* (ll. 8 and 16 of B). Consonants are doubled in a number of cases where one would not expect them[2] according to grammatical rules:—*agamm-ėḍuttu* (l. 3 of B),—*āṛṛāll—eḍuttu* (l. 10 of B), *anantaramm-iḍum* (l. 13 of B), *śauśamm-uḍaiyān* (l. 15 of B), *bhaṭṭannāgiya* (l. 17 of B) where *m, l, m* and *n* are wrongly doubled. *Āñaiāl* for *āñaiyāl* (l. 16 f. of B) is a case where the ordinary

[1] See the Tamil grammar *Vīraśoḻiyam,* Damodaram Pillai's edition, p. 63.

[2] Compare Ep. Ind., Vol. VI, p. 321.

sandhi rule is ignored.[1]

The vulgar form *āchchidin* occurs for *ānadin* in l. 15 of B; *parichchu* (l. 9 of A) for *parittu*; *oḻinśa* (l. 9 of A) for *oḻinda; iṭṭiṇai* (l. 6 of B) for *ittuṇai;* and *añju* (l. 11 of B) for *aindu.* The word *śuddharānān* (in l. 7 B) is logically wrong. It must be either *suddharānār* or *suddhanānān.* The accusative *samvatsaravāriyaraiyum* is wrongly used (in l. 12 B) for the nominative °*vāriyar-āgavum.* The form *śeyyāginṟār* (l. 12 of B) is perhaps a mistake for *śeyyāninṟār,* which is a recognised verbal noun of the present tense. The reading seems to admit of no doubt. But it is not impossible that the engraver has corrected *ki* into *ni. Paniraḍu* (l. 1 of A), if it is not a pure mistake, is almost the same as the Hale-Kannaḍa *panneraḍu.*

The Chola king Parāntaka I, in whose reign the two sub-joined inscriptions were engraved, was a strong and powerful ruler. He took Madura, the Pandya capital, and defeated the Pandya king Rājasimha.[2] The capture of Madura was perpetuated by the title 'conqueror of Madura' (*Madiraikoṇḍa*), which is found already in inscriptions of his 3rd year=909-10.[3] His proper name was Parakēsarivarman, and, in order to distinguish himself from his grand-father Vijayālaya, who must have borne the same name,[4] the epithet 'con-

1 See my remarks on the Madras Museum plates of Jaṭilavarman in Ind. Ant., Vol. XXII, p. 68, f., and Professor Hultzsch's notes on the Śīyamangalam inscription in Ep. Ind., Vol. VI, p. 320.

2 South-Ind. Inscrs., Vol. II, p. 379.

3 See the *annual report* on Epigraphy for 1906-07, Part II, paragraph 32.

4 The Chola kings were called Rājakēsarivarman and Parakēsarivarman alternately.

queror of Madura' was added. That he actually conquered the Pandya country is proved by the inscriptions of his reign found in the Madura and Tinnevelly districts. In the north, his dominions extended as far as Kāḷahasti in the North Arcot District.[1] In the west an inscription of his reign has been found at Somūr in the Coimbatore district.[2] The Western Ganga king Pṛthivīpati II, whose dominions lay partly in the Mysore State, was his feudatory.[3] Parāntaka claims to have uprooted the Bāṇas and to have presented their dominions to Pṛthivīpati. The Chola dominions in the west must have been strengthened by Parāntaka's marriage with the daughter of the Kēraḷa king.[4] Inscriptions belonging to the latter part of his reign add the conquest of Ceylon to that of Madura.[5] We may therefore conclude that he at least made a victorious inroad into the island of Ceylon.[6] Parāntaka I. claims also to have defeated the Vaiḍumba king,[7] whose dominions appear to have been in the Cuddapah district.[8] But

[1]*Annual Report* on Epigraphy for 1903-04, p. 25, No. 230. There is is also an unfinished inscription of his reign in the temple at Kāḷahasti.

[2]No. 68 of the Government Epigraphist's Collection for 1890.

[3]South-Ind. Inscrs., Vol. II, p. 381.

[4]South-Ind. Inscrs., Vol. II, p. 379.

[5]*Annual Report* on Epigraphy for 1904-05, Part II, paragraph 8.

[6]Parāntaka seems to have fought twice against the Singhalese. The first fight must have taken place in or before the fifteenth year of his reign, when Rājasimha-Pandya seems to have been defeated along with the "immense army despatched by the lord of Lanka", (South Ind. Inscr., Vol. II, p. 387). The second appears to have taken place towards the close of Parāntaka's reign and is referred to in his Tamil inscriptions (Annual Report on Epigraphy for 1904-05, paragraph 8). The Singhalese chronicle *Mahāvaṁśa* tells us that a Pandya king, who was attacked by the Chola, applied for help to Kaśśappa V., king of Ceylon (A.D. 929-39). This may be taken to refer to the second war, when Parantaka is reported to have invaded Ceylon. But, as the Mahavamsa is not very strong in its chronology, we cannot be quite sure on this point.

[7]South-Ind. Inscrs., Vol. II, p. 379.

[8]*Ibid*, Vol. III, p. 106.

unless this claim is supported by inscriptions of his reign found there, we cannot accept it. According to the later researches, Parāntaka I commenced to reign in A.D. 907[1] and continued until at least A.D. 947-8.[2] As we have seen that he conquered the Pandyas, befriended the Kēraḷas, and subdued the western Gangas, the only power that could give him any trouble was the Rāṣṭrakūṭa. The Rāṣṭrakūṭa king Kṛṣṇa II. (A.D. 888 and 911-12) was still ruling when Parāntaka ascended the throne, and his reign witnessed the accession of four Rāṣṭrakūṭa kings, among whom there appear to have been some internal dissensions. Of these five, two were at war with the Eastern Chāḷukyas of Vengi. Consequently no disturbance appears to have been possible from that quarter.

It may therefore be supposed that Parāntaka I was the undisputed sovereign of the greater portion of the Tamil country, if not of the whole of it. His frequent wars with the Pandyas, of which three are at present known,[3] only show his strength and determination to subdue his enemies. Though he was probably tolerant of all religions in his dominions, he is known to have followed the Śaiva creed, as he utilised all the booty acquired in his wars in covering with gold the temple of Śiva at Chidambaram in the South Arcot district.[4]

The foregoing facts warrant the belief that the Chola dominions enjoyed peace during the reign of

1 Ep. Ind., Vol. VIII, p. 261.

2 Annual report on Epigraphy for 1906-07, Part II, paragraph 31.

3 *Ibid* Paragraphs 32—34.

4 South-Ind. Inscrs., Vol. II, p. 379.

Parāntaka I and that he could therefore devote his time to questions of internal administration. Whether the king made the best use of his opportunity and what were actually the 'triumphs of peace' which the country owed to him, are matters on which our information is naturally imperfect. But we have reason to suppose that local administration was very near being wrecked in an important village not far from the premier city of the Chola dominions.[1] The rules regulating the constitution of village assemblies and the method of selection of committee members seem to have been lax, and unscrupulous and ignorant men appear to have taken advantage of the opportunity to embezzle communal funds, and would not render accounts. The king deputed one of his Śūdra officers, with special instructions, in A.D. 918-9, to set matters right. Owing, perhaps, to his want of experience and to the excitement of the villagers over the evil doings of the 'wicked men' of the village, the rules which he promulgated (A below) must have made matters worse, and the consequences of his mistakes were felt during the second year the rules were in operation. The king had to depute a Brahmaṇa officer of his from the Chola country to improve upon the system devised more than a year ago. Accordingly, on the sixteenth day of the fourteenth year of the king's reign (A.D. 920-21) a carefully worked out set of rules (B below) was framed and promulgated in order that the 'wicked men of the village might perish and the rest prosper.' The rules leave no doubt whatever as to who the wicked men were and wherein

[1] I.e. Conjevaram, sixteen miles north by west of Uttaramallūr.

their wickedness lay.[1]

It is here necessary to warn the reader against the impression that the Chola king Parāntaka I. started the system of village administration by assemblies and committees. Inscriptions prior to his reign bear ample testimony to their existence. The great men of the 'annual committee' are mentioned as the trustees of an endowment in an inscription of the Ganga-Pallava king Kampavarman (ninth century A.D.),[2] and village assemblies are referred to in several inscriptions of the Pallava period. 'The committee of the assembly' is spoken of in an inscription of Varaguna-Maharaja at Ambasamudram,[3] who reigned probably at the beginning of the ninth century A.D., while the *panchavārī* and *vāragosṭhi* (committee-assembly) are mentioned in Eastern Chāḷukya copper-plate grant[4] of the first-half of the tenth century A.D.[5] from the Kistna district.

1 These remarks seem to go much farther than a comparative study of the documents actually warrant. An evil may show itself and a correction may be applied without letting the evil go so far as to wreck the administration. The interval between the two documents is too short and the changes introduced are too minor to support the far reaching inferences drawn therefrom. See above.—*S. K.*

2 South-Ind. Inscrs., Vol. III, p. 9.

3 Ep. Ind., Vol. IX, p. 86 and foot note 9.

4 Ep. Ind., Vol. V, p. 138. These terms are capable of an entirely different interpretation in this document and in the S.I.I. I 37. The first term here is Pancha*vārī*, not *vāram*. This will be separately discussed elsewhere.—*S.K.*

5 The Tanjore inscriptions of the Chola king Rajaraja I (A. D. 985 to 1013) mention not less than 150 villages which had assemblies and 40 others where the villagers, as a body, seem to have managed their affairs. The system must have been in operation in thousands of other villages whose names and whose exact number remain to be disclosed by future researches. Neither the period nor the circumstances under which village assemblies arose in Southern India are known. But as the Greek ambassador Megasthenes—in his account of Indian administration as it obtained at his time, makes mention of six committees of five each, it may be supposed that the system was carried into Southern India by the Aryan immigrants and that slight alterations were probably made to

The system therefore seems to have been in operation almost throughout Southern India at the beginning of the tenth century A.D.

From the translation[1] which accompanies the text of both inscriptions, it will be seen that the later one (B below) dated in A. D. 920-21 is drafted with much greater care than the earlier one (A below). One point that is common in both is the implied indignation against the committee members who had just then vacated office and who appear to have brought the administration of the village into disrepute. They must have embezzled communal funds, and would not submit themselves to any sort of scrutiny. The wholesale condemnation in A of committee members who held office at the time the rules were made, is sufficient evidence on the point. This clause must have operated harshly during the second year of its introduction and must have restricted the choice within a smaller number, who might not possess all the requisite qualifications. In view of this difficulty better counsel prevailed in

suit the conditions of the South. It looks as if the system of administration by committees was employed only in villages. The few towns and cities which existed appear to have been governed differently.

'The number of committees of village assemblies does not appear to have been the same everywhere. Local conditions seem to have influenced the number very much. In the subjoined inscriptions provision is made for five committees:—'annual committee', 'garden committee', 'tank committee', 'the Pänchavāra committee', and 'gold committee.' But it is not said if it was a separate body, or if it was identical with one of the above mentioned five. Inscriptions found at Tirupparkadal near Kaveripak in the North Arcot District furnish the names of five more committees, viz., 'the great men of the wards-committee', 'the great men of the fields committee', 'the great men numbering two hundred', 'the great men of the village committee', and 'the great men of the *Udāsīna* committee'. (*Annual Report* on Epigraphy for 1904-5, Part II, paragraph 7.)

[1] In the Annual Report on Epigraphy for 1898-99, paragraphs 61 to 67, I gave a free translation of the later record (B) and in paragraph 68 pointed out the differences between the two.

A.D. 920-21, and the prohibition was restricted only to defaulting committee members and their relations.

The later inscription (B below) may be divided into the following sections:—(1) qualifications of committee members (ll. 2 to 4). (2) Disqualified persons: (a) defaulting committee members and their relations however remote (ll. 4 to 6); (b) incorrigible sinners and their relations however remote (l. 6); (c) outcastes until they perform the necessary expiatory ceremonies (ll. 6—7); (d) those who are mentally or morally disqualified (l. 7); (e) those who are themselves disqualified but do not transmit their disqualifications to their relatives (ll. 7—8). (3) Method of selection of committee members (ll. 9—11). (4) Number of committees to be appointed annually (ll. 11 to 13). (5) Two others which were perhaps not annually appointed (ll. 13—15). (6) Appointment of accountants (ll. 15—16). It will thus be seen that the document was drawn up with a definite plan and follows a natural order in the arrangement of its various parts.

The duties performed by the committees are not known precisely. The names of some of them indicate roughly their spheres of work. For instance, the tank committee was probably entrusted with the annual removal of silt, occasional repairs, investment of endowments made to tanks, and similar questions. The gold committee probably regulated the currency. Committee members were expected to take an active part in discussing questions brought before them. In fact, an inscription from the Telugu country refers to eloquence at committee assemblies as a special merit. The age restriction, the educational and property qualifications laid down, and the principle of membership by rotation are items which may commend themselves even to modern administrators. The method adopted for choosing committee members is one of casting lots, which was followed by all primitive communities.

A.—TEXT.[1]

1. Śvasti śrī[‖*](Madi)r(ai)-kon(ḍa kō=Ppa) rakēsarivammarkku yāṇḍu paniraḍu āvadu [‖*] Uttiramēruchchatu(r)vvē(d)immangalattu[2] sabh(ai)yō(m) ivv-āṇḍu mudal e(ṅ)gaḷ-ūr[3] śrīmukapr̥ aḍi añai.

2. yi(n)āl Tattanū(r-M)ūvē(nda)vēḷān irundu[4] v(ā)riyam=(ā)ga āṭṭ=orukkālum[5] samma(va)tasara-v(ā)riyamun=dōṭṭa-vāriyamum [6] (ēri)-vā(riya)mum iḍuvadaṟku vyavas(thai)śey—

3. da pariś=āvadu[|*]kuḍumbu mup(pad=āy) muppadu kuḍumbilum avvavakuḍu(ṁ*) bilā(rē)y kūḍi kā=ni(la)ttukku mēl iṟai-nilam[7] uḍaiyān tan manaiyilē a—

4. gam eḍuttukoṇḍu irup(pānaiy) ar(u)ba(du pi)rā(ya*)ttukku[8]-uḷ muppadu pirāyattukku mēl-

1 From two impressions prepared in 1898.

2 Read *chaturvēdimangalattu*.

3 The *akṣaraś śrīmuka* are Grantha.

4 In the *akṣaras va* and *ṇa* of this word, the length appears to have been subsequently inserted by the engraver; also the length *a* of *tto* in *āṭṭoru*.

5 Read *samvatsara*.

6 The remainder of the line is engraved over an erasure.

7 The *ai* of *dai* is unusual as it is made like the *ai* now added to *n*, l and ḷ; also that of *dai* in line 5.

8 The *Pi* is corrected from *tu*.

pāṭṭār[9] vēdattilum śāstrattilum kā(r)yyattilum nipuṇar-ennappaṭṭi=i—

5. ruppārai a(r*)ttha-śauśamum āt(ma)-ś(au)śamum uḍaiyār=āy mūv-(a)ṭṭini-pparam[10] vāriyaṅ=jey (di)l(ā)tt(ā)r (v)āriyaṅ=jeyd=olinda (p)erumakk[11] uḷukku[12]

6. [13]aṇiya [14]bandukkaḷ [15]allāttār(ai)=[16]kkuḍav-ōlaikku=ppēr tīṭṭi=[17] śadēri-vaḻiyēy tiraṭ(ṭi) pa(n) nirandu śēriyilum śēriyāl oru-pē(r-ām-āṟu) ēdum=uru (v=a)riyāttān=oṟu[18]—

7. bāla(nai)=kkoṇḍu kuḍav-ōlai (v)ānguvi(ṭ)tu=ppaniruvārum sama[19] (vatsa)ravāriyam=āvid=āgavum (|*) a(di)n minbēy tōṭṭavāriyattukku mērpaḍi ku(da)v-(ē)[20]—

8. [21]lai vāngi=ppanniruvarum tōṭṭa-vāriyam=(ā)vad=ā(ga)vum (|*) niṉṟa (a)ṟu(kuda)v-ōlaiy(u)m ēri-vāriya(m-ā*)—

9 Read *Mēlpaṭṭār.*

10 Read *i-ppuram.*

11 The *kku* is written as a group.

12 Read *makkaḷukku.*

13 The syllable *ni* is corrected from *na.*

14 Read *Bandhu°*, the writer seems to have inserted an *anusvara* between *ba* and *ndu.*

15 The initial *a* of this word is peculiar and resembles the Tamil *akṣara su.*

16 The *kku* is written as a group.

17 Read *tiṭṭi-chchēri°.*

18 The letter *na* of *no* looks like *na.*

19 The *akṣaras rum sa* are engraved over an erasure; read *samvatsara.*

20 The *ē* of *vō* looks like *ai;* read *kuḍav-ōlai.*

21 This line is a short one, beginning in the original just below *m* *samavatsara* of the previous line,

9. Vad=āgavum=appādu[22] kuḍav-(ē)lai[23] pa (ṛi)chchu v(ā)riyamñ[24] śeygiṅ(ṛa*) mūṅṛu (t)irattu v(ā)riyamum munnūr-a(rubadu)[25] n(āḷu)m (ni)ram (ba*) (v)āriyam oḻiṅ(śa)[26] anan(ta)ra(m) iḍu(m vā) r(i)yangaḷ (i-vya)vasthai(y-ō) lai*) ppaḍiyēy kuḍumbukku=[27]kkuḍav-ōlai-iṭṭu=[28]kkuḍav-ōlai pa(ṛich)chuk (ko)ṅḍ(ē)y vā(ri)yam (i)ḍuvad=āgavum (|*) vāriyañ=jeydār(k*)ku bandhukkaḷum ś(ē)rigaḷil a(nyōnya)mm(ē) * * * [29]

10. m kuḍav-ōlaiyi(|) pēr eḻudi i(ḍa)ppaḍādār=(ā)gavum (|*) panjavāra-vāri(ya) ttukkum ponvāriyattukkum[30] muppadu kuḍu(m)b(i)lum mup-(padu) kuḍa(v-ō)lai iṭṭu śēriyāl o(ru)ttarai=kkuḍav-ōlai paṛi(t)tu panniruvarilum (a)ṛuvar (pa)nja (vāra*)vāriyam= [31]āvid-āgavum (|*) aṛuvar p(on)-vāriyam=āvidāgavu(m)[32] (|*) [33]samavatsaravāri-(ya*)m allātta[34]—

[22] Read *°vad-agavu=muppadu.* [The correct reading probably is āgavum-appāḍu.—*S. K.*]

[23] There is some unaccountable space between the *akṣaras da* and *ve,* which may be occupied by an indistinct *v,* though it is gramatically wrong; read *kudav-olai.*

[24] Cancel the palatal *n.*

[25] Read *munnurr-arubadu;* the syllables *ba du* are written over an erasure.

[26] Read *olinda.*

[27] The syllable *kku* is written as a group.

[28] The syllable *kku* is written as a group.

[29] Perhaps *me avaru* is the intended reading.

[30] The syllable *kku* is written as a group.

[31] Read=*avad-agavum.*

[32] Read=*avad-agavum.*

[33] Read *samvat.*

[34] A cross is here entered in the original to show that the writing which at first sight appears to be in continuation of this line has to be read after line 11.

11. variya(n)gal (o)rukkāl śēydā(rai pi)nnai a-(v)vāriyattukku kuday-ō(lai) iḍa=pperuttidāgam[35] (|*) (i)-ppariśēy=ivv-āṇḍu mudalcha(ntr)ā(ditta)vat e(ṅ)ṟum (ku)ḍav-ōlai (vāri)yamēy iḍuvadāga[36] Dēvēntran cha(kra)vatti[37] (śrī)[38] Vīranārāyaṇan śrī-Parāntakadēvar=āgi(ya) Parakēsariva(r)mar śrī-mugam a(ru)ḷuchchēydu[39] va(rakka(āṭṭa—

12. śrī-āñaiyināl Tattanūr-Mū(vē)nda(vē)ḷān= uḍan=irukka nam gramattu(u du)ṣṭar koṭṭu[40] śiṣṭar varddhi(tti)ḍuvar=āga (vyava)-sthai śey(dō)m (Ut)-taramē(ru*)[41]chcha(turvv)ēnimangalat(tu) sabh(ai)-yōm (||*)—

A.—TRANSLATION.

(Lines 1 to 3).—Hail! Prosperity! In the twelfth year (of the reign) of king Parakēsarivarman, who conquered Madirai (i.e. Madura),—We, (the members of) the assembly of Uttiramēru-chaturvēdimangalam, made[1] the following settlement, in accordance with the order conveyed) in the royal letter (addressed) to our village,—Tattanūr Mūvēndavēḷān sitting (with us) and convening (?) the committee,[2]—for choosing once

35 Read **perādad-āgavum.*

36 Read *iduvad āga.*

37 The syllable *tti* is written as a group.

38 The symbol transcribed here by *śrī* is damaged and the existing traces look like *pri* or *vri* which gives no sense.

39 Read *aruḷichcheydu.*

40 Read *keṭṭu.*

41 Read *chāturvēdi.**

1 The wording of line 12 seems to show that the settlement was made by the assembly, though the point is not quite clear here.

2 *Vāriyam* is apparently the same as *vāra* or *vāri*, which Professor Kielhorn has translated by 'committee'; Ep. Ind., Vol. V, p. 138.

annually from this year forward (members for) the 'annual committee', 'garden committee', and 'tank committee':—

(Lines 3 to 6).—There shall be thirty wards;[3] in (these) thirty wards, the residents of each ward shall assemble and write down names for pot-tickets (*kuḍav-ōlai*) from among (the residents) who have not been on (any of) the committees for the last three years[4] and who are not close relations[5] of the great men (just) retired from the committees.[6] (The name may be put down of any) one,[7] who owns more than a quarter (*veli*) of tax-paying land; is living in a house built on his own site; is below the age of sixty and above thirty; is known to be learned in the Vedas and *śāstras* and to be conversant with business; possesses honest earnings and has a pure mind.

(Lines 6 to 9).—(The tickets bearing the names) shall be collected in (each) street (*śēri*); (one) pot-ticket shall be caused to be drawn by a young boy, who cannot distinguish any forms,[8] and thus one name

3 According to Winslow *kuḍumbu* means 'a bunch or cluster of fruits, flowers, etc.' The word appears here to be used in a wider sense than the Sanskrit *kuṭumba*, 'family.' I have, therefore, tentatively translated it by 'ward'. [It would be very much better to translate the term *śēri* by ward, and *kuḍumbu* by group.—*S. K.*]

4 Literally 'on this side of three years'.

5 The prohibited relations are specified in detail in the later inscription.

6 This wholesale condemnation of the men who had (just) retired from the committees is altered in the later inscription, where the prohibition is restricted to defaulting committee members and their relations.

7 Anybody possessing these qualifications who came under the proviso mentioned in the preceding sentence would, of course, not be chosen. His name could not be written on the ticket.

8 I.e., who knows no writing and cannot distinguish one ticket from another.

obtained for each of the twelve streets.[9] The twelve men (thus chosen) shall constitute the 'annual committee'. Subsequent to this,[10] pot-tickets shall be drawn for the 'garden committee' similarly and the twelve men (thus chosen) shall be the 'garden committee.' The remaining six pot-tickets shall represent the 'tank committee.'

(Line 9).—The three committees[11] doing duty (after their appointment) by drawing thirty pot-tickets (shall continue) for full three hundred and sixty days. The committees to be appointed after they retire shall be chosen by allotting pot-tickets to (each) ward (*kuḍumbu*) and by drawing pot-tickets according to this order of settlement. The relations of those who have been on the committees..........reciprocally in the streets..........names shall not be written on the pot-tickets and put (into the pot).

(Line 10).—For the '*Panchavāra committee'* and the 'gold committee' thirty pot-tickets shall be allotted to the thirty wards and one man (shall be chosen) in each of the (twelve) streets (*śēri*) by drawing pot-tickets. Out of the twelve (thus chosen) six shall form the '*Panchavāra* committee' and six the 'gold committee.'

(Line 11).—Those who have once served on (any of) the committees other than the annual committee shall not have pot-tickets (with their names) put (into

9 The method of drawing tickets is fully described in the later inscription.

10 The original had *adin minbey*, which means literally 'before that.'

11 Literally 'three kinds of committees.'

the pot in choosing men) for that committee subsequently.

(Lines 11 to 12).—The royal letter which the lord of gods,[12] the emperor, the glorious Vīranārāyaṇa, the glorious Parāntakadēva *alias* Parakēsarivarman, was pleased to issue to the effect that committees should from this year forward be invariably chosen in this way (by drawing) pot-tickets, for ever and as long as the moon and the sun, having been received and made known to us,—We, (the members of) the assembly of Uttaramēru-chaturvēdimangalam, made (this) settlement,—Tattanūr Mūvēndavēḷān sitting with us by royal order,—in order that the wicked men of our village may perish and the rest prosper.

B.—TEXT.[1]

1. Śvasti śrī (||*) Madirai-koṇḍa kō Parakēsarivanma(r*)kku yāṇḍu padinālāvadunāḷ padināru (||*) Kāliyūr-kōṭṭattu tan-kuṟṟu[2] Uttaramēruchchatu(r*)vvēdimangalattu sabhaiyōm ivv-āṇḍu mudal (e)ngaḷukku Peru(m)ān-aḍigaḷ Emberumān śrī-Vīranārāyaṇan śrī[3]Pārāntakadēvan (śrī)-Parakēsarivanmaruḍaiya śrīmukham varakkāṭṭa śrīmukhappaḍi ā—

2. jñaiyināl Śoḷa-nāṭṭu=Ppurangarambai-nāṭṭu Śrīvanganagar=Khāranjai-Koṇḍaya - kramavitta-bhaṭṭan=āgiya Somaśiperumān irundu vāriyam=āga āṭ

[12] This title, which is repeated in B, is meaningless, because no king, however great, could be called the 'lord of gods.'

[1] From two impressions prepared in 1898.

[2] Read—*kūṟṟu.*

[3] Read—*Parāntaka*

(ṭ.= [4]o)rukk(ā)lum [5]samavatsara - vāriyamu(m*) tōṭṭa-vāriyamum ēri-vāriyamum iḍuvadarkku vyavasthai śeyda pariś=ā(va)du (|*) kuḍumbu muppada-muppadu kuḍumbilum avvava kuḍummilā[6]—

3. rē kūḍi=kkā=nilattukku mēl iṟai-nilam=uḍaiyān tan manaiyilē agamm=eḍuttukkōṇḍ=irruppānai eḻubadu pirāyattin kīḻ muppattaindu pirāyattin mērpaṭṭār mantrabrāhmaṇam vallān ōduviytt=ariyvānai=kkuḍav-ōlai iḍuvid=āgavum (|*) arai-kkā=nilamē uḍaiyān=āyilu(m*) oru-vēdam vallān=āy nālu bhāsyattilum oru-bhā—

4. ṣyam vakkāṇitt=ariyvān avanaiyun=guḍav-ōlai eḻudi=ppuga iḍu-vad-āgavum (|*) avargaḷilum kā(r*)yyattil nipuṇar-āy āśāram=uḍai-yārānāraiyēy koḷuvid=āgavum (|*) a(r*)tthaśauśamu(m*) ānmaśauchamum uḍaiyār=āy mūv-āṭṭin=i-ppuram vāriya(n)=jeydilāttārai koḷvad=āgavum (|*) eppērpaṭṭa vāriyangaḷum śe(y)du kaṇakku=kkāṭṭāḍē iṟundāraiyum ivargaḷukku-chchiṟṟ-avai=ppēr-avai ma—

5. kkaḷaiyum ivargaḷukku attai māman makkaḷaiyūm[7] iva(r*)gaḷukku-ttāyōḍu uḍappirandāḷaiyum[8] ivargaḷ tama(p)panōḍ=uḍappirandānaiyu(m) tannōḍ = uḍappirandān-aiyum ivargaḷukku = ppiḷḷai kuḍutta māmanaiyum ivargaḷ brāhmaṇiyōḍ[9]-uḍappiran dānaiyu[10] tannōḍ=uḍappirandāḷai vēṭṭānaiyu(m*)

[4] The syllable *to* is corrected from *me*.

[5] Read *samvatsara*.

[6] Read *kuḍumbi°*.

[7] Read *makkaḷaiyum*.

[8] Read *°pirandānaiyum*.

[9] The syllable *ni* is corrected from *na*.

[10] The syllable *nai* appears to be corrected from *lai;* read *°pirandānaiyum*.

uḍappiran(dā)ḷ makkaḷaiyum tan magaḷai vēṭṭa maruganaiyum tan tamappanaiyum

6. tan maganaiyum āga i=chchuṭṭa * * * * *[11] bandhukkaḷaiyum kuḍav-ōlai eḻudi=ppu(ga) iḍa=p(pe)rāttār=āgavum (|*) agamyagamanattilum, mahāpādagangaḷ(i)ḷ munb=āḍain(ta)[12] nālu mahāpādagattilumm=eḻuttu-paṭṭāraiyum iva(gaḷu)kkum mun śuṭṭappaṭṭa ittiṇai bandhukkaḷaiyumkudav-ōlai eḻudi (i)=ppuga (i)ḍa=pperādā (r=ā)gavum (|*)sa(msaṛ)g-ga(pa)*(ta)rai[13] prāyaschittan=jeyyum-aḷa(vu)m

7. kuḍav-ōlai iḍādad=āgavum * * * * * diyum sāhasiyar=āy=iruppāraiyum kuḍa-(v-ō)lai eḻudi=ppu-gav=iḍa=pperādār=āgavum (|*)paradrāvyam[14] apa-harittānaiyum kuḍav-ōlai eḻudi=ppugav=iḍa=pperādar=āgavum (|*) e(ppē)rppaṭṭa kaiyyūṭṭu(n)=gonḍān kṛ(ta)-prāyaśchittan[15] = chaiydu śuddhar =ānānaiyu-(m)[16] avvavar prāṇān(t)ikam

8. vāriyattukku-kkuḍav-ōlaiy[17]=eḻudi puga(v=iḍa=pperādad=āgavum) * * pādagamñ[18] seydu[19] prāyachchit(ta)ṅ=jeydu śuddhar=(ā)naraiyumgrāma-kanḍ agar=āy[20] pṛāyaśi (ttaṅ)=[21] chedu śu(d)dhar=

11 The missing portion is probably *ppaṭṭa ittiṇai*, as in the later portion of this line.

12 The syllable *nta* is a group in the original; read *aḍainda*.

13 Read °*patitarai*.

14 *Read dravyam*.

15 The syllable *ncai* is a Grantha group in the original; read *jeydu*.

16 Read either *śuddhan=ānānaiyum* or *śuddhar-ānaraiyum*.

17 A second superfluous *lai* is engraved below the line beneath the *lai* of *ōlai*.

18 Cancel the palatal *n*.

19 The *a* of *pra* is entered below the line.

20 Read *prāyaśchittan*.

21 The syllable *nce* is a Grantha group in the original; read=*jēdu*.

ānāraiyu(m*) agamyagamanam[22] (śe)du prāya(śchi)-ttamñ[23]=cheydu[24] śuddhar=ānāraiyum āga i-chchuṭṭap-paṭṭa an(ai)yvaraiyum prāṇā(nti)kam vār(i)yattukku kkuḍav-ōlai eḻudi(i)=ppugav=iḍa -pperādad=āga—

9. vum (|*) āga i-chchuṭṭappṭṭa[25] ittanaiy-varaiyum nīkki-i-mmuppadu kuḍum(bilu)m kuḍav-ōlaikku=ppēr tīṭṭi-i-ppannirandu śēriyilum=āga i-kku-ḍumbum vevvēṛēy vāy-ōlai pūṭṭimuppadu[26] kuḍumbum vevvēṛē kaṭṭi=kkuḍam puga (iḍu)vad=āgavum (|*) kuḍav-ōlai paṛikkum(bō)du[27] māhā sabhai=ttiruvaḍi-yārai sabālavirurddham[28] niram(ba)=kkūṭṭi-konḍu aṅr=uḷḷūril iṛunta[29] nambimār oruvaraiyum oḻiyā—

10. mē[30] māhāsabhaiyilē uḷum[31] manḍagattilēy iṛutti-kkonḍu a-nnambimār naḍuvēy a-kkuḍattai (nam-(b)imā(gi)[32] viddhar-āy[33] iṛuppārr[34] oru-(na)mbi mēl nōkki(e)llā[35]-jjanamun=gāṇum-āṛṛāll[36] = eḍuttu-kkonḍu nirkka[37] pagalēy=[38]antaram=ariyādann[39]

22 The letter *śe* is Grantha in the original.
23 Cancel the *m*.
24 The syllable *nce* is a Grantha group in the original; read *jeydu*.
25 Above the two letters *tta* is an erased *lai*; see note 9, above.
26 The akṣara *du* is corrected from *m*.
27 Read *mahāsabhai—*.
28 Read *°vṛddham*.
29 The syllable *nta* is a group in the original; read *irunda*.
30 Read *mahāsabhai°*.
31 The letter *m* seems to be a correction from *var*.
32 Read *nambimāril*.
33 Read *vṛddhar° āy*.
34 Cancel the first *r*.
35 Cancel the first *j*.
36 Cancel the first *l*.
37 Cancel the first k.
38 The syllable *nta* is a group in the original.
39 Cancel the first *n*.

=orupālanai=kkondu oṛu-koḍumbu vān(giy) maṛṛ=oru-kuḍattukkēy pugav=iṭṭu=kkulaittu a-kkuḍattill[40] =ōr-ōlai vāngi maddhyasthan kaiyilē

11. (ku)ḍuppad=āgavum (|*) a-kkuḍu(t*)tav=(ō)lai madhyasthan vāngumbōdu anju viralum agala vaittu uḷḷangaiyilē ēṛṛu-kkoḷv (ā)n=āgavum (|*) avv-ēṛṛu vā(n)ginav=ōlai v(ā)śippān=āgavum (|*)[41] vāśitta avv-ōlai ang-uḷ[42]-(ma)ṇḍagatt=iṛunta[43] nambimār ellārum vaśippār=āgavum (|*) vāśitta[44] a-ppēr tīṭṭuvad=āgavum (|*) ipparišē[45] muppadu kuḍumbilu(m) orō-pēr k(o)ḷvad=āgavum (|*) i-kkoṇḍa (mu)-ppadu pērilumn [46]=tōṭṭa-vāriyamu(m)ēri-vāriyamum śeydāraiyum (vi)jyā-vṛddha(rai)yum[47]

12. vayō-[48] (vi)ddhargaḷaiyum [49]samavatsara-vāriyaraiyum koḷvad=āgavum (|*) mikku ninṛā-ru(p)[50] panniruvarai=ttōṭṭa-vāriyan=goḷvi(d=ā)gavum (|*) niṅṛa aruvarai=yum[51] ēri-vāriyam=āga =kkoḷvad=āgavum (|*) ivv-iraṇḍu (t)irattu vāriyamu(m) karai kāṭṭi[52] koḷvad=(ā)gavu(m) (|*)i-vāriyam śeygi(ṅ)ṛa mūnru (t)irattu vāriya-pperumakkaḷum munnū(ṛṛu-

[40] Cancel the first *l*.

[41] The syllable *śi* is Grantha in the original.

[42] The letter *ma* appears to be corrected from *ka*.

[43] The syllable *nta* is a group in the original; read *irunda*.

[44] The syllable *śi* is Grantha in the original.

[45] The letter *ś* of *śe* is Grantha in the original.

[46] Cancel the letter *m*; *nto* is a group in the original.

[47] The word *vṛddharaiyum* is perhaps an interpolation made subsequently by the engraver himself.

[48] Read *vṛddha°*.

[49] Read *samvatsara*.

[50] The engraver seems to have first written the letter *l* and then corrected it into *p*; read *niṅṛāruṭ=panniruvarai*.

[51] Cancel the second *m*.

[52] The akshara *va* of *koḷva* is entered below the line.

a)ru(ba)du n(ā)ḷum nira(m)ba-chcheydu oḻivad(ā) gavum (|*)vāriyan=jeyyagiṉṟārai [53]aparādan=

13. gaṇḍapōdu avanaiy=oḻ(i)ttuvad=āgavum (|*) ivagaḷ oḻi(nta)[54] anantaramm[55]=iḍum vāriyangaḷum pa(nniran)ḍu śēriyilum dhanma(kṛ)rttyan[56]=gaḍaik-kāṇum vāriyarē madhyastharai=kkonḍu kuṟ(i) kūṭṭ(i) =kkuḍuppar=āga(vu)m (|*)i-vyavasthaiy=ōlaip-paḍi-yēy * * * * (k)ku=kkuḍav-ōlaiy paṟittu-k(k)o(nḍē vāri)yam iḍuvad=āgavum (|*) panchavāra-v(āriya)t (tuk)kum pon-vā(ri)yattu—

14. kku - muppadu[57] = kkuḍumbilum[58] kuḍav-ōlaikku pēr tīṭṭi muppadu vā(y-ō)lai kaṭṭum puga (iṭ)tu mup(pa)du kuḍav-ōl(ai) paṟittu [59]muppadilum [60](panni)ranḍu pēr (pa)ṟittu-kkoḷvad=(ā)gavum (|*) paṟitta panniranḍilum a(ru)var p(o)nvāriyam aruvar panjavāra-vāriyamum āvānav=ā(gavum) (|*) piṟṟai ānḍum i-vāriya(n)gaḷ kuḍav-ōlai paṟikkumbōdu i-vvā-riyangaḷukku munnam śe—

15. yda kuḍumb=aṉṟikkē[61]niṉṟa kuḍumbilē karai paṟittu-kk(o)ḷ(va)d=āgavum (|*) kaḷudai ērināraiyum kūḍalēgai śeydānaiyum kuḍav-ōlai (e)ḻudi=ppuga iḍa=pperādad=āgavu(m*) (|*) madhyastharum arttha-śauśamm[62] = uḍaiyānē kaṇakk = eḻuduvān = āgavum

[53] Read *jeyyāniṉṟārai*.

[54] The syllable *nta* is a group in the original.

[55] The *nta* of *ananta* is a group in the original; cancel the first *m*.

[56] Read °*kṛtyan*.

[57] The second *pa* is corrected from *ta*.

[58] *Kuḍumbi* is corrected from *kummili*°.

[59] The letters *dilu* are engraved over an erasure.

[60] The letter *ni* is engraved over an erasure.

[61] The first *k* of *anrikke* is entered below the line.

[62] Cancel the first *m*.

kaṇak(k)=eḻudinān kaṇakku=pperunguṟi=pperu-makkaḷōḍu kūḍa=kkaṇa(k)ku(k)kāṭṭi śuddhan āchchidinpinn=aṅṟi.maṟṟu=kkaṇa—

16. kku-ppuga perādān=āgavum (|*) tān eḻudina ka(ṇakku)=ttānē kāṭṭuvān=āgavum (|*) maṟṟu=kkaṇak(ka)r pukku o(ḍu)kka=pperādā(r) āgavum (|*) i-ppariśē ivv-āṇḍu mudal chantrādittavaṟ[63] eṅ(ṟ)um kuḍav-ōlai-vāriyamē iḍuvad=āga Dēv(ē)ntran[64] chakrava(r*)tti (pa)ṇḍitavatssalan[65] kunjaramallan śūraśūḷāmaṇi kalpakaśaridai[66] śrī-Parakē(sa)ri(pa)nma(r ka)[67] śrīmu(kha)m[68]=aruḷuchchēdu varak(k)āṭṭa śrī-ā(ñ)aiā—

17. l Śoḻa-nāṭṭu-Ppurangarambai-nāṭṭu Śrīvanganagar=Kkaranjai-K(o)ṇḍaya [69](kra)mavitta-bhaṭṭann[70]=āgiya Somāśīperumān=uḍan [71](i)rundu i-ppariśu śeyvikka na(m) grāmattukku [72]a(bhyu)tayam=āga duṣṭar keṭṭu visistar va(r)ddhippad=āga vyavasth(ai) śeydōm Uttaramēru-chchaturvēdimangalattu sabhaiyōm (|*) i-ppariśu kuṟiyuḷ irundu p(e)rummakkaḷ paṇikka vyavasthai eḻudinē(n) madhyasthan

18. Kāḍaḍippōt(ta)n Śivakkuri [73]Irājamallamaṁkaḷapriyanēn ||—

63 Read *candradityavat*.

64 Read *Devendran*.

65 Cancel the second.

66 In the original *Kalpakaśari°* is Grantha; read *°charitai*.

67 The corresponding passage in line 1 has *°vanmaruḍaiya*.

68 Read *aruḷi°*.

69 The akṣara *kra* of *kramavitta* appears to be written over an erasure.

70 Cancel the first *n*.

71 The letter *i* is corrected from Grantha *ma*.

72 In the original, the letters *abhyu* are Grantha; read *abhyudaya* .

73 An *akṣara* is erased before *ja* in the original.

(Lines 1—2). Hail! Prosperity! On the sixteenth day of the fourteenth year of king Parakēsarivarman, who conquered Madirai (i.e. Madura),—Whereas a royal letter of His Majesty, our lord, the glorious Vīranārāyaṇa, the illustrious Parāntakadēva, the prosperous Parakēsarivarman, was received and was shown to us, we the (members of the) assembly of Uttaramēru-chaturvēdimangalam in its own sub-division of Kāliyūr-kōṭṭam,—Karanjai Koṇḍaya-kramavitta -bhaṭṭan *alias* Somāśiperumān[1] of Śrīvanganagar in Purangarambai-nāḍu, (a district) of the Chola country, sitting (with us) and convening (?) the committee in accordance with the (royal) command,—made[2] a settlement as follows, according to (the terms of) the royal letter, for choosing once every year from this year forward (members for) the 'annual committee,' 'garden committee', and 'tank committee':—

(Lines 2—3). I.[3] There shall be thirty wards.

II. In (these) thirty wards, those that live in each ward shall assemble and shall choose for 'pot-tickets' (*kuḍav-ōlai*) anyone possessing the following qualifications):—

(a) "He must own more than a quarter (*vēli*) of tax-paying land.

(b) "He must live in a house built on his own site.

[1] The word *somāśi* is a tadbhava of the Sanskrit *somayājin*.

[2] The wording in line 17 makes it likely that the settlement was actually made by Somāśiperumān and the village assembly very probably agreed to carry it out. [*Śeyvikka* seems to imply that the assembly did so under his presidency (vāriyam).—*S. K.*]

[3] This and the other marginal numbers and letters are not in the original, but are added for the sake of convenience.

(c) "His age must be below 70 and above 35.

(d) "He must know the Mantrabrahmaṇa[4] (i.e.) he must know (it) by teaching (others).[5]

III. "Even if one owns only one-eighth (vēli) of land, (he shall have) his name[6] written on the pot-ticket to be put into (the pot), in case he has learnt one Veda and one of the four *bhāsyas* by explaining (it to others).

IV. Among those (possessing the foregoing qualifications)—

(i) "only such as are well conversant with business and are virtuous shall be taken and

(ii) "one who possesses honest earnings, whose mind is pure and who has not been on (any of) the committees for the last three years[7] shall (also) be chosen.

(Lines 4—6.) [8]"One who has been on any of the committees but has not submitted his accounts, and all his relations specified below shall not have (their

4 I.e., the Mantras and Brahmanas, not merely the Chandogyabrahmana which is also called Mantrabrahmana.

5 This is the literal meaning of the phase *ōduvitt-arivān*. But the author perhaps wants to say 'one who can teach (others)' in which case the expression must be *oduvikka arivan*. The word *vakkānitt-arivān* in line 4 below is also similarly used.

6 The original has *avanai*, i.e., him. But to make the sentence intelligible I have translated the word by 'his name' in the light of what follows.

7 See note 6 on page 138.

8 The writer uses the plural here, but subsequently lapses into the singular number about the end of the next line. I have for the sake of uniformity used the singular.

names) written on the pot-tickets and put[9] (into the pot):—

(1) The sons of the younger and elder sisters of his mother.[10]

(2) The sons of his paternal aunt and maternal uncle.

(3) The uterine brother of his mother.

(4) The uterine brother of his father.

(5) His uterine brother.

(6) His father-in-law.[11]

(7) The uterine brother of his wife.

(8) The husband of his uterine sister.

(9) The sons of his uterine sister.

(10) The son-in-law who has married his daughter.

(11) His father.

(12) His son.

(Lines 6—9.) A. "One against whom incest[12] (*agamyagamana*) or the first four of the five great sins[13] are recorded; and

9 The words *puga iḍa* may also be translated 'to appoint in order to enter (the committee).'

10 The original has *śiṛṛ-avai* 'younger mother' and *pĕr-avai* 'elder mother.' As paternal cousins would be differently described, I have taken the words to refer to maternal cousins.

11 Literally 'the uncle who has given his daughter (in marriage).'

12 If a man guilty of incest performed the prescribed expiatory ceremonies, the prohibition against his relations was removed; see clause 1 of this paragraph (on next page).

13 The five great sins are:—(1) killing a Brahmana, (2) drinking intoxicating liquors, (3) theft, (4) committing adultery with the wife of a spiritual teacher, and (5) associating with any one guilty of these crimes; Manu, XI, 55.

B. "All his relations above specified[14] shall not have (their names) written on the pot-tickets and put into (the pot).

C. "One who has been outcast for association (with low people) shall not, until he performs the expiatory ceremonies, have (his name) chosen for the pot-ticket.

D. "One who is foolhardy,........shall not have (his name) written on the pot-ticket to be put (into the pot).

E. "One who has stolen the property of others shall not have (his name) written on the pot-ticket to be put (into the pot).

F. "One who has taken forbidden dishes (?) of any kind[15] and who has become pure by performing the ghee expiation (?)[16] shall not to the end of his life have (his name) written on the pot-ticket to be put into (the pot) for the committees.

G. "One who has committed..........sins and has become pure by performing expiatory ceremonies;

H. "One who having been a village pest has become pure by performing expiatory ceremonies;

I. "One who is guilty of incest and has become pure by performing expiatory ceremonies; all

[14] This evidently refers to the foregoing enumeration of relations.

[15] Manu (XI, 57), declares this as equivalent to drinking intoxicating liquor.

[16] *Krtaprayaschitta* is perhaps a mistake for *ghrtaprayaschitta*. Manu prescribes the drinking of hot ghee as an expiation for sins more than once; see, for instance, XI, 215. [This means one who has performed the prescribed expiatory ceremonies. The Tam. equivalent *prāyaschittam—śeydu* occurs in the same sense.—*S. K.*]

these thus specified shall not, to the end or their lives, have (their names) written on the pot-ticket to be put into (the pot) for (any of the) committees."

(Lines 9—11). "Excluding all these, thus specified, names shall be written for 'pot-tickets' in the thirty wards and each of the wards in these twelve streets (of Uttaramallūr) shall prepare a separate covering ticket for (each of the) thirty wards bundled separately. (These packets?) shall be put into a pot. When the pot-tickets have to be drawn, a full meeting of the great assembly[17] including the young and old (members), shall be convened. All the temple priests (*nambimār*), who happen to be in the village on the day, shall, without any exception whatever, be caused to be seated in the inner hall (where) the great assembly (meets). In the midst of the temple priests, one of them, who happens to be the eldest, shall stand up and lift that pot, looking upwards so as to be seen by all people. One ward (i.e., the packet representing it) shall be taken out by any young boy standing close, who does not know what is inside, and shall be transferred to another (empty) pot and shaken. From this pot one ticket shall be drawn (by the young boy?) and made over to the arbitrator (*madhyastha*). While taking charge of the ticket thus given (to him), the arbitrator shall receive it on the palm of his hand with the five fingers open. He shall read out (the name on) the ticket thus received. The ticket read (by him) shall (also) be read out by all the priests present in the inner

17 The assembly here gets the epithet *tiruvaḍiyār*, 'their majesties, which is omitted in the translation.

hall. The name thus read out shall be put down (and accepted). Similarly one man shall be chosen for (each of) the thirty wards."

(Lines 11—13.)" Of the thirty men thus chosen, those who had (previously) been on the 'garden committee' and on the 'tank committee', those who are advanced in learning, and those who are advanced in age shall be chosen for the 'annual committee'.[18] Of the rest, twelve shall be taken for the 'garden committee' and the remaining six shall form the 'tank committee.' These (last) two committees shall be chosen by showing the *karai*.[19] The great men of these three committees thus (chosen) for them shall hold office for full three hundred and sixty days and (then) retire. When one who is on the committees is found guilty of (any) offence, he shall be removed (at once). For appointing the committees after these have retired, the members of the 'committee for supervision of justice' in the twelve streets (of Uttaramallur) shall convene an assembly (*kuṛi*)[20] with the help of the arbitrator. The committees shall be appointed by drawing pot-tickets......according to this order of settlement."

18 The accusative *samvatsara-vāriyaraiyum* has to be taken in the sense of *samvatsara-vāriyar=āga*.

19 *Karai* in Tamil means 'stain, bank, shore, border, speech.' The expression *karai-kāṭṭi*, which is here used, must be synonymous with *karai-parittu* in line 15. These two terms appear to denote some method of selection easier and shorter than the tedious one of pot-tickets described at length in the inscription. Perhaps they mean something like 'oral expression of opinion,' which may be derived from the meaning 'speech,' given for the word *karai* by Winslow. [Karai-kāṭṭi=by public announcement, as in Tolkāppiyam. *S. K.*]

20 For this meaning of the word *kuṛi* see South-Ind. Inscs., Vol. III, p. 17; compare also *perunguṛi* in line 15.

(Lines 13—16). "For the '*pancha-vāra* committee'[21] and the 'gold committee', names shall be written for pot-tickets in the thirty wards, thirty (packets with) covering tickets shall be deposited (in a pot) and thirty pot-tickets shall be drawn (as previously described). From (these) thirty (tickets) twelve men shall be selected. Six out of twelve (thus) chosen shall form the 'gold committee' and the (remaining) six the '*pancha-vāra* committee.' When drawing pot-tickets for these (two) committees next year, the wards which have been already represented (during the year in question) on these committees shall be excluded and the selection made from the remaining wards by drawing the *karai*.[22] One who has ridden on an ass[23] and one who has committed forgery shall not have (his name) written on the pot-ticket to be put (into the pot)."

"Any arbitrator who possesses honest earnings shall write the accounts (of the village). No accountant shall be appointed to that office again before he

21 Professor Kielhorn translates *pancha-vāra* by 'committee of five,' Ep. Ind,. Vol. V, p. 138. But as the number of members of this Committee is fixed at six later on in this inscription this translation cannot be accepted. Perhaps it supervised the five committees (*pancha-vāra*) of the village. It is possible that originally there were only five committees in a village and the work of these was supervised by the *panchavāra* committee. In the Telugu country it appears to have been a special honour to be placed on this committee and this honour was probably due to its supervising the work of the other committees. Later on, the number of village committees seems to have been increased and there appear to be more than five committees. Even after this alteration the original name *pancha-vāra-vāriyam* given to the supervising committee was probably retained unaltered.

22 See note 3 on page 144.

23 Riding on an ass is apparently a punishment for some offence. It is implied in Manu (XI, 202) that driving in a wagon drawn by an ass is a sin.

submits his accounts[24] (for the period during which he was in office) to the great men of the big committee and (is declared) to have been honest. The accounts which one has been writing, he shall submit himself and no other accountant shall be chosen to close his accounts."

(Line 16). "Thus, from this year onwards, as long as the moon and the sun (endure), committees shall always be appointed by 'pot-tickets' alone. To this effect was the royal letter received and shown (to us), graciously issued by the lord of gods, the emperor, one who is fond of learned men, the wrestler with elephants, the crest jewel of heroes, whose acts (i.e., gifts) (resemble those of) the celestial tree, the glorious Parakēsarivarman."

(Lines 16—17.) "At the royal command Karanjai Koṇḍaya-kramavitta-bhaṭṭan *alias* Somāśiperumān of Śrīvanganagar in Purangarambai-nāḍu[25] (a district) of the Chola country sat with (us) and thus caused[26] (this settlement) to be made."

(Lines 17—18.) "We, the (members of the) assembly of Uttaramēruchaturvēdimangalam, made (this) settlement for the prosperity of our village in order that wicked men may perish and the rest may prosper."

[24] The word *kaṇakku* is unnecessarily repeated after *kūḍa* in line 16.
[Out of three, the middle repetition goes with assembly, meaning assembly for accounts. *S. K.*]

[25] According to the large Leyden plates, which also mention Vanganagar (l. 141f.), this district belonged to Arumoḷidēva-vaḷanāḍu.

[26] The later settlement appears to have been actually drawn up by the king's officer and formally accepted by the assembly.

At the order of the great men sitting in the assembly, I, the arbitrator Kāḍaḍippōttan Śivakkuri-Rājamallamangaḷapriyan thus wrote the settlement.

V. VENKAYYA.

[These valuable documents are reproduced above as the late Rao Bahadur V. Venkayya published them. A revised edition of these is in course of publication by me in the Epigraphia Indica.]

LECTURE VI.

The General Extent of the Chola Empire and the Divisions Constituting the Empire.

The rural administration pictured above from the *disjecta membra* of details collected from the large number of inscriptions of the Cholas that are still available to us for study, is likely to be taken, as it has often been, as applicable only to comparatively small kingdoms with a narrow extent, and unsuitable to larger areas and the vaster extent of territory which usually constitute kingdoms and empires in modern times. The differences in extent and area of the political units constituting empires and kingdoms in modern times have the advantage in these particulars; but it can be said justifiably to be due to the annihilation of distance by the application of steam and electricity rather than to anything peculiar to the character of modern political institutions. Even so, the Chola empire in its greatest extent comprised a vast area, not insignificant even from the modern point of view. It may be said roughly to have comprised within it the whole of the present day Madras Presidency excepting the regions of North Malabar and South Kanara on the one side and the hilly parts, commonly called Malnad, of Mysore. This even for a modern kingdom would be regarded as a comparatively large extent notwithstanding the fact that means of communication have improved beyond all proportion. Having regard to the times therefore and the means of communication available, the Chola empire may be described as vast in extent, and prosperous and efficient from the point of view of the character of its administration. A successful rural administration of a vast empire conducive to the prosperity of the people on the one side, and to the building up of the resources of the Government on the other, must be judged a satisfactory political organisation for the attainment of the highest ends of the existence of a state.

This empire was well divided into provinces and divisions, and territorial units of a smaller character on quite an intelligible and rational scale. No effort was apparently made to divide the empire into divisions of any geometrically or arithmetically perfect divisions as was attempted by revolutionary France. The divisions here followed the divisions of history, and the provinces mainly were the older political divisions or kingdoms, and continued as such or were given new names, though the old designations were still retained alternatively as a matter of convenience. But even in a comparatively small particular as that when the name was altered and a new title was actually given to a division, the practice, when references were made to these, was to give the older and the newer name together in formal documents, indicating a respect for the conservative habits of the people and a care to avoid confusion in transactions connected with them.

Of this extent of the Chola empire, the portion extending from Nellore to as far as Vizianagaram, perhaps even a little farther north, had a long anterior history. The Chāḷukya viceroyalty constituted in the seventh century under the great Western Chāḷukya ruler Pulikēsin, became the Eastern Chāḷukya kingdom when the early Chāḷukyas of the West were overthrown by the Rāshṭrakuṭas in the middle of the eighth century. Thereafter it continued as an independent kingdom and retained that position even under the Cholas when Rājarāja brought it under his authority by treaty, the arrangement being sealed by a marriage alliance between the two royal families. The political subordination of this northern division is in evidence in the freedom with which the Cholas were able to march through their territory to the extreme north, and otherwise deal with them as though they constituted an integral part of the empire. The rest of the territory under the Cholas had become more thoroughly incorporated in the empire, and constituted the larger divisions generally called *Manḍalam.* The Chola empire consisted of the Tonḍamanḍalam, which had the alternative name Jayamkonḍaśoḷamanḍalam, Śoḷamanḍalam itself, Pānḍiyamanḍalam with various other names at different times, Kongu-Manḍalam, and Malai Nāḍu, Gangappāḍi, Nuḷambappāḍi, which was otherwise called Nikarili Śolappāḍi and even Īḷam (Ceylon), which had the name Mummuḍiśoḷa Manḍalam. The first of these main divisions constituted the territory dependent upon Kānchī when it was a kingdom; the rest the Chola country proper, the territory of the Pandyas with their capital at Madura, the Kongu country with its capital at Karūr, the Malabar country of British Malabar, Travancore and Cochin; a considerable part of south Mysore went by the old name Gangappāḍi; east Mysore or the Ganga country, sometimes called Ganga-maṇḍalam, otherwise Nikarilisōḷa Maṇḍalam and Ceylon or Mummuḍisōḷa Maṇḍalam; these were the larger divisions or provinces that constituted the empire. Each one of these provinces or Maṇḍalams was divided into smaller divisions, which in the Chola, Pāṇḍya and even other countries generally went by the name Koṭṭam (Ghoṣṭa) following the older division that prevailed in the Toṇḍamaṇḍalam country previous to the age of the Chola ascendancy, this territory having been divided into 24 koṭṭams commanded by as many fortresses. Below these was the smaller division, something between the district and the taluk of modern times, which went by the plain name Nāḍu. A subdivision of this Nāḍu was the rural unit consisting of single townships where townships of importance were concerned. But more often rural areas, were divided into groups of villages, of which perhaps the larger or the more important township constituted the centre or headquarters, and the rest of the group dependent thereon as it were, but enjoying the same rights as the central township.

On the general lines indicated above, the Chola administration under Rājarāja consisted of seven divisions, and as many as about five smaller divisions not exactly on a footing with the main divisions. Each one one of these main divisions, corresponding to the major provinces indicated above, was sub-divided and divided again. For instance, Chola Maṇḍalam proper consisted of nine divisions, perhaps about as big as our modern districts, and each one of these divisions contained as many as ten or eleven, and in one case, 22 smaller divisions which have come down to us. It must be remembered that we are not taking the information from any complete official register maintained at the headquarters. Unfortunately not a single one of these documents has come down to us. We have to collect our information only from chance remnants, and we ought not therefore to generalise too quickly from the information available to us. Another division shows as many as 17 sub-divisions, so that it is not at all likely that the divisions of which we gain our knowledge from the scraps of information that have survived to our times is complete in any one case. But the general impression that these give us is that they were divided into manageable divisions of a systematic character, more or less equal in extent and consisting similarly of a number of sub-divisions not widely different so as to assure efficiency of control by the supervising officers of the divisions. Having regard to the fact that, imperfect as the information that has come down to us is, there is evidence of a systematic organisation we have to take it that the more mechanical divisions and the responsibilities that they involved were made as far as may be equal. Without attempting to be more complete, where such completeness is impossible, we may say that the general organisation in the matter of divisions and sub-divisions was much about the same that we are accustomed to in modern times. But when we come to surveys and land measurements, and the apportionment of land for purposes of culvation, we do find the details carried so far as to indicate a minuteness of organisation for revenue administration that the presumption that the administration was highly organised generally, would not be far from the truth.

It is on such a division of the rural localities that the general administration was based and the very backbone of that general administration was in the administration of the rural localities. It is in this department of the administration that the rulers of Tamil India show themselves at their best in the completeness with which they carried the devolution of power, which amounted to the people being left to administer their own affairs in the best interests of the communities occupying the localities concerned. As we have seen above, the administration, such as it was, was carried on practically by the people subject in the last resort to control by divisional governments, and the government at head-quarters; but even where the control was exercised, it was exercised with the willing co-operation of the people, so that the difference between self-government and the government by an administrative organisation placed over them can hardly be said to have been felt at all. It is to carry on this rural administration that an administrative practice has been growing, which had reached a stage under the early Cholas, that the practice might be gathered together in a set of rules, and probably the circulars of Parāntaka referred to above were circulars, which had this particular object in view. The laying down of the rules therefore is not necessarily the beginning. It is much rather in an advanced stage of that administration that the practice got to be generalised by prescribing the rules of general application for purposes of use in new localities and for the attainment of a certain amount of uniformity.

That the rules laid down for elections, etc., by Parāntaka I, were generally acted up to after their issue may be taken for granted from the several details we get in a large number of records of the period following. For a specific instance however, we might refer to No. 583 of the epigraphist's collection for 1904 bearing date equivalent to A. D. 1234-35. This records the dismissal of the village accountant and the debarring of all his relations from holding office, almost on the lines indicated in the documents embodying the rules. It was not always that matters were allowed to go so far before royal intervention was called for. There are many other instances on record of intervention by superior authority for various items, and there seems to have been general accord between the authority at head-quarters and his subordinates in the provinces on one side, and the assembly which administered with autonomous powers on the other. Among the large number of records that have come down to us, we do not hear of cases in which the intervention of the authority of the one party was resented by the other, although we have instances of a large number of cases of interventions in various forms taking place. We may refer to some of them which are typical of the power of intervention that the central authority exercised over the government of rural areas in the provinces.

In regard to the general method of carrying on business at the head-quarters, we may take the following as a general statement of the position. Usually matters relating to the provincial administration, or, as a matter of fact, all matters relating to administration generally were brought to the notice of the king, or the emperor for the time being, by a particular officer, whose function it was to do so. This was the case whether the emperors were in their capitals, or out in camp in the course of their progresses through the dominions. The records that have come down to us usually state it that the emperor was seated in a particular part of the palace, which is carefully mentioned, when the royal Secretary, as he is called, an officer corresponding to the Private Secretaries of modern times, brought up the matter which required royal orders. When the matter came up in the final state after the necessary enquiries and investigations had been made, the king issued his orders by word of mouth after hearing the documents read out to him. Particularly when he was out in camp and matters of dispute came to him, he generally made arrangements for holding an enquiry; the parties concerned were summoned and enquiries were made, which apparently were recorded, and he issued orders then and there, or on a subsequent occasion when the matter was formally brought up before him by the Secretary. In every case, the verbal orders of the king were put in writing by the Private Secretary, whose function it was to take down the orders of the king. This officer went by the name Tiruvāyk-keḻvi (the one that heard the order issuing from the mouth of the king). The order was passed on to the department presided over by an officer who is called Viḍai-Adhikāri, the officer whose function it was to issue orders, in other words the head of the office of issue. But before orders even of the king could issue, and when it was ready for issue in this department, it had to be submitted, probably to a council, and, in token of such submission, had to be approved and counter-signed by two officers of importance, namely, a high dignitary, *Perumdaram,* called Īrāyiravan Pallavayyan in the days of Rājarāja and his son, and the Chief Secretary, Ōlai Nāyakam, and then it was issued to the party concerned through the provincial office. It was received at the head-quarters of the provincial governor, dealt with by his office in a manner almost similar, and from there issued to the particular party concerned.

This would perhaps be best illustrated by the following extract taken from one of the Karūr inscriptions, which gives the details more or less fully and perhaps exhibits the procedure clearly. 'Being graciously seated in the royal bathing hall within the palace at Gangaikonḍa Śoḻapuram (the king) granted with libations of water, the village of Pākkūr in Vengāla nāḍu, a district of Adhirājarājamanḍalam, (and) was pleased to order that this village, excluding the tax-paying lands in the possession of the ryots, should become tax-free temple land from (the year) which was opposite to the third year (of his reign) including revenue, taxes, small tolls, eḻuvai, ugavai, the three fines called manṟupāḍu, danḍam, kuṟṟam, everywhere where the iguana runs, the tortoise crawls, an ant-hill rises and sprouts grow, the grass for the calves and the lands enjoyed in full by the great village; that (this village) should pay to (the God) Mahādēva of Tiruvānilai (temple) at Karuvūr in the same nāḍu, the revenue hitherto paid by this village, namely 303½ *kaḷanju* and one and one-twentieths *manjāḍi* of gold; and 3,531 *kalam,* 1 *tūṇi* of paddy, and that this village should be entered in the revenue register (vari) as tax-free temple land from this year forward.

'Accordingly the Royal Secretary, Vānavan Pallavaraiyan, the lord of Tāḷi Tiruppanangāḍu and the lord of Nērivāyil in Paṇaiyūr nāḍu, a district of Kshtriya Śikhāmaṇi' vaḷanāḍu, having written that the king had been pleased to order (thus), and the Chief Secretary, Achchudan Rājarājan alias Toṇḍamān, the citizen Uttamachoḷan alias Rājarāja Brahmādhirājan, Araiyan Vīrarājēndra Mangalapperaraiyan having unanimously approved (of this document), Vīrabhadran Tillaiviḍangan alias Villavan Rājarājan ordered, "Let it be ẹntered in our register in accordance with intimation received." In accordance with this order there was a meeting of a number of members, but here the record of their deliberations is unfortunately obliterated. 'Our revenue officers having entered (this) in the revenue register in accordance with the royal order let it be engraved upon copper and on stone (that this village was given) as tax -free temple land to the God Mahādēva of Tiruvānilai temple for the expenses of burnt-offerings, oblations and worship.'[1]

That was the ordinary way in which the government at head-quarters took note of what was taking place in the distance, sanctioning that which deserved to be sanctioned, examining that which had to be examined, and issuing final orders one way or another after

1 Ancient India, pp. 177-8; S. I. I. III, pp. 38-9;, Pt. 1, No. 20.

satisfactory examination. An inscription known as the Madras Museum Plates[1] of the sixteenth year of Uttamachola, the uncle of Rājarāja, shows the details of this procedure even more clearly. The matter related to a deposit of 200 pieces of gold with two sections of weavers in Kānchī for certain services to the temple. The king was seated in the royal palace at Kachipēḍu, in the decorated hall on the southern side of it. The *Adhikāri* of the locality, or the governor of the place, by name Śoḷa Mūvēnda Vēḷān begged that orders may be vouchsafed in regard to the disposal of the revenues to the temple of Vishṇu at Ūragam in the town of Kachipēḍu. The revenues under reference refer to taxes upon articles sold by weight and articles sold by measure as well as the various other incomes accruing to the temple from lands purchased in the ward Tunḍuṇukkachēri of the same town as well as sums of money laid out at interest. The incomes accruing from these various items had not been budgeted for various purposes, and the request was that orders might issue in regard to the matter. The king ordered that the said officer himself might frame the budget for the necessary distribution and that the carrying out of this arrangement may be left to the inhabitants of two wards of the town by name Kambulāmpāḍi and Atimānappādi. In accordance with the disposition thus made by that said officer, as set down in writing on stone, the order was given effect to as from the 22nd year of the king Kō Parakēsari Varman. The first item of this arrangement was that the Sabhas of Kūram and Ariyar Perumbākkam who had been lent

[1] S. I. I. III. Pt. iii, No. 128; pp. 265.

250 gold *kalanju* had every year to measure out, by way of interest, 500 *kādi* by the golden measure of 8 *nālis* in use in the village; (2) the Sabha of Ulaiyūr, according to the document set out in a stone inscription, for the fifty *kalanju* of gold that they received, had to measure out 150 *kadi* of paddy as interest; (3) in accordance with the record placed upon stone, the Sabha of Olukkaippākkam for the 24 *kalanju* of gold that they had received, had to pay annually four *kalanju,* four *manjāḍi* of gold. The total income thus derived was appropriated for the various services to the temple. The whole of the details are given here for the daily, periodical, and annual requirements of the temple in all their variety. But there is one point which may be of interest to note in this whole list. Provision seems to have been made for the supply of oil by one quarter of the town which went by the name Śolāniymam; two communities of people named Tōlachēviyar (those whose ears were not bored), and Ēlākkaiyar (those whose hands never accepted anything in gift) who had to supply something to the temple had completely vanished from the locality. What they had to do was allowed to be done by those that had occupied the particular ward from outside. These had to supply at the rate of one *nāli* and one *ulakku* of oil, and two *nālis* of rice per house per month. In lieu of these services that they were asked to render, they were to be freed from all kinds of dues that they would have had otherwise to pay to the town. This arrangement was finally put into force as from the 18th year, obviously of Uttama-chola, in accordance with the arrangement made by the citizens of Kachipēḍu. In accordance therewith, this

God is to accept these dues as detailed above. The people of this ward were to maintain the accounts of the temple, and the man that was in charge of the accounts was to draw one *kuṛuṇi* of paddy every day, and two *kaḷañju* of gold every year as remuneration. Then follows the arrangement for certain other services to the temple annually.

Whatever of defects there may be in the administration of the affairs of the temple were to be supervised by the 18 *Nāṭṭār*, whose "orders in regard to the matter shall be final." The accounts of this temple were to be audited annually as soon as the festival should be over by the mayor of this town, those that were in charge of the annual management and the inhabitants of the two wards of Ēṛṛuvaḷichēri and Kanjakalpāḍi jointly. The inhabitants of the two last wards were to take the funds from the temple treasury and make the necessary arrangements for carrying out the details of this settlement. The assembly of the whole town was to control those that superintended the management of the temple, those whose function it was to keep guard over the temple and those who had to maintain the accounts of the temple. They were to see that the temple was not taxed by the authorities. In case they should not be able to obtain the services of a proper *Nambi* (a temple priest) for conducting the *puja* (worship) of the temple, they were to appoint instead a Brahman well versed in the Veda. Having been thus ordered by those in authority, the *madhyasta* of Vīrappāḍi of this city by name Mangaḷāḍittan of "the forty-eight thousand" wrote out this proclamation.

In this important document, which runs through all the details of the administration of a temple, by no means a new foundation, we find the intervention of the king is called for by the officer responsible as for as we could make out from the document, on his own initiative; and the king accepts the invitation of the officer to lay down a scheme, as it were, of arrangements for the conduct of the affairs of the temple throughout the year. He does it, however, through the officer himself, and the arrangement has reference to various details, which affect all the departments of temple administration and of the people or the bodies who had the conduct of the ordinary temple business throughout the year. The intervention there of royal authority seems to have been free and unfettered, and notwithstanding this freedom of intervention, we see that the various bodies who had the government of the locality in its various departments are invoked to do whatever comes within their purview and in their particular department, although the arrangement is prescribed by royal authority. There is no exhibition of jealousy on one side, or undue interference on the other. Royal authority does come in as a matter of course, but seems to operate with due regard to the susceptibilities of the local authorities, and nothing is done except through the particular branch of the local authority.

Another record[1] relating apparently to the reign of the same ruler, Uttamachola, is of very great importance as throwing light on another side of the administrative organisation of the Chola empire in its earlier days.

1 S. I. I. Vol. III, Part iii, No. 128.

This refers to a gift that was made to the temple of Tirumālpuram (Tirumālpēru) made in the 21st and 22nd years of the Chola king who died at Tonḍaiman-Āṟṟūṟ. This grant refers to lands in Śiṟṟiyāṟṟūr belonging to Maṇayilnāḍu of Maṇayilkkoṭṭam and brought in an annual revenue of

1. Puravu, 3,000 *kadi*
2. Iravu, 561 *kadi*
3. Gold, 26½ *kaḻanju, 1 manjāḍi.*

This land which belonged to one Śangappāḍikiḻān was purchased from him, and his ownership rights were transferred accordingly. The grant was actually made in the 21st year of the ruler, Tonḍaimān-Aṟṟūr-tunjina Dēva, and the land was made over in the 22nd year after the boundaries were marked in the usual ceremonial fashion. The whole of this grant was made a *Brahmadēya* gift and was entrusted to the Sabha of Puduppākkam, itself a *Brahmadēya* village belonging to Puruśaināḍu in Maṇavirkoṭṭam. This transaction had somehow failed to be entered in the register of tax paying lands. This omission was rectified in the fourth year of Parakēsarivarman, who captured Madura and Ceylon, Parāntaka I. It was allowed to continue in possession of the Sabha at Puduppākkam as before, and the Sabha was paying the said quantity of paddy and the amount of gold accordingly. For some reason or other, the Sabha of Puduppākkam ceased to make these payments from the 36th year of Pārantāka I, but continued to be in the enjoyment of the land all the same. A complaint was preferred pointing out this unjust misappropriation by the Dēvakarmis (those in temple service), Uṇṇāḷigai Uḍaiyār (those in charge of the sanctum of the temple), and the Panmāhēśvaras, the Śaiva Brahmans of the locality to the king. The king happened to be in camp at the time in Kacchippēḍu, the modern Conjeevaram, and was at the time in the ground floor of the golden hall of his palace. Śoḷa Mūvēnda Vēḷan, having heard the complaint of these people communicated it to the king. The king immediately summoned these three bodies connected with the management of the temple at Tirumālpuram, as also the Sabha at Puduppākkam against whom the complaint was made. On enquiry and investigation it was discovered that the Sabha of Puduppākkam was guilty of having misappropriated this property, which once belonged to Śangappāḍikiḻān, and which had been made over to the temple in the manner described above. The king ordered accordingly, that the Sabha of Puduppākkam be fined by being made to pay annually a *Puravu* of 3,000 *kadi* of paddy, upon the land which belonged to Śangappāḍikiḻān, and which had been transformed into a gift to the temple, as from the fourteenth year of his reign, the land being made over to them as a *Brahmadēyam.* They were also made to pay on the same land what they have had till then to pay under the arrangements originally made, of *puravu,* 3000 *kadi, iravu* 561 *kadi* and gold 26½ *kaḻanju* and 1 *manjāḍi,* in all making a total payment from them on the land, which once belonged to *Śangappāḍikiḻān* of *puravu* 6,000 *kadi, iravu* 561 *kadi* and gold 26½ *kaḻanju* and 1 *manjāḍi.* This was to be entered in the tax register as a *Dēvadāna* and *Brahmadēya,* free from the payment of taxes to the government. It was so ordered by the king, and the superintendent of the audit department, Parakēsari Mūvēndavēḷān, the President (Tam. Naḍuvirukkai—Sans. Madhyasta), Trayambaka Bhaṭṭa; the Śola Mūvēndavēḷān, having been the Agñapti and recorder of the verbal orders of the king, the Secretary Aṇṇāttūr Uḍaiyān, the Uttara Mantri Bhaṭṭālakan, wrote out the order. The chief Secretary Śoḻa Mūvēndavēḷān accepted it. The supervisor of our affairs Parakēsari Mūvēndavēḷān ordered that it may be entered in the tax register according to this order. A certain number of officers were present and were witnesses to this order which was promulgated as from the 218th day of the fourteenth year of the reign.

The officers that were present and the procedure that was actually adopted for recording and carrying out the order are of considerable importance as giving us an idea of the actual staff at the headquarters and their methods of work. When the order was actually passed and taken down as above, the necessary entry was made in the accounts and arrangements made for the conveyance of the land as *Devadana* and *Brahmadeya* to the inhabitants of Pudupākkam. The officers that were present are noted below, and they constitute what is generally called in these inscriptions the *Uḍankūṭṭam*, which would mean literally the body of officers in immediate attendance, corresponding to the *Amātya Parishad* or the *Mantri Parishad* of Sanskrit writers. These were (1) Puravuvari Śembiyan Uttaramantri alias Tanḍipūdi, the headman (talaimakan) of Iraiyānkuḍi, (2) Aḍigaḷ Nakkan, the headman (Kiḻavan) of Pavvattiri, (3) Udayadivākaran (*a native of*) Pēraraiśūr, (4) Vīrābharaṇa Mūvendavēḷan alias Venṛān Karpagam of Kaḷanivāyil, (5) the Varipottagam Tāḷi Śandiraśēkaran the headman of Tirunalūr, (6) the Mukaveṭṭi Araiyan....of Paḷanakkuḍi, (7) Aḍigal Vīraśoḷan of Viṭṭār, (8) Pāngan Kaḍamban of Iṛaiyānśēri, (9) Krishnan Rājādittan of Mukkuṛumbu, (10) Ninṛān Nakkan of Śāttanūr, (11) the *Puravuvari* of Tonḍaināḍu, (2) Araiyan Śivakkoḷundu of Śiruguḍi, (13) Kunṛādi Tiruppori of Śembākkam, (14) the *Varippottakakkaṇakku* ....Tāḷi of (Mē)-Nāraṇamangalam. (15) Paranjodi Paṭṭālagan of Nerkunṛam, (16) the *Variyil-īḍu* Śuvaran Śāttan of Uḍaiyūr and (17) the *Paṭṭolai* Rājavijayābharaṇan of Kurichchi,—being present[1] They form a body of seventeen officers in this instance and the offices mentioned are (1) Puravuvari, the head of the Department of Survey and Settlement; (2) Kiḷavan of Pavvattiri, the headman; (3) Varipottakam, the keeper of the tax register; (4) the Mukhaveṭṭi, the Directing Officer or head of village watch; (5) the Puravuvari, Settlement Officer, of Tonḍaināḍu; (6) Varippottakakaṇakku, the head accountant of the revenue department; (7) Variyil-īḍu, the officer in charge of entry into the revenue register of actual collection, and (8) the Paṭṭōlai, the writer of despatches. Besides these eight officials there were nine others present, who must have been acting as members of council holding no office or portfolio in

1 S. I.I. Vol. III, Part III, p. 292-293.

the administration. Of these Puravuvari as has been already explained is the register of holdings, and apparently there was a general officer at headquarters, as also officers of that department for each division as the two happen to be mentioned here. There is one headman mentioned here, the headman of Pavvattiri. Pavvattiri must have been not far from Gūḍūr in the Nellore District, and why that particular headman was present on this particular occasion is not explained to us. Pavvattiri was of course included in Toṇḍai-nāḍu. Probably he was there at headquarters on business, and was present at the time that this actual order happened to be issued. He could not be regarded as a regular member of council. Then there is the *Vari-Pottakam,* that is the tax-register. The two, *Puravu-vari* and *vari-pottakam,* were apparently separate registers and there were two separate departments for these. The bearing of this is to be clearly understood. *Puravu* is a term that had remained so far unexplained. It means actually, as some of the recently published inscriptions[1] make it clear, an individual holding consisting of a number of plots of land scattered over various large fields in a particular village, constituting the holding of one man, or one property, and forming a single item of taxable land. The register of holdings, therefore, would naturally contain details as to what constituted each holding and to what payment it was liable; whereas the other is a department which had reference to the actual revenue paid and maintained a register recording in it the actual revenue, to which a holding was liable as ascertained by the actual area cultivated, which

1 S. I. I. Nos. 346, 348, &c.

may be more or less, owing to various causes, than the measurement noted in the *Puravu* register. Some bits may lie uncultivated; some bits may have lands added to them by reclamation; some bits which had not been brought under cultivation for one reason or another when the survey was actually made, may have been brought under cultivation. These were several reasons that brought about a variation of the actual cultivated holding from the holding as registered in the general register of holdings. Hence it is that this had to be treated separately, and a separate department maintained for it. When we come to the third division, *Varikkaṇakku,* perhaps we have here another department, which maintained the register of land revenue collected, and yet to be collected, from each separate holding. Then comes the fourth department, *Variyil īḍu,* whose function must have been the posting of the register of revenue paid by noting down against each holding the actual payment made. Thus we come upon four separate departments of revenue accounts. The others concerned are the officer in charge of the king's affairs, perhaps corresponding to a revenue commissioner; then the other that is called arbitrator (a kind of chairman), whose function it was perhaps to see to the adjustment of dues whenever they should arise, or otherwise to see to it that the various departments worked in proper co-operation. There must have been undoubtedly the Chief Secretary and the Secretary; the Secretary's function was to submit papers and obtain orders, the Chief Secretary maintaining a supervising control over all official transactions that took place. Others present are mere witnesses to the transaction and no more. This was the position at the headquarters of the sovereign generally as other records make it clear, and in this case, he happened to be in camp away from the headquarters, the only difference between this and the headquarters being perhaps a smaller staff here than at headquarters. The other possible difference would be that the persons other than the officials here present would be naturally different, and it may be perhaps in larger number at the capital.

The first extract made above gives an idea that the provincial government was constituted almost like the headquarters government with perhaps a comparatively smaller staff. It will be clear from the extract that the provincial government acts the part of an intermediary between the headquarters and the locality concerned, and has otherwise no particular character of its own. The headquarters government exercises power in revenue administration not as an external authority whose intervention is called, but as an authority whose function it is to exercise the power. The fact of its exercise through the local authority, however, clearly indicates that it is a devolution of power. The headquarters government, or the king, handing over the authority to the village assembly, various matters of the administration connected with the locality in fulness, and seeing to it that the power that was thus devolved was not unnecessarily interfered with either by himself, or by his provincial officials. This has reference so far only to the administration in the revenue department and departments allied to it.

Even so, the genuine co-operative spirit and the complete cordiality with which decisions were accepted, though usually the case, it would not be in keeping with facts to assume, prevailed in every case. Differences there were, and sometimes acute differences. Official orders and arrangements were not always carried out with alacrity for one reason or another, and led necessarily to a certain amount of acerbity. But even here there is hardly evidence of any inclination to call into question the good faith on the one side as well as the other, which would exhibit want of confidence and is fruitful of trouble in consequence. Two typical instances may be given here of how such shortcomings in the administration were met. The first instance is that of an omission like the one previously recounted, perhaps graver in point of the interests involved. This is on record in an inscription of Vīrarājēndra, and is dated in his fifth year, which would give us a date A.D. 1067. It comes from Tirumukkūḍal,[1] and has reference to a grant to the great temple of Vishṇu in the village. While the emperor was seated on the throne called Rājēndrachōla Māvali Vāṇarājan in his palace at Gangaikonḍacholan, eight of his executive officers submitted the following report to him; Seventy-five *kaḻanju* of gold which the residents of Vayalaikkāvur, a *Dēvadāna* village of the temple of Mahāvishṇu at Tirumukkūḍal, used to pay, for the *Śāla* of the temple (school or hospital), had been stopped since the second year "of the king who conquered Iraṭṭapāḍi 7½ lacs (the territory of the Chāḷukyas), saw the back of Āhavamalla twice on the field

1 No. 186 of Appendix B, 1916.

of battle), and brought peace and prosperity to the world." The king referred to in this statement is the immediate predecessor of Vīrarājēndra, and his second year would mean about A.D. 1057, that is, just about ten years before the date of the report. The king on hearing the report issued orders granting, as a rent free temple gift, land yielding the 75 *kaḻanju* mentioned above. He added to this the taxes of the village, viz., Vayalaikkāvur, amounting to 72 *kaḻanju* and 9 *manjāḍi* including all taxes, and therefore constituting a total incidence of revenue upon the village of 147 *kāḻanju* and 9 *manjāḍi* in gold. The taxes are put together in various groups. One class *Kīḻiṟaippāṭṭam* (minor taxes or dues) including *Ūrkaḻanju* (the gold to be paid to the township, or for the township), *Kumārakachchāṇam* (seems to be a tax in gold to be paid to the prince, or something like that), Vaṇṇār-pārai (the stone of the washerman, perhaps a professional tax on the washerman using the stone for washing), *Taṭṭārpāṭṭam* (a tax on smiths, silver smiths in particular and other such fee). The other taxes following are not given a distinct name, but perhaps we shall have to classify them as *mēl-īrai* as opposed to the *kīḻ-irai,* the major demands, viz., one *Vēlikkāśu* (that is the *kāśu* or gold piece that had to be paid on each *vēli* of land), *Tingaḷ Mērāmu* (something that had to be paid every month), *Muttu-Āvaṇam* (which literally means of course the pearl market or bazaar, which may mean a tax upon the jewellery in the shops), *Tarippuḍavai,* the *sāri* on the loom that perhaps means a tax levied on each cloth for women as it was completed on the loom). The next *Valangai-Iḍangai*

Maganmai (a sort of poll-tax upon the right hand and the left hand castes), *Daśavandam* (the tenth tax); this seems to be the ten per cent. market dues on things brought and sold in the market. *Māḍaikkāśu* seems to be a seniorage due upon coins, *maḍai* meaning a gold coin; and the last item mentioned here is *Vīra-śēlai,* the cloth of the warrior, whatever that may signify. So then what the order did was not merely to rectify the omission by restoring the gift of whatever was collected upon land under cultivation, but it was also made to include the royal dues other than land revenue, pure and simple. That is the first point to note.

The second point is that the fact of the omission was brought to the notice of the king by his eight officers, whoever they be. How was this the function of the eight officers? The details of procedure do not happen to be given to us in the inscription. From what we know from other records generally, it would seem that the matter about which complaint had been made and the proceedings in regard to which must have been initiated, must have arisen either by a complaint, from the locality, or the temple concerned, or by a report of the auditing officer on the occasion of his investigation into the accounts of the temple. In this case, it rather seems to be perhaps the result of a complaint by the temple management, as an auditor could not have taken ten years to discover it. Whichever way it came, the matter seems to have concerned eight departments each of which had to look in and examine as to the truth of the facts, and when on such examination they found the allegations true, they apparently submitted a joint report that the facts were as stated. This implies the following procedure. A complaint was made and investigation in all its details was ordered. The investigation was undertaken by the department directly concerned, certified to as correct by the auditing departments and ultimately the report was agreed to by all the departments concerned directly or indirectly and in one way or another with the transaction. The eight departments therefore would be represented by their heads, and they would be chiefly departments associated with the revenue, accounts and perhaps local government also. Once the matter had been brought to the notice of the king in that complete form in which it seems to have been, there remained nothing for the king to do except to pass orders and he passed orders accordingly, the order consisting of course of two parts. The first part is the restoration of the grant, and the next is an additional grant; this was to make up the inadequacy of the original grant to meet the expenses of the temple. The need for the additional grant is not clear unless it be that, in the course of the investigation, it was discovered that the 75 *kaḻanju* granted was not adequate to meet the requirements of the service for which the grant was originally made, and the need having been felt for an addition to this, nothing better could have been done than to have transferred the whole of the revenues of the village to the temple instead of a part, as it had hitherto been. As the inscription itself puts it, the original grant of the 75 *kaḻanju,* the amount according to the *Vari-pottakam,* the tax register, was restored; and to it was added the other incomes coming into the register of land taxes, the miscellaneous taxes, &c. The totalised revenue from these was asked to be added as registered and gathered up together in another department, which is named *aḍangal*, the total of revenue demands upon the particular village. In other words the land revenue of the particular village, and the other miscellaneous items of revenue payable to the king or government were both of them put together, and the village was made over in complete possession as a *Dēvadāna*, or gift to the temple, because the original amount proved to be inadequate to the carrying out of the service for which provision had been made. We therefore see here what an actual grant involved, and even as a restoration the matter was not disposed of in a perfunctory or haphazard fashion. The procedure adopted is again fully brought to our notice, and nothing was done without a proper investigation and responsible report. But that is not all. When the order had been issued actually six of the royal officers of the *Uḍankūṭṭam* (those in immediate attendance), and 33 officers belonging to the *Vidayil* (the Secretariat) communicated the order. It does not require 39 officers to communicate the order. What actually is the case again is that as many departments of various kinds, and sections of offices as were concerned in the matter had to take note of an important order like this. In addition to these 39 officers, there were present on the occasion ten officers of the *Puravuvari-Tiṇaikkaḷam*, that is the departments of survey and settlement alike. There were also present the officer in charge of the tax-register (*Varipottakam*); other officers present were (1) accounts officer clearly, the *Variyil Iḍu*, that is, the officer in charge of the revenue or taxes paid in; others whose functions do not appear to be quite clear are the *Mukhavetti* (the chief officer perhaps of the Vetti, village watch or of the free services. *Terippu* (the meaning is not clear), *Taravusattu* (that is the register of the classification of land), *Palanyāyam* (perhaps an officer in custody of the *mamool* or practice of the localitv) and others. The totalised amount of 147 *kalanju* and 9 *manjadi* is ordered to be converted at the rate of 16 *kalams* for each *kalanju* by the *Rājakēsari* measure, and other income in gold and under certain miscellaneous heads amounting to 216½ *kasu* and 2 *mā* (20th) were ordered to be assigned for the service in the temple. Among these was an annual festival on the birthday of Vīrarājendra, the *Āślēsha Nakshatra* in the month of Śravana. August-September in each year. There was the recital of the Vaishṇava scripture, Tiruvaymoḷi. The third was an annual festival in the month of Kārttika and under the asterism of Pūrvāshāḍa in honour of Vaiśya Madhava, who seems to have been responsible for the revival of the charities in the temple, and who seems to have put himself to the expense of constructing a grand hall for the temple called Jananātha Manṭapa.

This has reference merely to what may be regarded as a sort of omission which had remained unremedied for ten years of what was in origin a royal grant. What follows is a different order, more acute in point of character, the import of which has been to some extent misunderstood also. This is a case that has reference to what was done by the governor, or the viceroy of the locality, who carried out what was a general order of the monarch. The record has reference to the reign of the great Chola Kulottunga III, and comes from the temple at Tiruvottiyūr, the modern northern suburb of Madras. It is numbered 202 of Appendix B for the year 1912.[1]

I have appened my translation of this record to this lecture—

An officer of the locality by name or title Yādava-rāyar, in all probability Vīra-Narasimha Yādavarāyar, the ruler of Kāḷahasti and governor of Pottappināḍ, seems to have enjoyed the confidence of the monarch to the extent of having been the recipient of the high honour of being called *Piḷḷaiyār* or Prince. He imposed a tax called *Poṉvari*, obviously under orders from the headquarters, on all the lands in certain villages of the District at one quarter *māḍai* per *vēli* of land. Being a general impost of an extraordinary character, this must have been imposed by royal order, and probably the officer was simply putting into operation what was a general order of the monarch. But he seems to have neglected what was the usual practice, viz., the exclusion of uncultivated lands in villages from this general impost. Having promulgated the order imposing the tax, he commissioned a subordinate officer of his, by name or title Valaiyamaḻagiyān Paiyūr Nāḍāḻvān to collect the revenue thus imposed. The landholders of the

[1] I acknowledge with pleasure here my obligation to my friend, Pandit Dr. Hirananda Sastri, Epigraphist to the Government of India. who permitting my examining the transcript in original at the Office of the Assistant Superintendent for Epigraphy. Mr. S. V. Visvanatha was good enough to provide the facilities for my examining the documents. I have since been allowed to take copies of the transcripts through the kindness of Mr. K. V. Subrahmanya Aiyar,

village Punnaivāyil, which otherwise was known as Rājanārāyaṇachaturvēdimangalam, obviously a Brahman village, were also obliged to pay this tax. The tax could not be collected and the officer resorted to coercive processes, collected all that could be collected from out of the common funds of the Sabha, and for the balance due held the members of the village assembly responsible, arrested and put them to distress not merely, but threw them into prison. It seems however that in this coercive process he left out the Brahman members of the assembly, perhaps because they were usually not subject to this treatment. Eight or ten of these Brahman members are mentioned by name. It must be said to their credit that in these distressing circumstances they did not utilise their freedom to sleep over the matter, but exhibited a very commendable degree of public interest in setting about promptly to do what could be done to bring about the relief of their colleagues of the village assembly. What they did was, they put up to public auction in behalf of the village assembly 80 *vēlis* of land lying uncultivated in one of the hamlets of Punnaivāyil, and succeeded in selling it for 200 *kāśu* to a certain Pichchan-Duggai-āḷvān. They utilised the cash thus realised to pay up the dues and get their colleagues released. The record being a record in the temple which is concerned rather with the gift of the land thus purchased to the temple, does not proceed to state what happened as between the assembly and the governor. But the man who purchased the 80 *vēlis* of land seems to have intended it for a charitable purpose. He disposed of 20 *vēlis* by assigning them in parts to a Vishṇu temple, a Jaina Paḷḷi to a shrine of the local Piḍāri (village-deity) and by gifts among a certain number of learned Brahmans (Bhaṭṭas). The remaining 60 *vēlis* he dedicated, with the permission of the king, for the maintenance of a pavilion in the temple, called Vyākarṇadāna Maṇḍapa, at Tiruvottiyūr, and for the provision for the upkeep of teachers and pupils, who studied grammar in addition to the conduct of the annual festival concerned. This last provision involved two purposes. According to tradition Pāṇini is believed to have been taught grammar by Śiva himself, and it is this gift of grammar, particularly the 14 initial Sūtras called Māhēśhvara-sūtras made by Śiva that is under allusion here; and this is what is celebrated as a festival in the hall which was specially constructed for the purpose. But the thoughtful donor was not merely content with providing for a festival; he also made provision for the continuous cultivation of the subject, and made arrangements for teachers to teach the subject and students to learn it in the *manṭapa* all the year round. Both these are involved in the gift of the 60 *vēlis* of land.

Reverting to the dispute between the governor and the assembly, which is our particular purpose, the error seems to have been on the part of the governor; but the persistence in the error is unusual, and we are not able to explain from the document itself how it came about. The resistance on the part of the village assembly to the degree shown here in this case is also not very usual. But in this case they were undoubtedly in the right, as numbers of such exemptions actually allowed, have even come down to us. It must have been perhaps the result of a misunderstanding of the order; and it was possibly misplaced enthusiasm in the carrying out of the order, that failed to admit an appeal to the headquarters as to what exactly was the import of the order. Another inscription almost in the same place in the temple, but referring to the third year of Rajaraja III, the immediate successor of Kulottunga, indicates the possibility of errors like this. There the question relates to a vast extent of land, the revenue of which was assigned to the temple. But the doubt seems to have arisen, for what particular reason we do not know, whether it was an *Iṛangal* or a *Nīngal,* two technical terms. Iṛangal would mean the abolition of the taxes on the land and making it tax-free. Nīngal would simply mean the assignment of the taxes, and the transferring of the income therefrom to another body or person. The reference was made to the king at the time when he happened to be present in Tiruvottiyūr whether what was intended by the royal order was the abolition of the taxes, or their transfer to the temple. The king gave it out, of course after reference, that it certainly was not an abolition, but a mere transfer of the revenues to the temple, and what was ordered was that it should be removed from the register of rents due to the government and transferred to the register of lands paying revenue to the temple. This indicates that errors like that were of actual occurrence, and the usual method of rectification was by reference to the authorities concerned. Mistaken enthusiasm in carrying out royal orders may lead to consequences of a serious character. The illustration above referred to exhibits the possibility of such error, and at the same time shows a commendable public spirit in the members of the assembly who took it out of the impasse to which it had come by the hasty action of the royal officer. This Yādavarāyar is referred to in other inscriptions as an enlightened and liberal-minded governor generally.

TRUNK ROADS.

We have had occasion already to point out in our study of the inscriptions in Uttaramallūr that these rural localities were provided with official machinery for looking after roads. Their functions were not merely confined to the maintenance of the roads already made, but seem to have involved the making of new roads as well. These apparently were roads which served the locality, and must have been those within the limits of the rural unit serving the purposes of catering to the needs of communication, ordinary and even industrial, of the locality concerned. But apart from these, we have reference to large trunk roads, which led across the whole length of the country far beyond the limits of the Tamil land. Of such we have reference from very early times to some of a very definite character. We have for instance the road called *Vaḍukavaḻi* in Tamil, *Āndhrapathā* in Sanskrit, and this consisted of two roads, a western and an eastern, as they are actually so distinguished. We have already referred to them as the two trunk roads that lead out of the regions of Madras northwards, one nearer the coast and the other into the interior up the plateau and across Mysore. Similarly we have reference to another called *Taḍikaivaḻi,* leading apparently to the division called Taḍikaippāḍi, which was composed of a considerable part of Eastern Mysore and parts of the districts, it may be of Bellary and Anantapur. We have a similar reference to the trunk road leading to Kōṭṭāṛu in the extreme south of the peninsula. There is also a road called *Konguvaḻi,* road through the Kongu country. These constituted the main thoroughfares of traffic from one region of the country to another, and cut through the whole of the Tamil country connecting the entire length of the interior regions with coast towns at salient positions serving the useful purpose of commerce overseas.

The local roads that we mentioned at the beginning were not merely village pathways but were themselves roads of considerable width, and could be described appropriately as roads in the modern sense of the term, as we get references to roads of 64 spans so that the local roads are not altogether mere village pathways. These trunk roads therefore must have been bigger roads than those, and must have been roads of importance taking one through the whole country and providing efficient means of communication not merely for passengers but even for heavy vehicular traffic. The reference to the road to Kōṭṭaru is made in connection with the great Chola king, Kulottunga, who is said, in that connection, to have planted colonies of military men in agricultural localities along this great road. The step was taken probably with a view to holding the Pandya country effectively in subjection, and this measure was taken as a matter of precaution against possible rebellion of the people of the recently subordinated country. The road is not spoken of as specially constructed for the purpose, but is actually referred to in terms which would suggest that it was a long existing road, and a well-known and well-used thoroughfare; and the colonies were planted along this famous thoroughfare. While therefore we are clear from the information that has come down to us that the roads in the rural localities were maintained by the rural administration, such as it was, no information has come down to us giving us details as to how exactly the great trunk roads were made and maintained, who was responsible for their administration. We are driven therefore to make out these inferentially. It is just possible that the roads were in part maintained by the rural unit wherever these main roads passed within the limits of a particular rural unit, and as they must have passed for the greater part of their way through rural units, a considerable part of it might have come within the competency of the rural unit. Wherever it transcended these limits, the roads must have been made by either the provincial or by the central government, and maintained in an efficient condition for purposes military as well as commercial. Records have come down to us giving us intimation that armies were marched to and fro across the whole length of the country, and this could not have been done without roads, and it would be wellnigh impossible to presume that the roads were made each time for the occasion. It is however matter for regret that no information of a very explicit character has come down to us in regard to the maintenance and management of these roads.

When however we come to other la ge works of public utility, we come upon a number of references to the building of great temples with all their appurtenancees, such as charitable feeding houses, educational institutions, rest houses and the like. The great Rājarājēśvara temple in Tanjore is a well-known foundation of Rājarāja I himself. The temple at Gangaikoṇḍaśoḻapuram, the capital town itself that was constructed there and the huge tank to which we have been making reference already were all of them foundations of his son Rājēndra, the Gangaikoṇḍachola. The temple about four miles from Kumbakonam called Tiribhuvanam is similarly a foundation of Kulottunga III, who had the alternative title Tṛubhuvana-Vīra, from which the temple takes its name. Other temples were undoubtedly older, and extensive works of repairs and renovation in addition to mere donations for particular purposes and on particular occasions, were made by rulers themselves in their individual capacity and occasionally perhaps even as public gifts. Public gifts however to these and the expenditure of public funds certainly were not the rule. They were very exceptional.

Associated with these and perhaps to some extent independently of them, were educational institutions, such as colleges with hostels attached to them, and hospitals even were provided for. These were as much private foundations as the others. Occasionally either the whole provision, or part of the provision, was made from public revenues. Detailed accounts of two such educational institutions, hostels attached to them and the foundation of a hospital are set forth below as they have come down to us in inscriptions.

Larger Irrigation Works.—

It was already pointed out that ordinary irrigation works of a minor character, and even those of a comparatively larger character, came within the purview of rural administration, certainly so far as their upkeep was concerned, whatever be the way these were brought into being. We have, at least in a few cases, information as to how these have been brought into existence where they were of a specially large character, and it would be worthwhile taking note of these. Among these we may note first of all that the principal channels of irrigation that exist in the Trichinopoly and Tanjore Districts and constitute the irrigation resources and the means of the agricultural prosperity of the Districts, existed in times anterior even to the great Chola king Rājarāja, that is, in the centuries before A.D. 1000. It is old tradition that says that it was the ancient Chola Karikāla that was responsible for the damming of the Kaveri at the Grant Ancient and making very many of the distributory channels that carry the waters of the Kaveri all over the delta. It may be that the tradition is true substantially. But we note here a few channels that bear names which are referable to the time of the great Cholas, whose period of rule is what we are considering at present. There are some even referrable to later times. Of this last one good example is furnished by the stream called Tirumalairājan, which reaches the sea about seven or eight miles north of Negapatam at a place called Tirumalairājanpaṭṭinam. This last city was the capital of the Vijayanagar prince Tirumalai Raja, and the stream probably ook its name from him and may actually owe its exi tence to his enterprise. But the stream next after it on the Nīḍā-mangalam road, about half a mile from it, goes by the name Muḍikonḍān, a well-known title of Rājarāja. Either the canal was made by Rājarāja himself, or by somebody in his reign, who honoured it with the name of the ruling sovereign for the time being. But the other channels, big and small, seem all of them to be of an older date, and must have been in existence and in a useful and flourishing condition in the time to which we are referring. Channels that could be thus marked out are comparatively few, while those with older names and possessing the character of old irrigation works are, as compared with these, many. There are two channels, however, which call for particular attention. They both of them bear the name Vīraśoḻan, probably after the name of a prince-governor, or of the ruler himself. The Cholas were in the habit of conferring titles upon their relations on the occasion of their accession to the throne, and several princes received titles, and sometimes one and the same prince received different titles on different occasions. The identification of the holders of these titles is therefore not a matter upon which we could feel certain. Even admitting possibility of error, we are not likely to be in error by many generations in these cases. A prince Vīraśoḻan was administering important provinces for the Cholas and we know of a great Chola king Vīrachola, Vīrarājēndra as he is called in full style. The channels under reference may be due to the one or the other, and it may be even both. In any case they are not divided widely apart in point of time. The first is a channel which takes off from the Kaveri just a short distance below Kuṃbakonam and reaches the sea near Tranquebar. The Kaveri itself reaches the sea about twenty to twenty-five miles further north. This portion of the delta is considered one of the most fertile tracts because of the fertility carried to a very great extent by the new channel called Vīra-śoḻan. There is another Vīraśoḻan, however, its full name being Vīraśoḻa Vaḍavāru, popularly known now-a-days by the latter part of the name Vaḍavāṟu, northern stream. It is a canal which runs close to the walls of Tanjore on its northern side taking off from the Veṇṇār some way north of the town. It is a smaller river than even the previous one, but the real importance of it consists in this. It leads the water of the Veṇṇār to a distance of ten to fifteen miles south of the course of the Veṇṇār itself, and serves the purpose of irrigating a comparatively small area on the way. The main purpose of the channel however seems to have been to store the flood waters of the river in an artificial tank in the village called Vaḍuvūr ten or twelve miles from Mannarguḍi. From this tank channels are taken out, and they irrigate a comparatively lagre area of the more arid parts of the Tanjore District, bringing into wet cultivation lands which otherwise should have been dry lands and no more. This has therefore to be regarded as a channel deliberately made for the purpose of feeding the tank from which the irrigation of the dry parts of the district is made possible.

In respect of these irrigation canals, there are two possible methods of bringing them into existence. It is not beyond the administrative enterprise of the rulers, or the co-operative labour of the subjects, provided there is an organisation behind then to bring this into existence. We have no definite information whether these were constructed by the rulers as special works carried out at their own expense, or at the expense of the public treasury, for either of which it is quite possible to quote examples from inscriptions. It would also be possible in these cases to utilise the labour of the various localities through which the streams pass to get the people to construct the channels so far as it passed through the rural areas with which they are concerned, provided either the prince or the potentate found the means to make the head works and such other of the appurtenances either at his own expense or at public expense. Records have come down to us to give the information as to how exactly these were carried out. Another large scheme of irrigation must be mentioned here, and we have full information concerning it. The Chola country proper is not one which depends for its irrigation upon tanks. But as was remarked already, there are arid parts of the country even within the area of the present Tanjore District where river irrigation is well nigh impossible and storage tanks are a matter of necessity. The tank adverted to in connection with the Vadavār has relation to the southern extremity of the district.

The northern end of it is similarly under the same need. The country on the northern bank of the Coleroon for some distance is of about the same character and would have remained uncultivable but for special irrigation works of this character. Just in that locality a site has been chosen for the construction of a big irrigation tank, one of the largest irrigation works in

India, by the early Chola ruler Rājēndra I, son of Rājarāja. This was a tank in the immediate vicinity of the Chola capital Gangaikoṇḍaśoḷapuram on the trunk road from Salem and further north along the north bank of the Coleroon river and proceeding now-a-days to Madras. It is not the position where the natural advantages for the construction of irrigation tanks exist, as in other favoured localities for this kind of work, the country being flat there and having comparatively few hills worth the name. The physical advantages for constructing such a work are not obvious. But the existence of differences of level have been utilised along with certain other favourable features to plan out a big tank with a bund on the lowest side running as long as 16 miles. The total area of the tank must have been very large if the water had been impounded by a bund of this great length. No note of its actual size had been made anywhere. But two channels of water were made to feed the tank. One of these took off from the Coleroon higher up and brought the water to the tank. To supplement this source of supply another channel was taken off from the northern stream Veḷḷār, which sometimes is very destructive in its floods, and that was similarly led into the tank. The waste weir of the tank was just about the middle of the long bund of 16 miles from which the waters were led through the southern parts of the Chidambaram Taluq to where at present one big irrigation tank with 64 sluices supplies that part of the district with water for irrigation. This is the well known Vīraṇam tank. This huge irrigation work was constructed about the same time as the famous Bhojpur Lake of Rājēndra's contemporary, the great Bhoja of Dhar. We are told in the Sanskrit part of the Tiruvālangāḍu plates that when Rājēndra the Gangaikonḍachola returned from his northern invasions with all the spoils of war that he collected in a prolonged and distant campaign, he wished to signalise the victorious campaign by a monument, usually a tower of victory. He just chose this form of celebrating the event and made this "big tower of victory", the very big irrigation tank and called it Chola-Gangam, the Ganga (or the Ganges) of the Cholas, and that was to serve the purpose of a pillar of victory. This was quite close to the capital that he built for himself with all the appurtenances of a royal residence, which remained the capital, if we may say so, of the Cholas and their successors the Pandyas till their power was overthrown by the early Muhammadan invasions. The following extract from Pharoah's Gazetteer of the middle of the nineteenth century gives an idea of the tank as it existed at that time, and provides us with a glimpse of the city as well.

"It may also be mentioned that in the Woodiarpolliem talook there is an embankment sixteen miles long running north and south, provided with several substantial sluices and of great strength, which in former times must have formed one of the largest reservoirs in India. This huge tank or lake was filled partly by a channel from the Coleroon river, upwards of 60 miles in length, which enters it at its southern end, and partly by a smaller channel from the Vellaur, which entered in on the north. Traces of both these channels still remain. The tank has been ruined and useless for many years, and its bed is now almost wholly overgrown with high and thick jungle. It is said traditionally that its ruin was wilful and the act of an invading army. Near the southern extremity of the bund there is a village now surrounded by jungle, called Gungacunda-pooram. Immediately in its vicinity is a pagoda of very large size and costly workmanship, and close by, surrounded and overgrown with jungle, are some remains of ancient buildings, now much resembling the mounds or "heaps" which indicate the site of ancient Babylon, but in which the village elders point out the various parts of an extensive and magnificient palace. When this palace was in existence Gungacundapoorum was the wealthy and flourishing capital of a small monarchy, and the great tank spread fertility and industry over miles and miles of what is now trackless forest. It has often been projected to restore that magnificent work, and supply it by a channel from the upper annicut; but hitherto this scheme, like so many others for enriching the country, has remained in abeyance for want of Engineer officers to make the necessary examination. At some future time it may be prosecuted to a successful issue; till then this most fertile tract must remain covered with jungle and almost bare of men; and the few inhabitants will still point with pride to the ancient bund as a monument of the grand and gigantic enterprise of their ancient sovereigns, and compare it contemptuously with the undertakings of their present rulers. Speaking of the noble temple of Gungacundapoorum, it must not be omitted that when the lower Coleroon annicut was built, the structure was dismantled of a large part of the splendid granite sculptures which adorned it, and the enclos ng wall was almost wholly destroyed, in order to obtain materials for the work. The poor people did their utmost to prevent this destruction and spoliation of the venerated edifice, by the servants of a government, who could show no title to it, but of course without success; they were only punished for contempt. A promise was made indeed that a wall of brick should be built in place of the stone wall that was pulled down; but unhappily it must be recorded that this promise has never been redeemed."

This as we know definitely from Rājēndra's inscriptions is a work of the monarch constructed out of the resources of the monarch himself from the plunder and other spoils of war that he brought with him from a prolonged successful campaign as far as the banks of the Ganges striking the river in the region between Benares and Patna. This invasion was what gave him the name Gangaikoṇḍa Chola. He felt so proud of his achievement that he perpetuated the memory of it in this beneficent work, giving it the name that would remind us of its origin unless the name itself is forgotten as it actually happened to be in this case.

Educational Institutions.—

Rājēndra, the Gangaikoṇḍachola, whose pride in his conquests did not make him oblivious of the public good even in the erection of a victory memorial by him, was a peculiarly enlightened monarch, whose partiality for literature is in such evidence in the composition of the Sanskrit *Praśasti* in the Tiruvālangāḍu-plates handed down to us as one of his many inscriptions. From a place called Eṇṇāyiram in the South Arcot

District comes an inscription giving an account of an educational foundation of his, which gives us an idea of his notions in this particular department. Reference has already been made to several educational foundations by private individuals for various purposes beginning with the foundations for the cultivation of the science of grammar, for which provision was made by a lady in Uttaramallūr. We noted the provision that was made for the study of Prabhākaram, the work of a school of Mīmāṁsa at Kumbhakonam. We also similarly referred to the provision for the teaching of grammar in the temple of Tiruvottiyūr. There are also references to provisions made for the purpose of teaching the Śiva Dharma and Siddhānta. These are but stray references to individual foundations for these particular studies, and give us no idea of what like a college, or what might even well be called a University, was organised like. This inscription of Rājēndrachola at Eṇṇāyiram gives us details, from which it is possible to reconstruct something like an institution of the kind that prevailed in the early eleventh century. We shall find that that is not a solitary instance. The inscription referring to this foundation contains the usual introduction, in which the vast conquests of Rājēndra in the north (Uttarāpathā) are detailed, of course with a certain amount of gusto. He took part in the invasion himself, directly or indirectly, and his glorious return from a war of conquest is described in eloquent terms. The inscription could not have been earlier than A.D. 1023 from the details of the conquests given. The main purpose of the inscription, however, was provision for a particular kind of worship to the Paramasvamin at Eṇṇāyiram "in a fearsome form" in order that success may attend the arms of the king engaged at the time in the distant invasion. This is almost a clear indication that the inscription must be of date A.D. 1023-24 and not very far beyond, the utmost being possibly a year later. The provision was made by the assembly of Rājarājachaturvēdimangalam, the other name for Eṇṇāyiram, and it was made in behalf of the temple of Rājarāja-Viṇṇagar, the chief Vishnu temple in the locality. The really permanent object of the gift was the maintenance of a college for Vedic study and of a hostel attached thereto.

Vaidic studies were carried on according to immemorial tradition by students going to a teacher, remaining in residence with him engaged in rendering such services to him as his own children would render unto him, and receive instead the instruction that he had to impart to them. As time advanced and perhaps the demand for education grew, educational institutions apparently came into vogue, where education of a comparatively high degree, so long as it happened to be of a secular character, could be acquired without the rigours of the residential system that the other involved. When a student had attained to the degree of having completed the study of the Śāstras so-called, that is the auxiliary sciences which are essential to the understanding of the highest learning, Vēdānta as it is called, he then moved on individually to an expert for completing his education by acquiring the higher learning. Even so it was not perhaps quite insisted upon that he lived as a member of the family of his teacher. It was possible for him to make his own arrangements for living, only attending the teacher's convenience for purposes of education. Education, therefore, whether it be on the secular side, or on the philosophical and religious, had outgrown the system of individual teaching to resident pupils by the teacher. But the kind of education that had to be imparted, was none the less that it could not be conducted with efficiency unless students and teachers could be made to congregate at one locality, where suitable arrangements could be made for the residence alike of the teacher as of the pupil. Institutions for this purpose, therefore, were generally of a residential character. The purpose, however of colleges and college buildings were served by the large temples, and these as a matter of course had to make some provision for imparting education in philosophy and religion. They had halls set apart for the purpose; sometimes provision also of a separate character was made with this object. Provision or no provision, any teacher could go and teach in one of the temple halls in any branch of Vaidic learning in which he was an expert to such pupils as wished to go to him. But in certain of the bigger temples, there were regular *Pāṭasulas,* which were more completely organised than these institutions, and this foundation in the reign of Rājēndra has apparently reference to one such in the great temple at Eṇṇāyiram. The grant under reference made provision first of all for a number of minor services connected with the daily worship of the temple. These were (1) the chanting of the Tamil hymns of the Āḻvars known by the collective name Tiruvaymoḻi. Four Brahmans were appointed to do it, and they were allowed three *kuṟuni* of paddy for each day, making a total of one *kalam* of paddy. To meet this particular expenditure of about 360 *kalams* a year land, measuring half a *vēli* and two *mās*, was set apart; (2) in the *Maṭa* attached to the temple, 25 Śrīvaishṇava Brahmans were to be fed everyday. For meeting this item of expenditure, a similar allotment of twelve *mās* (about four acres) of land was made; (3) a seven days' festival was to be conducted every year in the *Nakshatra Anurūdha* in the month Jēshṭa (Āni, Anusham), and 1,000 Vaishṇava Brahmans and *Dāsas* were to be fed among those that came to witness the festival. The provision made for this was 60 *kalams* of paddy and three *kaḻanju* of gold in cash; (4) there was to be a special car festival and the God was to be taken in procession on a car. On the occasion cloths used to be presented to mendicants. For the festival itself, cloths for the God, for bathing the image and other incidental expenses, provision had to be made. For all these sundry expenses, another twelve *mā* of land was set apart, and cash provision was also made, although the amount is not definitely stated. These miscellaneous items apart, the rest of the income from the total grant which was a large one, was to be spent on the maintenance of the educational institution attached to the temple.

For the purpose of this, a hall Gangaikoṇḍaśoḻa Manṭapa was set apart. This college provided for the education of 340 pupils, and instituted for teaching them fourteen professorships in all. The arrangement was somewhat as follows. Rig-Veda was taught by three professors. Yajurveda was similarly taught by three other professors. There was one professor set apart for Chandōga Sama Veda. One other professor was set apart for the Talavakāra Sama Veda. There was one professor for teaching Vājasanēya or the white Yajurveda. One professor was set apart for the Baudhāyanīya Grihya Sūtra and Kalpa Sūtra, and the Kāthaka. In this Vedic school proper 230 bachelor students attended and learned the *Apūrvam,* as it is called, the Vedas. There was a secular side to this school, and in this department there was a professor for Rūpāvatāra with forty pupils of his own. There was a professor for Vyākaraṇa with 25 pupils of his own. There was a professor for the Prabhākara, the text of one school of Mimamsa, with 35 pupils of his own. There was a professor for Vēdānta with ten pupils of his own. These together made a department of four professors and 110 students. For each of the bachelor (Brahmachārin) students the daily allotment was six *nāḻi* of paddy, that is three quarters of a *paḍi* of paddy per day. For the more advanced students, that is the seventy pupils reading the higher subjects, grammar, etc.—*Sattira,* who learnt the *Ōttu* (Veda)—the provision made was one *kuṛuṇi* and two *nāḻi* of paddy per head. The professors who expounded Vyākaraṇa, Mīmāmsa and Vēdānta each received one *kalam* of paddy a day. The professor of grammar is here called *Nambi,* which means one who was engaged in temple-worship, a class which in these days is not remarkable for its learning. The professor for Rūpāvatāra was rated at about a quarter of these, and received three *kuruṇis* of paddy. Any teacher that expounded the Veda received one *kalam* and one *tūṇi* instead of one *kalam* of the other professors. The ten professors of the Veda seem to have received between them something like 16 *kalams* on the whole, although that is not stated in so many words. The total expenditure for these establishments was 10,500 *kalams* of paddy for the year.

In addition to this provision of grain or payment in kind, there was also a cash payment, a practice which obtained till within living memory. The highest cash payment was, though we do not know the reason, for the professor of Vyākaraṇa who received eight gold *kaḻanju* a year. It seems to have been rated at one *kaḻanju* for each chapter of the grammar that he had to expound, Pāṇini's grammar being composed of eight such chapters. There is provision for 12 *kaḻanju*, but the name of the person who received it is obliterated in the record. But the twelve chapters for which he received gold pieces are mentioned. It looks probable that it is the twelve chapters of the Pūrvamīmāṁsa, and therefore the 12 *kaḻanju* of cash probably went to the Pūrvamīmaṁsa professor of Prabhākara. The remaining other professors and the seventy advanced students received each half a *kalanju* of gold, thus making a total gold payment of 61½ *kaḻanju* of gold. To meet the total expenditure therefore of 506 *kalams* of paddy and 61½ of *kaḻanju* of gold that was required, the temple was to be put in possession of land measuring 45 *vēlis* in the village Māmbākkachēri, otherwise called Pavitramāṇikkanallūr, a dependent suburb of Ānāngur, otherwise Rājarājanallūr, and Mēlakkūḍalūr, otherwise Purushanārāyaṇanallūr. The king approved of this disposition suggested by the assembly of Rājarajachaturvēdimangalam of Eṇṇāyiram, and ordered in the presence of Kāḷi Ekāmranar, the head of the village, that the two villages should be entered in the account books as liable only to 1|16 *mā* (apparently of gold, and one *padakku* of paddy and nothing else. This arrangement is what is usually called a Veda *Vṛitti* and *Adhyayanānga,* the first indicating that it was provision made for learning the Veda, and the next a provision made for learning the Tamil Prabandam.

Another record in the same locality, which unfortunately has been built in at the beginning and at the end, and therefore available to us only in part, has reference to the maintenance of a hostel. We are not sure whether it was connected with the college, or was meant to be a separate institution. There usually was a hostel attached to such colleges and this may have been one such. The provision made here was to feed 506 Brahmans classified in three groups, Brahmans proficient in the Vedas, Brahmans in general, and Śrī Vaishṇavas. The large number of Brahmans in general seems to have been composed of those that could sing the Tirupadiyam, those that formed the Ghosṭi for *Adhyayanam,* those that could recite the Tirupugaḷ and those that uttered the Mantra called Shaḍyagyam. This document, however, contains a distinct provision which seems to refer to the school already described. On the day of the *Jayanti Ashṭami,* the day called Śrījayanti or Krishnajanmashṭami now-a-days, Brahmans who had completed the study of Rig, Yajus and Sama Vedas, received what is called a *Jātaka Dakshina* (presentation on the birthday). This consisted of a gold flower and a ring in token of their having attained to the proficiency of a study of each one of these Vedas. For this feeding house, the merchants as a community or guild, which collected the market dues, were to supply excellently husked rice at the rate of 2 to 5 of paddy for 50 Brahmans. Apparently by this proportion 2 to 5, they were to supply two *kalams* of rice necessarily for five *kalams* of paddy. But what the 50 Brahman students stands for is not clear. The Urvariyam (village supervision committee) had to see to it that the daily supply of fire wood required for the hostel was provided by the village. There seems to have been another class of merchants in the locality, and they are described as the Brahman and the Valanjiya merchants whose place of business seems to have been in the south bazaar. They received a certain amount of money and agreed to supply sugar and other things in lieu of the interest on the sum deposited with them. Excess of ghee, milk and curds received at the temple was ordered to be made over to the hostel.

We have reference in another inscription to a similar but smaller feeding house called Śālai, which fed daily 50 Brahmans and 10 Śivayogis, who were also provided with oil for their weekly baths. This inscription also makes provision for a teacher conducting a free school (*Dharmapaḷḷi*), and other provision for the maintenance of three water-sheds. Here in this we get a more or less complete idea of the character of the educational institutions attached to temples. We get a still more clear idea from another inscription of Gangaikoṇḍachola's son and successor, Rajādhirāja.

These give an idea as to what these institutions were like, how they came into existence and what beneficent purposes they were intended to serve. It ought to be borne in mind that these by no means exhaust the means for education or the maintenance of public health. These are merely specimens of the way in which these supreme needs of society were served. There probably were other means for which provision local and general existed. But no information of a general character has come down to us in regard to them.

The next item of general administration is the question of an army and navy. These undoubtedly were subjects which clearly transcended the power of local authorities and were entirely under the control of the government at headquarters.

The educational institution organised in the reign of Rājādhirāja, is, in many particulars, almost exactly the same as the one described before. But it is so complete in itself that it may be quite worthwhile describing it. Along with this I am including the provision for a hospital that was made under Rājādhirāja's successor, a brother of his by name Vīrarājēndra. The two institutions are more or less connected with each other in regard to their character, and will give an idea of the provision made for two kinds of educational institutions and a hospital even of a general character. The first of these relates to what is perhaps now an obscure village in the South Arcot District, Tirubhuvani, by process of abbreviation from Tribhuvana Mahādēvi Chaturvēdi Mangalam and is dateable in A.D. 1048. The record details a charitable foundation attached to the temple, to which the name given was

Rājēndraśoḻan Uttamāgram. This was established in the temple by the general Rājēndraśoḻa Māvali Vāṇarāja for the health of king Rājēndrachola. It seems as though this is one of the kind of gifts oftentimes made by well-meaning friends and officers for the good health and prosperity of the ruler for the time being. We have instances of these in which even a ruling monarch sometimes makes provision of this character for the welfare of an important officer of the state. But that is not our concern at present. The provision made here relates to the charitable gift of land measuring 72 *vēlis* calculated to yield an annual rental of 12,000 *kalams* of paddy, apparently the quantity of paddy that was required annually for the maintenance of this institution. On the day specified the great assembly of the village met in the pavilion of the great temple of Vīranārayaṇa Viṇṇahar Āḻvār, that is, Vishṇu of the temple Vīranārayaṇa, erected by one Śembiyan Ombala Nāṭṭu Vēḷar, and made the arrangements by which this charitable work could be carried out from year to year. The whole grant provided for offerings, worship, etc., on a scale of munificence to the two principal gods in the temple. The main image was named Vīṟṟirunda Perumāḷ Aḻagiya Maṇavaḷa (the beautiful bridegroom who was pleased to be seated) and the other Narasinga. The assembly provided for the conduct of the festival in the asterism *Punarpūśaṁ* in the month of *Māśi*, on the Jayanti Ashṭami day, on the great *ekadasi* in the month Mārgaḻi (Vaikunṭha Ēkādaśi) and the four important *vishus* of Uttarayaṇa, Dakshiṇāyana, Aypisi and Chittirai, for the feeding of Śrī Vaishṇavas and for reciting the Tiruvāymoḻi.

Excepting the detail that it provides for a large number of festivals in the temple, the general character of the items happen to be the same, viz., festivals, feeding of Sri Vaishṇavas on a large scale, and the ceremonial recital of the sacred Tamil texts of the Vaishṇavas, the Tiruvaymoḷi. They set apart from the total income of 12,000 *kalams* of paddy, 2475 *kalams* annually for these festivals and purposes connected with the festivals. The rest they appropriated for the maintenance of an educational institution, which followed in detail the same classification as the one founded by Gangaikoṇḍachola noticed above. The particulars given are more complete in this case, and the details may be noted. The first for the Vedic section there were as before three teachers for the Rig-Veda, three teachers for the Yajur Veda and one for Chandōga Sāma, one for Talavakāra Sama, one teacher for Apūrva, one teacher for Vājasanēya (Śukla Yajurveda), one for the Bodhāyana and one for Satyāshāḍa Sūtra. It will be noticed that this makes a total of 12 professors instead of the ten of the other institution. The two new ones are the professor for teaching Apūrva, and another one for teaching Satyāshāḍa Sūtra. The whole allowance for these is set down at four kalams of paddy. (2). In the next department, there was one professor each for expounding (1) the Vēdānta, (2) Vyākaraṇa, (3) Rūpāvatāra, (4) Śrī Bhārata, (5) Rāmāyaṇa, (6) Manu Śāstra, (7) Vaikhānasa Śāstra making seven professors in all, of which it is only the first three are as in the other school, the last four are additions.

So far as students were concerned, there were sixty students each for Rig and Yajur Vedas making a total of 120; and there were twenty for Chandogasama and fifty for other Śāstras together making a total of 190 students. The total provision of daily ration for these people was made and set down as 11 *kalams* and 10 *kuruṇi* and four *nāḻi* of paddy. In the next section, the advanced students, there were seventy of them, receiving instruction in Vēdānta, Vyākaraṇa and Rupavatāra. The daily provision for these seventy is not specifically mentioned. The total provision for the whole body of them, viz., 260 students and 19 professors is set down as 9525 *kalams* of paddy a year. Including the previous appropriation for the festivals, etc., the total annual supply was to be 12,000 *kalams* of paddy which were to be measured out by those that cultivated the 72 *vēlis* of land purchased and made over for this particular purpose. An important additional stipulation was made that even when general classifications of land were undertaken, these 72 *vēlis* of land should not be revised even in the matter of the *taram* (the class to which the lands actually belonged). (2) That on this land, no other taxes or other obligations should be imposed other than the *Eri Ayam* (dues for maintaining the tank), *Pāḍi Kāval* (the dues for keeping care over the village lands) and *Ēri Āmanju* (free services that had to be rendered for keeping the irrigation tank in condition). (3) the professors who gave instruction in the Vedas, the Bhaṭṭas, who expounded the Sastras and the students who learnt the Vedas, etc., were exempted from certain payments or obligations. It is very unfortunate that the rest of this huge record should have been damaged. It is very likely that it would have added a great deal more of useful information, adding to the knowledge that we posses of the real character of these institutions.

These institutions normally were residential institutions, as was stated already, and wherever these institutions existed, provision had to be made for hostels for the maintenance of the students and other appurtenances necessary for the residence and convenience, both of the students and the teachers alike. From an inscription of Vīrarājēndra, who was another son of the great Gangaikoṇḍachola, we get an idea of a hospital that was instituted for the benefit of these students. Such hospitals, of course, are mentioned, and a few details of their organisation happen to be given. But in this record we get a complete account of what a hospital was like in those days. The provision for this hospital and the other items combined with it seem to have been old. But from the second year of Rajendra, the predecessor of this monarch Vīrarājēndra, for some reason or other, the payment failed to be made to the Śala of the temple at Tirumukkūḍal. This payment was a cash payment of 75 *kaḻanju* of gold, which the residents of Vayalaikkāvūr, a *Dēvadāna* village had to pay to the temple of Mahāvishṇu at Tirumukkūḍal, to which the land was apparently gifted. It is said in this record that the eight executive officers of the king brought this failure on the part of the village to the notice of the monarch, who ordered that the grant be restored, as it was made by his predecessor, making the village pay the 75 *kaḻanju* of gold; but he added to the grant, the taxes due from that village. The two items together made a total in *gold* of 147 *kaḻanju* and 9 *manjāḍi*. This was converted into paddy at the rate of 16 *kalams* per *kaḻañju*, measured by the Rājakēsari measure, the standard dry measure. Other income in gold under certain miscellaneous heads amounted to 216½ *kāśu* and 2 *mā*. These were assigned for various services in the temple, such as the annual festival on the *Āślēsha* in the month of Śravaṇa, which was the birthday of Vīrarājēndra Dēva, the recital of the Vaishṇava Tiruvāymoḻi and the festival in each year in the month of Kārttikai under the asterism Pūrvāshāḍa. This marked the birthday of the Vaiśya Mādhava, who not merely revived the charities in the temple, but also constructed the surrounding halls and a special *manṭapa* called Jananatha Manṭapa.

HOSPITAL VĪRAŚOḶAN.

This Jananātha Manṭapa actually served the purpose of a school for *Vaidic* learning provided with a hostel for students and a hospital (*Ādula Śālai*). The students (*Sattirar*) were provided with food, oil for bath on Saturdays and the oil for lamps. The hospital went by the name Vīraśoḻan, and was provided with fifteen beds for sick people. For the maintenance of this hospital, the following provisions were made: (1) a doctor in whose family the privilege of administering medicine was hereditary; (2) a surgeon (*Śalliyakkriyaipaṇṇuvān;* (3) two servants, who had to fetch drugs, supply fuel and do other services for the hospital; (4) two maid servants for nursing the patients, and (5) a general servant (*Viśan*) for the school hostel and hospital. The following stock of medicines was also provided for:—

1.	Asahārītaki	.. 2 paḍis.
2.	Gomūtrahārītaki	.. 2 padis.
3.	Daśamūla Hārītaki	.. 1 paḍi.
4.	Bhallataka Hārītaki	.. 1 padi.
5.	Gandiram	.. 1 padi.
6.	Balakōranḍa Tailam	.. 1 tūni.
7.	Another Tailam, the name of which is partially gone	.. 1 tūni.
8.	So another Tailam	.. 1 tūni.
9.	Uttamakarṇādi Tailam	.. 1 tūni.
10.	A special preparation of ghee	.. 1 padakku.
11.	Bilvādhighritam	.. 1 padakku.
12.	Manḍūkara Vaṭakam	.. 2000
13.	Dhrivaṭṭi	.. 1 nāḻi.
14.	Vimalai	.. 2000
15.	Tāmrādi	.. 2000
16.	Vajrakalpam	.. 1 tūṇi and 1 padakku.
17.	Kalyānalavaṇam	.. 1 tūni and 1 padakku.
18.	Other drugs required for administering these.	

This is so far as the supply of medicine is concerned. It is needless to add that the quantity of rice required for feeding the patients and perhaps the servants was provided for. Cow's ghee for making Purānasarpi, and oil for burning throughout were also provided for. For the sick inmates of the Jananātha-maṇṭapa, pure water was brought from Perambalūr and supplied scented with cardamoms and *kuskus*. The provision made in this unique institution so far, by no means implies that this was the only one that existed. The detailed provision that is made gives the clearest possible indication that people were accustomed to such institutions, and there was the knowledge what these institutions required by way of staff, medicinal requirements, and other things that were required of a special character and the ordinary supplies of articles for maintenance. It seems as though this was but one of the many institutions that existed for the purpose of looking after the ailing, and providing treatment. We may not be perhaps quite justified in inferring from these that hospitals for the treatment of the public existed. It would be all the same hazardous to assert that they never did, as hospitals in this country were of common occurrence not only in the days of the humane emperor Asoka of the Mauryas, but even in the days of Hindu rule under the Guptas where such institutions were maintained as stated by the Chinese traveller Fahien. Exceptional as these institutions seem to be, they cannot be regarded as so rare; and it may not be too much of an inference if we took it that most of the bigger temples had similar institutions attached to them. The provision made for education of this character must have been ample and met the needs of society adequately. It would have been welcome if we had the material to describe in as much detail institutions that existed for general education of a secular character. Unfortunately we have none such, having regard again to the actual character of the sources of information that have escaped destruction and have come down to us. But even so, the one or two details that peer out occasionally give enough to make a negative statement far from true. Such provision as existed for secular education probably was of a character, such as we were accustomed to till within very recent times, and to which reference has been made even by the organisers of the British Government early in the 19th century on the eve of the formation of the Madras Presidency.

ARMY AND NAVY.

From what has been said in connection with the administrative organisation of the Cholas, military affairs proper appear to stand out clear, except for mere accidental references to foreign wars and conquests. During the period with which we have to deal lasting over perhaps a millenium in all, internal wars, that is, wars between different parties within the kingdom or the empire is a comparatively rare occurrence. These are heard of only when dynastic revolutions take place and they were so far as this part of the country is concerned few and far between. A certain number of undoubted references however come to our notice scattered through the very large number of records that we have. In some cases they happen to be merely incidental references such as we have had to mention in the course of our account of the rural administration itself. But with the advent of Rājarāja, the end of the tenth century, things assume a different aspect; not that the character of history changes, but the method of recording that history seems to undergo something of a radical change. Inscriptions of these monarchs like the inscriptions of the others are not documents intended to serve the purpose of history specially. They may be regarded more as documents of rights to property, etc., and had purely that object in view. The real historical matter that goes into them goes into them more or less by accident. With the advent of Rājarāja, truly entitled to the distinction "Great" usually given to him, he gives additional evidence of his originality in the innovation that he introduced in this line. While we have examples of *Praśastis* in the Sanskrit inscriptions elsewhere, referable as early as to the Gupta time, perhaps Samudragupta's claim to have originated this would be about as substantial as that of Rājarāja, Rājarāja seems to be the first South Indian ruler that introduced this innovation. We have very elaborate Pallava documents, but none of them give us a historical introduction, such as the inscriptions of Rājarāja and his successors seem of set purpose to provide. In fact that special kind of a composition in Tamil called *Meykīrti,* literally "true glory", the really glorious deeds of the ruler or rulers, or much rather the ruling family, has been brought into fashion, and these introductions supply us with a valuable source of historical material.

A study of the reign of Rājarāja or Rājēndra, or any of the successors of these great rulers could be made chronologically from these introductions alone. In these we get an account of their wars, particularly wars carried on against their neighbours and enemies, and these, of course, could not be carried on except with the aid of an army organised and maintained on a basis for war. These are the proverbial three arms of war, the fourth having perhaps died out by becoming useless. These three constituted (1) the elephantry, (2) cavalry, and (3) infantry. The chariots, drawn by four horses and two alike, seem to have fallen into desuetude ; at any rate, we have not come upon any kind of a reference to that particular arm, though the term *Chaturanga* still continues in use. There is nothing in these records to show, however, that Rājarāja originated the army, or that he gave it even an original or even a revised organisation in particular. The army, however, was regarded as an important factor to be organised and maintained in a condition of efficiency, and is sometimes referred to in the inscriptions of his successor Rājēndra as 'a great warlike army'. Perhaps the army could be treated as an important branch of the administration, and some special trouble was perhaps taken to maintain the forces constituting it in a condition of efficiency ready to be put on a war footing at short notice. We get the names of as many as 31 divisions of these collected from incidental references. The 31 could hardly be regarded as exhaustive, nor have we the details to give us an idea as to the actual number that these 31 contained. For instance, there is one division that is spoken of as *Ānaiyāḷ*, (Elephant-men), that is, soldiers fighting from the back of elephants. These need not be mistaken for the *Mahuts* as they are referred to separately as *Ānai-pāhur,* which would mean elephant-driver. Then there is a division called *Terinda Villikaḷ* (expert archers). Probably this was a division, which was maintained distinctly as a division of bowmen. There is another division, which is called *Udanilai-Kudirai-Śēvakar*. The latter term would simply mean horsemen. The former *Udanilai* means that their position was near the sovereign. It would mean horse-guards constituting the bodyguard of the king, implying naturally that there were other horsemen, whose function was not particularly guarding the person of the king. Another division that is referred to, to which reference must be made, is called *Andaḷagattāḷar*. It seems to be men or soldiers detailed for guarding the fort. Then we come upon a large class divided into as many as 25 divisions of infantry. Of these divisions *Aṇukkar* and *Meykāppār* seem to refer the first to the infantry constituting the bodyguard, and the others, two or three called *Mēykāppār* with the term *vāśal* before, meaning merely the palace guard. These guards were given separate distinguishing names. One division goes by the name *Parivāra Meykāppār*, which seems to imply that they were to accompany the king as personal guards. The next class is called *Aṇukkavāśal Kāppār*, the guards of the inner palace gates. Another division is called *Kēraḷāntaka-vāśal-kāppār*. The first part of the name Kēraḷāntaka seems to have been derived from a title of the king, which means nothing more than that, among the palace guards, this division went by this distinguishing title. Then there are a number of divisions called *Parivārattār*, that is, those that accompanied the king. All these four separate divisions are named as such. Then there is a division called *Parāntaka-Kongu-Vāḷar* the last word would imply that they were swordsmen. The first may be disposed of as a title from which the regiment drew its name. The second word Kongu seems to imply that these were a people drawn from the Kongu country. There is also a *Mūlaparivāram,* which would mean the main body of the hereditary forces of the crown referred to in the *Kuṛaḷ.* Then there is a *Kālavar,* described as *Śirudanattu-vaḍuka-kālavar. Kālavar* would mean infantry, *Vaḍukar* would mean the Telugu-Kanarese people from whom the regiment was raised. The term *Śirudanam* and its correlative *Perundanam* are not clearly understood. *Śirudanam* and *Perundanam* seem to stand for the two bazaars (big bazaar and the small bazaar), which have got their analogues almost in every city of any age in India, and which obtains all over in the Tamil country and the Kanarese country, and I believe even in the Telugu country. But the terms have a peculiar use also, when they are made to apply to streets of dancing girls, and then the division is based on the fees that have to be paid for these public women. But these terms, however, occur in combinations as *Perundanattu Perumākkaḷ,* and in such combinations, the meaning intended seems to be what is stated first.

There are two divisions which go by the peculiar name *Paḍaikaḷilār* translatable as military men, more or less, without any specific distinction whether they belonged to the infantry, or cavalry, or the elephant corps. One of these divisions is called *Valangai Paḷam Paḍaikaḷilār.* This would mean ancient military men of the right-hand caste. We have not come upon any corresponding left-hand, although the correlative divisions *Valangai* and *Iḍangai* are well known, and their sub-divisions are of frequent reference. The other division is called *Palvahai Paḷan Paḍaikaḷilār,* which would mean many kinds of military men, similarly ancient, perhaps hereditary. Probably this involved men in military service, perhaps not as soldiers, but as camp followers required for various kinds of work. Then we come upon 14 divisions, of which 12 are described as *Vēlaikkārar* and (2) as *Velaikāra Paḍaikaḷ.* Several of these are given the attribute "expert" (*terinda*), and all of them are distinguished by a special title derived from one or other of the titles of the king, or prince with whom they were particularly connected, and the two divisions which are called *Vēḷaikkāra paḍaikaḷ,* one of them belongs to the *Perundanam,* and the other belongs to the *Śirudanam.* The *Vēḷaikkārar* that are described here are all of them of the *Valangai* kind, and we do not come upon an *Iḍangai* among them. What indeed is the actual significance of the term *Vēḷaikkārar* is not clear, but that they constituted a class of military men is certain. These figure in the history of Ceylon as mercenary troops engaged by the Ceylonese monarchs, and, at one time when the rulers proved themselves weak, they took the power into their own hands and played the part of the famous Praetorian Bands in the empire of Rome. While one could understand easily their mercenary character in Ceylon, it would be difficult to imagine that they were all mercenaries in the Chola country. The *Vēlaikkārar* seem to have been a powerful community of merchants, who carried on trade generally in countries outside of their native territory. This gave them perhaps an opportunity to develop in them the spirit of soldiering, as they had to be fighters as well as traders if they pursued trade, of course of the Sārthavāha (Tam. '*Sāttu*') kind moving in caravans. If they went great distances, they must be prepared not merely to carry on trade and earn profits, but to earn and hold possession of what they earned, against robbers and other dangerous pests of the highway. This class perhaps served usefully for raising the soldiery from, and these regiments were raised from among them. They apparently followed other professions as well, as we have a reference to a few of them taking to the profession of music and being employed as musicians in the temple at Tanjore on a salary of 75 *kalams* of paddy per year. These regiments sometimes were treated as a corporate body with joint responsibility. They had sometimes to manage some of the smaller shrines on their own joint responsibility. There are instances in which they borrowed money on their joint responsibility from the temple, though we are not informed in what manner they actually applied the funds.

Numbers of officers are under reference, and among them in the reign of Rājarāja two stand out prominently. The first one of them is called *Kuravan Ulahaḷandān,* which was his name, the former probably indicating a title and not the caste. But he had the title *Rāja Rāja Mahārājan.* The other one is called Krishnan-Raman, meaning Raman, son of Krishna. He had a title *Mummuḍi Śoḷa Brahman Mahārājan,* a Brahman. These are both of them described as generals, and they must have been very distinguished in their profession, as otherwise the title *Mahārājan* would not have been given to them, *Mahārājan* in the case of a *Non-Brahman,* and *Brahma-Mahārājan* in the case of a Brahman. This title entitled their wives also to call themselves *Mahārājiyār,* generally written in *Mārāśiyar.* The latter Krishnan-Raman continued to be, throughout the reign of Rājarāja and the earlier period of that of his son, holding the position of Chief Secretary in the civil administration called *Olai Nāyakam* briefly, or in full *Tirumandira Olai Nāyakam.* A number of these secretaries are mentioned with high titles, and most of them hold high positions in the civil administration bearing the responsibility of great offices. They seem to have been at the same time, at least a great many of them, generals of rank as well. They may have been all of them actually military men or no. It is just possible that like the Mansabdars under the Mughals, these were officials, whose rank is indicated on the military basis, as in the case of Mansabdars.

The details given above such as they are perhaps prove that a standing army was maintained, divided into a certain number of units, each unit being characterised or distinguished by a certain feature in its duty, or by attachment to a particular ruler, prince or general. But each one of these divisions must have had its staff of officers, and otherwise provided with an orderly organisation. We have no reference whatever to anything like a general levy, and possibly we shall have to presume that it is only the standing army that went and fought, the ordinary inhabitants of the territory going free from war service, except of course, when they had to stand on their defence and do what they could to defend themselves and the country when their own homes were actually invaded perhaps an abnormal occurrence in Hindu India.

NAVY.

In respect of the navy, we are in the unfortunate position of having no direct material bearing on the question. During the period so far covered in the course of these lectures, we have references to sea-going and over-seas commerce. Expressions and comparisons, etc., in literature give evidence of familiarity with sea-going and knowledge of places across the Bay of Bengal at any rate, in the early centuries of the Christian era. The Chinese traveller Fahien, who was in Ceylon and left on his return journey for China overseas, makes the remark that on the eastern shores of the Bay of Bengal, there were settlements of Indians, whom he found to be generally Hindu with very few Buddhists. So colonising by Hindu inhabitants of South India seems to have been more or less general. We have an inscription in Koettei in East Borneo, which seems to be inscribed upon the sacrificial pillars of a Brahmanical sacrifice that was celebrated there and the inscription records the details of the gift made at the sacrifice by an Indian Raja. Other evidence of colonisation are found in plenty in the islands as well as in the Easternmost Peninsula of Asia in regard to contact with India, though much more work is required before anything like a specifically chronological statement could be made regarding them. But this inscription is datable, though it does not actually carry a specific date. It is referred, on grounds of paleography, to the territory of the Pallavas, because the script is the Pallava *grantha* character, and is generally ascribed to the fourth century or thereabouts. We have another inscription at Takopa now in the Malay Peninsula referring to the construction of a Vishṇu temple dedicated in all probability to Vēṇugopāla, the construction of a tank called Nāraṇam, as it is put down in Tamil, and the placing of this public institution in charge of certain communities of Indian merchants. Among them figures the famous *Maṇigrāmam* thereby indicating that the colony probably proceeded from the west-coast. On the western side, there is considerable evidence of a brisk commerce. The whole of the evidence seems to indicate the coming of foreign ships to carry the articles of commerce from the coast. But we are not altogether without evidence that Indian fleets were maintained principally for purposes of commerce, but sometimes taking part even in the operations of war. There is a specific instance of a fleet of a Chera king, which attacked a Yavana fleet, defeated and partially destroyed it; brought in prisoners of war from among the mariners, and punished them in a characteristic fashion. That is the first reference that we have to a navy, understanding it in a rather freer sense than the modern technical usage would warrant. It would perhaps be too much to imagine that they had a fighting line of ships, as distinct from the commercial merchantmen. Perhaps it was one flotilla of ships, which, as occasion required, plied in the work of commerce, discharged the duties of a fleet of transports for carrying soldiers across, and when occassion demanded it, even served the purpose of a fighting line of ships. The next specific item of evidence we have of ships put to a warlike use is in a statement that Hiuen T'sang makes regarding a navy that was sent by the great Pallava Narasimha Varman in the 7th Centuary A.D. Narasimha Varman had a fugitive ruler of Ceylon at his court, who actually assisted him in his wars and rendered yeoman service in the capture and destruction of the Chalukyan capital, Badami. In return for this loyal service, the Pallava monarch felt it his duty to equip an army and send it for his friend's assistance against the usurper-ruler in Ceylon. This Ceylon fugitive was known by the name Mānavarma, and the army fitted out for the invasion in his behalf is said to have been carried across by a fleet of 300 transports from "the port of Kanchi" to the landing place in Ceylon. A fleet of 300 transports carrying soldiers must be prepared to fight on the sea, if the occasion demanded it. It must therefore be taken that these transports had sufficient equipment to do the fighting in case of need, as even in the case of ships going on commerce, a certain amount of fighting they had to be prepared for, and there are actual references to this particular point in literature. So this Mānavarman invasion of Ceylon—or rather two invasions the first having failed, the second having succeeded in placing him on the throne—is the first specific evidence that we have of fleets of ships being put to warlike use within historical times, and on a statement of undoubted historical authority. It cannot be regarded as a mere solitary instance; it is a solitary reference, however that has come down to us, which does not necessarily mean that that is the only occasion in which a naval enterprise of the character called for the equipment of a navy.

The Takopa inscription already adverted to seems to refer to the period following that of Narasimhavarman and Mānavarma, and while the name of the king is not clear, it seems to be one of these Pallava monarchs that is under reference. But the really most important part of the inscription is where at the closing part of the document it mentions that the charitable foundation,—the temple and the tank—was placed under the protection of people constituting three divisions or communities of Indian origin. The three divisions are mentioned as *Śēnāmukhattār, Chāpattār* and *Maṇigrāmattār.* All these three terms are obscure in regard to their significance, notwithstanding the fact that they are, more or less, wellknown terms. Without entering into a discussion in regard to these here, the term *Maṇigrāmam* seems to be a community of merchants, and the term itself is regarded as a title capable of being conferred upon distinguished individuals of the mercantile and other communities as well, the title carrying along with it certain privileges and ceremonial adjuncts, such as a parasol, a palanquin and the carrying of torches and the band. *Chāpattār* would similarly mean a community it may be a community of military men—constituting a portion of the army. *Chāpattār* is a term applied also to the Cheras as carrying the bow for their national royal insignia, and *Chāpattār* would therefore mean merely bowmen in the sense that they carried the flag of the bow, implying that they were a part of the Chera army, which seems to be the more probable significance here rather than that division of the army consisting of bowmen exclusively. *Sēnāmukham* in *Sēnāmukhattār* is similarly a term of technical import. *Sēnāmukham* is usually a division of the army, that part of it that went forward, making way as it were for the main division to follow. It has also a significance that this part of the army constituted the body of the king in the sense, of course, that the army it is that provides the king with his physical strength. It has got a third meaning, namely, a protective outwork thrown in front of the gates of a fortresses, and by transference a part or section of the army that mounted guard over these. Whichever it is, we may be clear so far that probably this is another military community. If so the question would arise why there should be any such community at Takopa from the West coast, and why a temple constructed for the use of foreigners should be placed under the military. The inference is simple that possibly it was a colony of merchants from the West coast of India, and the temple and the tank there were placed in charge of the whole community constituting the colony of which a substantial part happened to be members of the military profession. We cannot go further on the material available to us; but as far as is clear to us this record justifies our taking it that such colonies containing military men were not unusual in the age of the later Pallavas of Kanchi.

When we pass out of the age of the Pallavas and come into that of the Cholas early in the tenth century we seem to be on clearer ground. The first signal achievement of the new dynasty is the conquest of Madura, and that was followed soon after by the conquest of *Īḻam*. *Īḻam* is purely a name for Ceylon. A conquest of Ceylon by the Cholas would be an impossibility without a fleet—a fleet of transports to carry the army across—as in the instance given under the Pallava Narasimha Varman. When we come to the reign of Rājarāja, we seem to be transported at once, as if without a transition, to a navy proceeding to the West Coast and inflicting a crushing defeat upon the Chera fleet at Kāndalūr. It is one of the most signal, and withal early, achievements of Rājarāja. Such a naval achievement on the part of the Chola implies two things;—a powerful navy that can sail round the coast of South India—a bit of navigation not regarded as easy in those days—and inflicting a defeat worth boasting of upon the Chera fleet, which was ready to receive them. The second fact is that the Cheras maintained a fleet of some considerable strength, and to bring them under subjection to the Chola, it was essential to defeat it on the sea; in other words, the Cheras would have to be regarded as a nautical power and could not be subdued otherwise than on the sea. That the Cholas were under the necessity to maintain a fleet not only for this particular purpose, but probably for other purposes as well, becomes clear when we come to the reign of Rājēndra the Gangaikoṇḍachola. It is strange that among the large number of inscriptions that have come down to us and the mass of material providing information upon all other details of history there should be no reference to the navy as such in the inscriptions. It is, however, possible to understand why, if we remember that among the large number of inscriptions that have come down to us, far the largest number have reference to temples and grants to temples and documents of that kind where it would normally be difficult to expect references purely of a royal or governmental concern, such as the maintenance of a navy would be. That perhaps would account for the absence of information, although we may yet come upon references to these. As a matter of fact, a number of inscriptions of Rājēndra do mention in some considerable detail his overseas invasion, and the manner of the introduction of these does not give one to understand that it was taken to be anything novel or extraordinary. This naval enterprise is described almost in the same manner as the other details relating to war, and therefore gives us to understand that, to the inscription writer at any rate, it was a thing quite familiar.

Rājēndrachola's main object in the distant northern invasion that he undertook seems to have been more or less a continuation of the war that his father had begun against the ruler of Kalinga. It was already pointed out that on the coast side, Rājarāja had to undertake military operations against the Eastern Chāḷukyas during the period of interrugnum in their territory. He so far succeeded in the enterprise that he placed a particular ruler upon the throne and entered into a treaty with him—a treaty sealed even by a marriage alliance. The two dynasties ever after remained allies in this fashion and at peace with each other during the rest of their history. It was this treaty that gave Rājarāja the facility to carry on a war against the further northern power of the Kalingas, as it was possible for him to march across the territory of the Eastern Chāḷukyas with the same facility with which he could carry his army across his own Chola country. So he undertook a war against the Kalingas with a view merely to bring them into subordination to him.

It must be borne in mind that these wars of conquest among Hindu rulers were wars, which had merely the object of getting the acknowledgment of suzerainty with a view perhaps to obtain freedom of action and even possibly united action. The Kalinga rulers at the time happened to be a new dynasty that had achieved prominence and were gradually working their way up to make their kingdom a powerful one by bringing into it all the divisions of Kalinga, sometimes spoken of as the three Kalingas, and almost as often, as seven (Sapta Kalingas). The war therefore was of a protracted kind, and when, in the eleventh or twelfth year of his reign, Rājēndra found it necessary to undertake an invasion of Kalinga, he had to carry his war on through the whole of the extensive territory of the Kalinga kings extending his operations further north to the banks of the Ganges. As a matter of fact, the general in charge of the expedition is said to have struck the Ganges somewhere about the region of Bihar, it may be between Patna and Bhagalpore, and carried his army down along the banks of the Ganges to where it reaches the sea, and having finally defeated the Kalinga king there, marched back to Rajahmundry, where Rājēndra was encamped at the time having led another army in support of the previous one. The two together attacked the capital of Kalinga, and, after putting on the Kalinga throne, a new king on terms of treaty, organised and sent out an invasion across the sea to the country of Kaḍāram, where at the time a powerful dynasty of kings was holding rule over an extensive territory. This invasion was undertaken against the Mahārāja of Śrī Bhoja, and either he himself or his capital is described as Śrī Vijaya, both of them identified from Chinese history to have had reference to the ruler and the capital Palambang in Sumatra. This dynasty had already come into touch with the Cholas as a predecessor of the ruler at the time had already sent a mission—diplomatic mission—to Rājarāja and obtained his permission to build a Buddhist *Vihāra* to be called Chūḍāmaṇi Vihāra in his own name, in Nagapatam, and that relationship was kept up when another embassy came in the reign of Kulottunga I, a grandson of this Rājēndra and obtained his permission to acquire two villages and make a grant of them to the same Chūḍāmaṇi Vihāra.

This naval invasion of Rājēndra gets described not exactly as a naval invasion, but incidentally of course among a description of his achievements in a large number of inscriptions both in the Tamil country, and even in the southern parts of Mysore. The drama Rājaśēkhara Vilāsam in Kanarese is said to have been based on this great exploit of Rājēndrachola. Rājēndra's son claims conquest of Kaḍāram, which need not mean a separate invasion and may be no more than the part that the prince played in the invasion sent out by the father; and even Kulottunga lays claim to a conquest of Kaḍāram. It seems doubtful again whether there was a separate war against Śrī Bhoja in the reign of Kulottunga. It may possibly be that as a young prince he also took part in the great invasion of Rājēndra. Whether these subsequent invasions were separate invasions or no, does not affect the position that the Cholas felt the need of maintaining a navy, and a navy organised even for such distant expeditions as the one that had been sent against the powerful nautical empire of Śrī Bhoja, which from its central position in Sumatra, laid claim to authority over an extensive region of the peninsula across, and possibly islands in its immediate neighbourhood. In the age of the Cholas therefore, there was a navy, probably of the same organisation as before, but with a successful war or two on the High Seas to the credit of the navy. It is not possible for us to say whether there was a separate navy on a war footing as distinct from the commercial marine.

During the century of Pāṇḍya ascendency that followed this great dynasty of the Cholas of the south, the same organisation seems to have continued. There is evidence, however, that in the last period of it, perhaps even earlier, Arab enterprise was gradually superseding the Hindu in this particular field. This process of supersession must have gone on for some little time when we find actually that, in the reign of Māravarman Kulaśēkhara, whose reign covered the last quarter of the 13th century and the first decade of the fourteenth, powerful Arab merchants were settled in coast towns of the Pāṇḍya country and even held important customs offices under Pāṇḍya rulers. An Arab from the Persian Gulf by name Abdur-Rahman-ut-Taibi, a horse trader, had the farming of the customs revenue for the port of Kāyal, and held the position of officer of very high rank in the court of the Pāṇḍya, and the Pāṇḍya entrusted a mission that he had to send to China to this Arab, instead of sending a mission as before headed by his own officer as did Rājēndra, the Gangakikoṇḍa Chola and Kulottunga, his grandson. This seems to indicate clearly the manner in which this gradual supersession of the Hindus by the Arabs took place at least in regard to the more distant overseas enterprise. It is from now that the archipelago gradually passes from the hands of its own rulers, natives and colonists from India, into the hands of the Arabs, and during the next two or three centuries the process of Islamisation goes on till at last in the 16th or the 17th century practically the whole region had become Muhammadan—a character that it maintains to the present times. By all accounts, the inhabitants are now all Muhammadan, but the whole of their intellectual culture seems to be Hindu, as their dramas and dances, their temples and treatment of literature alike bear witness to.

GENERAL CHARACTER OF THE ADMINISTRATION—AT HEADQUARTERS.

We described already in the previous sections the work of the king, his council, and his ministers at headquarters, in connection with several grants made to temples and institutions. The account there given must necessarily be of a partial character and cannot give an insight into the working of the machinery of administration at headquarters in all its departments. As a matter of fact our information in regard to it, notwithstanding fullness in certain directions, is defective considered as a whole. The administration of the army and the navy seems to have been entirely a matter for the king, his council and ministers, and does not appear to have reached beyond that administrative circle of the immediate entourage of the monarch for the time being. Departments near allied to peace and war, foreign relations and diplomacy, and departments akin thereto seem to have been exclusively the field of the monarch and his council, speaking generally. All details belonging to the civil administration, whether it be directly administrative, or corrective of administration, came before the king in his council of administrative heads and others, associated with them in some stage, and others interested in the matter, so that the decision arrived at at the royal headquarters was ultimately the decision not merely of the headquarters, but of the headquarters and the body actually concerned, so that we may say generally that, in matters of internal administration, people usually had as much of a share as is at all possible to give them a share under any system of government. In matters other than the branches of the administration that could be included in this classification, people or their representatives appear to have had no direct voice except through the voice of the members of the council at the headquarters. The monarch seems to have exercised his power with the advice of his council, liable to no other check than that which he might receive from those members of the council and the heads of the administration whom he might consult. How complicated this administration was, and how far from being purely autocratic, could be seen from a detailed consideration of a large grant which has come down to us and which gives full detail of the working of this department. The document relates to the gift of a village to a temple in Tiruvālangāḍu, the hamlet which happens to be a railway station this side of Arkonam towards Madras in the M. S. M. Railway. There is a big Śiva temple there, and the grant is a provision for the general requirements of the temple. The village is called Paḻayanūr, which was ultimately made over to the temple. The order portion of the grant, apart from the *Praśasti,* is a Tamil document of 524 lines actually engraved on 21 copper-plates. The order proper takes up the first 145 lines. The following 281 lines describe the boundary minutely, taking it from feature to feature in all the four directions so as to avoid all possibility of mistake, or error for the future. The last 98 lines describe in detail the conditions of the gift consisting of one section called *parihāra,* that is the demands and the dues to which it was liable and the other *vyavastha,* the actual conditions or privileges normally enjoyable and actually to be enjoyed by the new holders of the land. The land actually belonged to a Brahman (Brahmadēya) village called Singaḷāntaka Chaturvēdi Mangalam. It had first of all therefore to be freed from the *Brahmadēya* (gift to Brahmans). Then the next process is its being brought down to *Veḷḷānvagai,* that is, villages under the ordinary arrangements for cultivating lands by the agricultural population of the locality; in other words lands directly taken over by the cultivators and cultivated by them (*rayatwar* in modern language), paying whatever was due to the government and the community under which they cultivated. Then as such, the village had again to be made over to the temple as a gift. This involved naturally the removal of such privileges as the village enjoyed when it was a Brahmadēya gift. As a Brahmadēya village therefore it paid for its share a revenue to the government 598 *kaḻanju,* 1 *kunṛi* of gold only, and the revenue due from Singaḷāntaka Chaturvedimangalam be reduced to this extent. It was to be made to pay as of old, the revenue of 3238 *kalam,* 7 *kuruṇi* and 5 *nāḻi* of paddy, and 193 *kḻanju,* 1 *manjādi* and 1 *mā* of gold including the revenue dues in kind and coin (*paḍi* and *paḷḷi*). It will at once be seen that what seems a very simple gift of a village to the temple involves a rather complicated administrative process in conveying the gift to the party. So the process begins with the various departments taking notice of it, and having to investigate and report how far the transfer would be possible and what there may be to be said against it. First of all two of the royal officers, whose function it is to supervise the administration, something like Commissioners or Inspectors-General, and two arbitrators testified that this royal writ transferring the *Brahmadēya* into a *Dēvadāna* was not open to objection. The royal order was received on the 88th day of the sixth year of the reign of Rājēndra, the Gangaikoṇḍachola. The officers above mentioned certified to the unobjectionable character of the proposed gift and the order was signed and got ready for issue by four Secretaries (*Ōlai-*

nāyakam) on the basis of the draft order received from the Secretary, who took it down as the order emanated from the sovereign. Three chief executive officers other than those, had to approve of the order and sign in token of their approval. Having passed through all these stages, the order was actually issued in the presence of two officers of the department of taxes (*Puravuvari Tiṇaikkaḷam*) and the officer in charge of the taxes register (*Varipottakam*), the *Mukhaveṭṭi* (the chief of the village watch) the officer in charge of the keeping of the accounts of the taxes (*Varipoṭṭaka Kaṇakku*), the officer in charge of the receipts under the head of taxes (*Varyil-īḍu*), the secretary in charge of despatches, and the divisional *Mukhaveṭṭi.* Along with the issue of this order, direction was given that two of the administrative officers associated with another middle man, perhaps not holding any office, be appointed to superintend the conveyance of the land.

The process of conveyance of the gift consisted in a she-elephant being driven round, as it were, along the boundary of the village, the principal inhabitants of the village walking behind it, a contingent of labourers marking the boundary at salient points by trees, or channels, or water-courses wherever they existed, by planting milkbush wherever there was no natural feature such as an old tree or an anthill, or by marking by structures of earth and stone, wherever that was required, thus marking the boundary and putting it beyond possibility of dispute. The whole process is what is called in Sanskrit *Kariṇībhramaṇa.* In Tamil it is described as *Paḍāhai Naḍattal,* which would mean the walking round the land involved. But the term *Piḍi-śūlndu* is also prefixed to it; that means the inhabitants of the village walked round the village in connection with the marking of the boundary, accompanying the she-elephant. In the doing of this, the neighbouring villages concerned were ordered to be present also. In this case one neighbouring village was in attendance by its representative, the Karaṇam of the village. The inhabitants of the village involved in the gift followed the she-elephant marking the boundary in the manner described. The royal writ (*Tirumukham,* Sanskrit *Śrīmukha*) was sent to the village concerned, the assembly of which went forward to receive it, and when received returned putting it upon their head. Simultaneously writs were sent to the other villages to assist in the process. Over 280 lines of this document are devoted to a detailed description of the circumambulation of the village by the officers and by the people of the district (*Nāṭṭār*).

It is not necessary for our purpose to go into the details of this description of the boundary. But there is one little point of interest, that in those days one high road passed from Tirupāśūr, near Tiruvellore to Mērpāḍi another railway station called in those days Rājāśrayapuram. This trunk road constituted the boundary for a small part of it. Among the *parihāras* mentioned are those we have already described in some of the Pallava grants in an earlier part of the work, which need not be gone into in any detail here. But the general statement that follows the specification of details is of interest. It concludes "these above detailed incidences of revenue, all that the king was entitled to demand and enjoy, was resigned by the king in favour of the god in the temple, and the temple management was authorised to receive and enjoy as the king had hitherto been doing. Therefore the term *parihāram* does not necessarily mean exemption, but much rather means the dues to which the locality concerned is liable. Then follows the conditions of the gift. These indicate the specific privileges that the village was bound to enjoy by itself, and as against the neighbouring villages, and these rights are specified and conveyed to them as privileges to which they were entitled even as against their neighbours. The whole of this process and the actual conveyance of the land took perhaps a little over a year, and was actually conveyed and completed on the 155th day of the seventh year of the king's reign. This is just one year and 65 days after the final order. It might seem a comparatively slow process. It must, however, be remembered that the order probably had to pass through divisional offices and a number of local administrative units, and the conveniences of all of them had to be consulted for conveying the gift ultimately. As a matter of fact, the order happened to be addressed to the headmen of the Brahmadēya villages and to the residents (*Ūrār*) of *Dēvadāna* (gift to God), *Paḷḷi Chanda* (gift to Jain Buddhist and other heretical institutions), *Kaṇimuṟṟūṭṭu* (lands given for reclamation to cultivation), *Veṭṭipēṟu* (that which was given in return for village services) and *Aṟa Sālā Bhogam* (cultivation on annual quit-rent). All these would have had to take some part or other. As was pointed out already, the people of the district (*Nāṭṭōm*) had to approve of it. The officers deputed had to carry out the transfer in their presence. The Singaḷāntaka Chaturvedi Mangalam, of which it was a part had to take note of the transfer. They contented themselves on this occasion by being represented by the *Karanattān* (accountant) of their village. The townsmen of the village unit (*Ūrōm*) were present in full, and the assembly of Nittavinoda Chaturvēdimangalam, a neighbouring Brahmadēya village were also present.

The king was seated in his private room in the upper story of his palace at Muḍikoṇḍa Śoḷapuram when the secretary submitted his report and was ready to take his orders. The king dictated the order on hearing the documents read to him, and the private secretary (*Tirumandiraolai*) took down the order as it emanated from the king. The formal request for the passing of the order was made by one Tirukkāḷatti Pichchan. The royal order was written by Uttamaśoḷa Tamiladarayan. Jananātha, the son of Rama, was the minister of the king; he saw the order being carried out. Under his orders, one Araneri, son of Nārāyaṇa, a native of Mangaḷavāyil and "of the fourth caste" did the business of taking the elephant. This describes the method of work at headquarters in some detail, and gives us an idea as to the character of the details into which these royal orders had to enter. We can infer from this what system of records should have been maintained from the indubitable bureaucratic details which are insisted on in the carrying out of these royal orders.

From the details so far given, it would be justifiable to make the inference that the monarch enjoyed full power in regard to the administration of the kingdom, over which he ruled. It is equally clear that he exercised this power to the uttermost extent possible in a manner that assured to him the willing consent of those his authoritative acts affected. It was a bureaucracy with the monarch at its head, possessed it may be of autocratic powers. The monarch as well as the bureaucracy uniformly operated through a popular agency, and assured for themselves the active co-operation of the people in carrying their orders into effect. Such a system of administration had perhaps its small beginnings in the remote past and took time to grow and perfect itself. We cannot say that we have the material to see the beginnings, but the survey made above gives us an insight into the processes of its growth and we could see clearly that with the coming of the Cholas to power, it had attained to a degree of completion, which shows the whole administration at its best under them. This system was followed without substantial alteration during the period of decline of the Chola power and under the Pāṇḍyas who had succeeded to their position in the century that followed. It was then that there came upon South India, as in fact over the whole of India in the preceding century, the cataclysm of Muslim invasions, which in their devastating character upset much, and otherwise disturbed the even tenor of the administration as we have seen it at work for a millenium. After near half a century of this disturbance came in the empire of Vijayanagar, which put an end to the disorder and confusion caused by these invasions and repaired much of the damages caused by the ravages of these invaders. We shall see in the following section that the administrative system continued under Vijayanagar substantially as it was in the four centuries from A.D. 800 to A.D. 1,200.

Administrative Institutions under Vijayanagar:—

The whole of the region with which we have been dealing in our study of the administrative institutions of this part of India passed in the first half of the fourteenth century under the rule of a power, which is generally known to historians by the name of its capital placed at one of the salients of its northern frontier. This was the famous city known as Vijayanagar with the alternative name, through much of its history of Vidyānagara or Vidyāraṇya Nagara, and of which the ruins of Hampi are the modern representative. This dynasty established itself in the particular locality under stress of circumstances, which gave to the administration itself as a whole, a new power and a new character, we may say. The early years of the fourteenth century saw the advance of the Muhammadan power into this distant *enclave* of India. The plunder carried by the first invasion only served to whet the appetite for more, and successive Muhammadan rulers wanted to make the accumulations in the temples and palaces of South India a milch-cow for their never ending requirements, good and bad. So during the quarter of the century extending from A.D. 1310 to A.D. 1335 there were a series of invasions, of which the later ones added the motive of conquest to that of plunder. The earlier invasions did not come in force, and therefore attempted to make up for the want of adequate force by perpetrating atrocities of such a cruel character as to strike terror into the inhabitants, and of unnerving the population for active resistance. The first invasions proved successful so far as to give them plenty of plunder. The first effort, however, at founding a southern principality in Madura with salient Muhammadan garrisons in important centres on the line of communication proved abortive through the exertions of a Travancore ruler, who in behalf of the Pāṇḍya for the time being, marched forth as far north as Nellore and turned the invaders out. But the Muhammadan pressure still persisted.

The province of Dēvagiri was founded by Mubarak Kalji, son and successor of All-ud-din, to which was gradually added the territory along the southern frontier such as the divisions of Sagar and Gulbarga, and this was gradually pushed forward into the Hoysala dominions to the extent of overturning the brave little state of Kampli and acquire possession of even the territories of the Hoysalas on the northern frontier, consisting of the present-day Kannada districts of the Southern Mahratta country. Early in the reign of Muhammad-bin-Tughlak, he sent out a number of invasions, and himself led two, in one of which he was able to send an army ahead and establish his power in Tamil India proper to such an extent as to constitute the province, known to Muhammadan historians as Ma'abir, that is, the Coramandel Coast region, not Malabar. The success that he was able to achieve the first time was not great enough to assure him permanence; but he put matters right for himself in the subsequent invasion that he had undertaken, and his authority prevailed over the country with its provincial headquarters at Madura and possibly Kaṇṇanūr, a suburb of Trichinopoly as an alternative, for a period of about seven years, A.D. 1328 to 1335. In the latter year his own provincial governor Jalal-ud-din Āḥsan Shah declared himself independent at Madura and founded a kingdom for himself in Ma'abir; and that was the Muhammadan Sultanate of which we have a series of coins. From these we are enabled to reconstruct the succession of rulers and the salient points of their history with the account furnished by the Algerian traveller Ibn Batuta, who happened to be in South India for a couple of years during the period, proceeding on his mission to China in behalf of Muhammad, the Tughlak sovereign.

It was by a supreme effort of the last great Hoysala ruler to conquer this Muhammadan kingdom and dislodge the Muhammadan garrisons from the salient positions in which they were planted that the new kingdom of Vijayanagar actually sprang. The Hoysala Vīra Baḷḷāḷa bent before the storm of repeated Muhammadan invasions in the belief that they were temporary raids, and were not intended to be of a lasting character of conquests. He was preparing at the same time for eventualities ever since Mubarak Khalji distributed the Mahratta country among "the Amirs of the Hundred" as they were called. He was in his own turn fortifying places on the northern frontier and putting them otherwise in a condition of defence, so that when the occasion offered, he might be sure of the frontier being efficiently held against new invaders to carry out his ultimate object of turning the Muhammadan garrisons out of the south. It was with this object in view that he transferred his residence from Halebid to Tiruvaṇṇamalai and held his position there on the high road leading towards Madura from the north. This was very soon after Muhammad bin Tughlak had made his conquests and created, as he thought successfully, the province of Ma'abir. The first Islamic governor of this province therefore had to maintain himself against the attacks of Vīra Baḷḷāḷa and was able more or less to hold his own. But the Hoysala attacks had been gradually closing nearer and nearer, and the case of the Muhammadan Sultans of Madura was made desperate after the first Sultan declared himself independent of Muhammad bin Tughlak. This necessitated more active measures on the part of the Hoysala monarch, as from what was known of the nature of Muhammad bin Tughlak, he was certain of marching down upon the south to re-assert his authority. It was at about that time that the northern garrisons were properly organised and put on a satisfactory footing from the point of view of the southern ruler. One outer salient was at Bankāpūr in Dharwar, wherefrom the western line of advance could be defended. The main centre of defence, however was Halabid, the capital of the Hoysalas and in order, the better to defend it, the village of Hampi, set over against the fortified position of Anegundi on the northern bank of the Tungabadra on the highroad of communication, was fortified and put in a position of defence as an outwork. This became the more necessary since the destruction of Kampli only about 2½ miles down the river. Another important garrison was placed at Udayagiri in the Nellore District to guard the eastern highway. As a second line of defence to this were probably set the palatine viceroyalties, under early Vijayanagar, of Araga in the Shimoga District, and Penugonda in the Anantapur District. Farther back of this was the next great viceroyalty, or Mahārājya, as it came to be called in the days of Vijayanagar, at Mulbāgal. Various important fortresses on the road and along this western frontier were also obviously garrisoned, particularly places like Adoni. Vīra Ballāla brought matters to a crisis by making a slow but successful effort to confine the Muhammadan garrison into Madura and destroy them, when he felt sure that Muhammad bin Tughlak was too much occupied with rebellions nearer home to think of making a renewed effort at invading the south. That was in the years following A.D. 1335 till his death. The Hoysala king fought and fell in battle against the Muhammadans, who were reduced to desperate straits, at Trichinopoly between the Muhammadan garrison at Kaṇṇanūr and their headquarters in Madura. This gave temporary relief to the Muhammadans at Madura, who continued for a little over twenty years holding a precarious position there while the death of Vīra Ballāla was followed by the transformation of the Hoysala kingdom into what became ultimately the empire of Vijayanagar.

When the new dynasty established itself therefore, its preoccupation was entirely to prevent the Muhammadans from effecting entry into this part of the country, and to carry out this object, the actual *raison d'etre* of their position, they had to strain their every resource towards this particular object of providing an adequate military force to guard the northern frontier extending across the whole width of the peninsula. For four full centuries practically they had maintained this struggle. During the first three centuries of the existence of the Vijayanagar empire, they were able to offer successful resistance and keep the tide of invasion on the whole satisfactorily out. But during the last century of the existence of this state, they gradually receded till at last about A.D. 1739, the last Hindu state which sprang out of Vijayanagar was defeated and the back of the Hindu resistance broken at Trichinopoly. The Muhammadan conquest of the south became something like an actual fact, and within a score of years of this achievement, Muhammadan rule over this locality itself was overturned, and after another half a century of confusion, and we might say, even anarchy, the British East India Company established itself gradually, and laid the foundations of the Madras Presidency at the commencement of the nineteenth century.

From this summary account, it would be clear that the preoccupation of the rulers of Vijayanagar was the organisation of their military resources, primarily with a view to the defence of the northern frontier. The development of military resources naturally implies attention to the sinews of war, and without these, the development of an efficient defence would be a feat impossible. While therefore they were occupied primarily with the business of developing the fighting resources of the empire, they had also to pay a considerable amount of attention to the development of the civil resources to maintain these; but it may be admitted without question that the amount of attention that they were able to pay to the organisation of a civil administration of a satisfactory character could not have been as much as that of their predecessors in the centuries previous to the Muhammadan invasions. Fortunately for them, however, there was a highly developed administration which had attained to its full development, and all that they had to do was to see that the administrative machinery, which had been perfected by their predecessors, were maintained in ordinary efficiency, so that they may have the benefit of the full resources of the empire for their particular purpose. They were therefore interested in keeping up the good administration that there was in the country, only repairing the damages that it might have suffered in the course of the repeated ravages by the Muhammadans during the half century of their raids. While therefore we hear from the records of Vijayanagar of much that they did by way of fighting wars to keep the enemy at arm's length and of developing the fighting resources of the country, what we hear of their administrative doings is comparatively subordinate to this main purpose. Even so, the records that have come down to us of their advance in that particular line redounds to their credit and exhibits an understanding of the spirit of the administrative arrangements with a laudable effort at maintaining these institutions undamaged.

As one instance of this effort at conservation of the administrative resources of the country, we have an illuminating example from what was done in the reign of the great Vijayanagar ruler, Dēvarāya II of the first dynasty, whose reign period was in the first half of the fifteenth century. Dēvarāya II was by far the greatest ruler of the first dynasty of Vijayanagar, and it was in his reign that the military resources were reorganised and developed to such a high degree as to inflict more than one crushing defeat upon his enemies across the northern frontier. The measure has reference to the rural division of Vaḻudilampaṭṭu in the Trichinopoly and Tanjore Districts. It was the headquarters of a rural unit itself, the division being called by its name Vaḻudilampaṭṭu-Uśāvaḍi. An inscription of date A.D. 1429-30 registers the decision arrived at by the inhabitants of a whole district called Parāntaka Nāḍu consisting of 98 sub-sects of the Right Hand (*Valangai*) and the 98 sub-sects of the Left Hand caste (*Iḍangai*). The subject matter of their deliberation was the various items by way of taxes and cesses and other dues payable by them to government (*Rājakaram-iṟaimuṟaimai*). The consideration of this matter was necessitated by the confusion into which the administrative arrangements had been thrown during the time of the temporary occupation of the place by Kannaḍiyas as they are called (Kanarese people, probably the Hoysalas, who were in occupation of the locality for a considerable length of time). The settlement to which they arrived followed the lines of the settlement adopted by the inhabitants of the other districts included in the division Vaḻudilampaṭṭu Uśāvaḍi. As the document itself states it, it was made into a *Jīvita Paṟṟu* of the servants, it may be, of the temple or of the king, since the district had been occupied by the Kannaḍiyas. As such, the collection of taxes due was not made by any single authority properly constituted. The lands were leased out to persons other than the cultivators in occupation at the time, and the revenue dues (*Puravuvari*) were collected obviously in an arbitrary fashion. The district is stated to have thus become ruined. The first item of the decision arrived at was that certain specified parcels of land were not to be alienated under any one of the following heads *panḍāravāḍai* (lands for the maintenance of Śaiva mendicants), *Aḍaippu* (usufructuary mortgage), *Otti* (simple mortgage), *Kuttakai* (lease), or *Śērvai* (service inam). The next was the general classification of assessment. What was to be the schedule of assessment of the lands appertaining to the district? This was laid down in the following schedule.

Rates of assessment on other lands were agreed upon :—

	Class of land.	Assessment in paddy on one vēli, including araśupēru, ilakkai, etc.	Other taxes, such as kāṇikkai, sammadam, paṭṭavaṭṭam, kāṇikūli etc., on each vēḷi.
	A1		
1	Paddyfields ..	50 *kalam* of paddy and ¼ *paṇam*..	20 *paṇam*.
2	Uncultivated waste (brought under cultivation) ..	40 kalam of paddy.	18 „
3	Forest reclaimed ..	20 kalam of paddy.	2 „
4	*Kaḍaippū* (flower for sale) lands and lands irrigated by baling water ..	20 kalam of paddy.	10 „
	B		
5	Plantain and sugarcane gardens in wet land ..	....	60 *paṇam* (including *araśūpēṟu*, *kāṇikkai*, etc.).
6	Plantain and sugarcane gardens in paḍukaitākku (river margin) ..	....	50 *paṇam*.
7	Marshes in which red lotuses are grown ..	....	40 „
8	Lands producing turmeric, ginger, onions, garlic, etc. ..	....	25 „
9	Lands producing brinjals (valudilai), pumpkins, etc. ..	....	30 „

	Class of land.	Assessment in paddy on one vēli, including araśu-pēru, ilakkai, etc.	Other taxes, such as kāṇikkai, sammadam, paṭṭavaṭṭam, kāṇikūli, etc., on each vēḷi.
	B.—(*Contd.*)		
10	Lands producing nellu, parutti (?), castor seeds, varaku parutti(?), mustard, Bengal gram, wheat. and kusumbai (Carthamus tinctorius), ērivāi, tāngalvāi and puḷudi, (lands producing) gram (kāṇam), lands producing paddy and (sambalādi) ..	....	20 *paṇam* (including *araśūpēṟu*, *nēr-ōlai*, etc.).
11	Lands producing gram, green pulse, tanipparutti, tani āmaṇakku, tiṇai, pani varahu, śāmai, etc. ..	....	1 *paṇam*.
12	Lands producing sesamum (taxed for first crop) ..	....	½ of the above?
13	Lands yielding vedikoḷundu(?) ..	....	200 *paṇam*.
14	Lands yielding oḷimuḍukoḷundu taxed for first crop ..	....	100 „
	C		
	Dry crops (vanpayiru).		
15	Every five areca palms yielding about 1,500 nuts per tree ..	....	1 *paṇam* (including *araśūpēṟu*).
16	Every cocoanut palm yielding not less than 40 fruits per tree ..	....	½ *paṇam*.
	N.B.—Tender trees which have not borne fruit, barren trees and trees in the backyards of houses are exempted ..	....	
17	Every jack tree yielding not less than 20 fruits per tree ..	....	Lost.
18	The surrounding (i.e., other) trees are not taxed ..	....	....
	D		
	House and professional taxes.		
19	Each house of a villager (Nāṭṭār) ..	....	3 *paṇam* (including *vilai-āśarudi*).
20	Each house of a follower of the *tantra* (tantirimār)[1] ..	....	1½ *paṇam*.
21	Each house of........makkal ..	....	1½ „
22	Verandahs with sloping roofs (i.e., sheds?) ..	....	½ „
	N.B.—Unoccupied houses are exempted ..		

[1]*Tantirimār*=administrative officials, as opposed to *mantirimār* (Councillors)—This has nothing to do with *Tantra*. *S. K.*

	Class of land.	Assessment in paddy on one vēli, including araśupēru, ilakkai, etc.	Other taxes, such as kāṇikkai, sammadam, paṭṭavaṭṭam, kāṇikūli, etc., on each vēḷi.

E

Workshop (paṭṭaḍai) taxes, etc.

23	Every Śeṭṭi-proprietor ..	....	3 *paṇam* (including *araśupēru, vaṭṭam, kaṇikkai*).
24	Every principal collector of tolls ..	....	4 *paṇam*.
25	Each (Kaikkoḷa) weaver with one working loom ..	....	4 "
26	Each (Kaikkola) weaver with one loom that does not? work (aḍaitari) ..	....	2 ".
27	Every shopkeeper who opens the shop in his house (manaikkaḍaiyār) ..	....	3 "
28	Every (Śāliya) weaver for each loom ..	....	9 "
29	Every judge (nyāyattār) ..	....	5 "
30	Each member on the village Council (manṛāḍi) ..	....	½ "
31	Each lace-loom in working order ..	....	3 "
32	Each lace-loom not? in working order ..	....	½ "
33	Each blacksmith, carpenter, gold and silversmith ..	....	5 *paṇam* (including *kottu, kiṛṛu, araśupēru, kāṇikai*).
34	Each chief potter ..	....	5 *paṇam* (including *tirikai āyam*).
35	Each chief barber ..	....	4 *paṇam* (including karivi āyam).
36	Each chief washerman ..	....	4 *paṇam* (including *kallāyam*).
37	Each kannakkāṇan (brazier) ..	....	6 *paṇam*.
38	Each chief oilmonger ..	....	20 *paṇam* (including *karu āyam*).
39	Each member of the Paraiya caste (exceptions being made in certain specified cases). ..	....	½ *paṇam*.

In regard to (A) lands allotted for wet cultivation, those that became damaged, after having been planted with paddy (*naṭṭuppāḻ*), those that yielded only blighted paddy. (*śāvi*), and those that are otherwise destroyed (*aḻivu*) should not be taxed. Lands under dry cultivation were similarly exempt under the three heads. The remaining holdings alone were to be charged with these dues at a reduced rate of 8½ in 10. We are not explained why this reduction was allowed. It was laid down however distinctly that if, on inspection, any of the lands excluded as above were found to have yielded one quarter of a crop, those lands were to be charged 1|3 of the produce as rent (*vāram*).

A somewhat similar order and referring to two divisions, namely, the division under Trichinopoly and that under *Vaḻudilampaṭṭu* has come down to us in No. 376 (b) of 1914 from Chidambaram. It is of date Śaka 1349, which would correspond to A.D. 1427, early in the reign of Dēvarāya II. This refers to one of those general irregularities caused by the upsetting of the established order by the disturbing influences which it is worthwhile noting down as indicating the desire on the part of the administration to restore things, as far as may be, to the condition before the disturbing invasions either of the Kannaḍiyas or of the Muhammadans that followed the Kannaḍa occupation. The document records "as we have been informed by the Māhēśvaras and Marudavāṇa-śivan that the king's officers in the villages belonging to the temples are unjustly collecting the taxes called *Kāṇikkai, Araśupēṛu, Karaṇakkar-jōḍı, Viśēshādāyam, Āḻamanju,* etc., representing these to be dues payable to the palace; that the villagers taking up on mortgage lands purchased, presented or otherwise owned by the temples, stubbornly refused to give back these lands to the temples, and that, as a consequence, the temple tenants have abandoned the villages causing thereby the stoppage of worship in these temples, we order the taxes mentioned above shall no longer be collected, the only payable tax, however, being the *Śūlavaripon;* that the worship, etc., in your temples shall be continued in future, under the direction of the said Marudavāṇa-śivan, and that temple lands shall in no case be let out on (long) lease, nor shall they be assigned to anyone as tax free, hereditary property, free gift or *Bhaṭṭavritti.*" In regard to this order, the points deserving of attention are (1) the king's officers demanded the usual royal dues from the lands under reference; (2) those that were in possession of the land claimed, what was the privilege of temple lands, exemption from the payment of these. Then arises the question that if they claimed the privilege they ought to make over the lands to the temples, which apparently they were unwilling to do, as they claimed the possession to have been due to purchase, presentation or some other manner of transfer. The result naturally would be an enquiry as to the legitimate character of the claim, and the order apparently is based upon such an enquiry. The investigation must have exhibited that the lands were actually temple lands and had been taken unduly in possession by those that were in temporary occupation. The consequence would therefore be neglect of cultivation of the lands as such by those to whom the temple let them out for the purpose, and their migrating elsewhere. The result is the order, which restored the lands to the temple, and put it on the footing in which it was before the disturbances. This reconstruction work was what engaged the attention of the first dynasty of Vijayanagar during the century to about A.D. 1450, and a number of similar instances could be quoted not only in the reign of Dēvarāya II but during the reigns of his predecessors and his successors not only of the first dynasty, but even of the others. Dēvarāya II, however seems to have set about it systematically through two of his ministers Lakkanna and Madanna, whose names figure as in charge of the government of various localities constituting practically the whole of the empire of Vijayanagar.

A specific tendency comes prominently to notice in about the same locality under an earlier governor known in epigraphical records as Virūpaṇṇa Oḍayar ordinarily, but as Virūpāksha in more formal style. The matter is of a judicial character and has reference to the dispute regarding the right of worship in the Kāmēśvara temple at Āragalūr. This is recorded in No. 413 (b) of the year 1914. Tirumalli Nāyaka, the governor of the locality had to intervene and give the award bringing about a settlement of the dispute. The order actually summarised the dispute itself as it was brought to his notice and contains his award, and is therefore quoted *in extenso;*—"(1) A has been enjoying for a long time the privilege of worshipping all the 30 days of the month in the temple, while actually only fifteen days belonged to him by right and the other fifteen days belonging (-ed?) to another person named B; (2) the privilege of B enjoyed by A without proper authority requires settlement; (3) in support of the latter part of the statement made in (1) there are records in the temples to prove that the fifteen days of B (now abandoned by him and enjoyed by A) have under orders been counted unclaimed (*Irangal*), and (4) this privilege of the fifteen days so declared unclaimed you have sold (on your own responsibility), 7½ days to a third person C and given him a sale deed; (5) by so doing, you have deprived the acquired right of A, enjoyed by him for the last eight or ten generations; (6) at this stage, the Nāṭṭār appear to have volunteered to settle the question of enjoyment (A being found issueless?) and to have called the parties to present themselves before them together with A; (7) you (the managers) were also required (under my orders) to be present on the occasion, to hear the case and to carry out the decision arrived at by the Nāṭṭār and to have in the meantime. during this period of hearing (by the Nāṭṭār) the worship of the temple performed by outsiders on payment; (8) A thus having appealed to me, while I happened to be present at Āragalūr to have his case transferred and give a just decision, I and the Nāṭṭār together advised the parties to put their case before the Mahājanas and issued an order to this effect; (9) in obedience to our order the *Mahājanas* and the *Agrahāras* of Kaḷattūr, Ālambalam, Ṣaḍayanpaṭṭu and Mattiyākurichi met together, heard both sides and decided that, although A may have been the hereditary holder of only fifteen days of the privilege, it was not fair to sell part of the disputed portion thereof to an outsider like C while the right to purchase (by virtue of long enjoyment) pri marily rested in A; (10) accordingly therefore, to this decision of the Mahājanas we order that A must continue to enjoy the full thirty days as before and that the sale deed you have given to C should be cancelled. The procedure adopted and the decision arrived at alike in this particular case, which was brought to the notice of the governor by the *temple* priest concerned, show clearly that, in point of judicial administration, the course followed under Vijayanagar happened to be almost exactly the same as under the Cholas of the eleventh century. The aggrieved priest invited the intervention of the governor. The governor intervened not by himself alone and exclusively in virtue of the royal authority vested in him and give a decision. He called in the assistance of the Nāṭṭār, whose decision was called in question, to help him. In the course of the enquiry it seemed to him that perhaps that that was not enough to settle a question of importance like the long standing right of temple worship. He therefore, and the Nāṭṭār together, felt it necessary to put the matter before a larger assembly of higher authority. Hence the Mahājanas and Bhaṭṭas of a number of surrounding villages assembled at their invitation and gave the award, which in effect states that the right of worship for the fifteen days which originally belonged to B and had been abandoned by him ought not to have been sold away to an outsider except with the consent of A, who had acquired a prescriptive right to pre-emption by having conducted the worship for a long time. Having that prescriptive right, he should have been given the option before any other party was allowed to come in even by purchase.

It is hardly necessary to go on multiplying instances. This process of rectification went on even in the succeeding reigns, and on the whole, the procedure adopted was almost exactly the same as in the previous regime. In certain cases we come upon a more active kind of beneficence which took the form of abolition of taxes that were oppressive, of which we have one remarkable instance, which made a great impression upon the people. It was the great Chola ruler, the first Kulottunga, that, for some reason or other, attained to the title *Śungadavirttachoa,* the Chola who abolished tolls. We have pointed out that one of the legitimate sources of revenue of a Hindu monarch was the income from payment of various kinds of tolls. It therefore is not a question of the removal of new taxes or imposts of that character. It was the removal possibly of certain of the legitimate items which might have become unsuitable by pressing too hard upon the people, that gave him the great reputation, which the people marked in this signal fashion. That that was not a solitary instance, and that such remissions were in practice even in the much harder times of the days of Vijayanagar, is in evidence in the following case. One great disturbing factor that seems to have intervened between the establishment of the rule of Vijayanagar, and of the times either of the Cholas or of the Pandyas, is the occupation of the Tamil counrty by the Kannaḍiyas under the Hoysala king Somesvara and his son Ramanātha for a period of about a quarter of a century. During the rule of these foreigners to the locality, there seems to have been a considerable amount of disorder introduced possibly through the ignorance of the new government and its agents, of the customs of the locality. Two instances come to our notice under the government of the famous Narasānāyaka, the father of the much more famous Krishnadevarāya while he was carrying on the administration of the whole empire in behalf of the two sons of his own master, Sāḷuva Narasimha I. According to No. 50 (C) of 1916, dated Śaka 1423, A.D. 1501, a record of the sale of lands by the Marava inhabitants of Vēlanguḍi, they had no means of discharging their revenue dues to government, because, as it is significantly stated "it was the period of occupation of the Kannaḍigas or Karṇāṭakas." That this was the case widely is in evidence from No. 247 (C) of the same year from Śrīmushṇam in the South Arcot District where the same kind of oppressiveness seems to have been experienced. But what is to our purpose here is that this record of Śaka 1426, A.D. 1504, refers to a revision of the rates and taxes by the chief apparently with a view to moderate the pressure of the incidences. It is stated that the rates of taxes "had become exhorbitant in the time when the country was in the hands of the Kannaḍiyas. The cultivators, owing to the oppression, had dispersed and the *Svarupa?* scattered." The chief therefore ordered (1) that the lands be measured annually by the standard rod of 34 feet (the royal foot of the Chola times); (2) that 15 *paṇam* (including all items of taxes) be levied on one *mā* of dry land, and 20 *paṇam* on one *mā* of wet land; (3) that towards *araiśupēru* (royalty due) 1|8th *paṇam* be levied on each tenant, 3 *paṇam* on each loom of *Seṭṭies*, 2 *paṇam* on each Kammāḷa aggriculturist, 3 *paṇam* on Kaikkoḷa weavers, and (4) towards the Iḍaitturai (probably grazing fee on lands between rivers) be collected 1|4 *paṇam* on each cow, 1½ *paṇam* on each buffaloe and 1|4 *paṇam* on each

8 sheep. Taking ten paṇam the equivalent of a varāha and one *ma* of land as equal to 1|20th of a *vēli,* the epigraphist notes that "this revised settlement of Trinetranatha Kachiya Raya, the chief under reference cannot be regarded as mild." More factors have to enter, in a comparison like this, for an opinion as to the character of the incidence being justifiable or otherwise. It is clear that the revision, milder or heavier in comparison, was obviously better than what it was under the disturbed times of Kannaḍa occupation.

We have another instance of heavy taxation under the great Krishnadevarāya in No. 246 (C) of 1916. An officer by name Śinnappa Nayakar, a brother of Adiappa Nāyakar, the Adapanayque of Nuniz, issued a circular to the agriculturists of a whole district containing 17 divisions, who had migrated to other places on account of excessive taxation. According to this circular, a permanent settlement of consolidated taxes was introduced of 28 *paṇam* on wet lands and 22 on dry lands for such cultivators as resided in the district. This was to be 20 paṇams on wet land and 15 paṇam on dry land if the cultivators were not resident in the division, the reduction being possibly to cover the expenses of locomotion. A further reduction to 15 paṇams on wet lands and 10 paṇams on dry lands was given to cultivators, who habitually resided outside and took up the cultivation of these lands, this high reduction being more or less offered as a temptation to bring the lands into cultivation even at a disadvantage. This would indicate probably that cultivating tenants were not to be had in plenty and cultivable lands had by all means to be brought under cultivation even at a disadvantage. Another document No. 388 (B) of 1916 dated Saka 1447 in the reign of Krishnadevaraya has reference to a settlement introduced by a Chennama Nāyakar. This has probably reference to land newly brought under cultivation by an irrigation tank having been either constructed, or repaired and brought into use. The arrangement was to divide the whole into five parts, of which three parts were to be distributed among the *Velamas* (the cultivating ryots), gods and Brahmans, and two parts to be distributed among Kāpus, whose function, in addition to cultivation, seems to have been the guarding of the village, a class of military tenants, as it were. 3|5 of the whole land were divided among people either actually engaged in cultivation or dependent on cultivation, and 2|5 were distributed among people, who in addition to cultivation had to do the duty of guarding the district.

This kind of a resettlement and reassurance of people to remain where they were and carry on their avocations as heretofore, we have evidence of even in the reign of Achyutarāya. There are a number of records particularly in the northern and north-eastern districts of the empire of Vijayanagar readily open to the incursions of their enemies, the Muhammadans of the Bahmani kingdom on the one side and the Hindus of the Kalinga kingdom on the other; and the whole region therefore was liable to be harried by the repeated incursions of these enemies and a considerable amount of unsettlement would have resulted therefrom. A record coming from a village called Kavaṭālam in the Adoni Taluq makes a reference to this. The whole *Sīma* or division was being evacuated by the cultivating inhabitants who betook themselves to the neighbouring districts, and it was discovered that their complaint was acts of injustice and perhaps undue demands from them. Ordinary enquiries not satisfying, a special commissioner was sent in the person of Salakraju Timmaraju to make an enquiry and give the people satisfaction. It will be remembered that Achyutaraya had two brothers-in-law. The one under reference here is the person who was the chief minister of Achyutaraya, and his deputation therefore shows the importance attached to an enquiry of this kind. He proceeded to Adoni, made the necessary enquiries and granted to the agriculturists terms satisfactory from their point of view, and arranged for their repeopling the villages that they had abandoned, to bring them under cultivation again. The document seems also to make provision for a certain number of service *inams* for various village services, indicating thereby a complete unsettlement of the village organisation. Similar cowles (or agreements) are found in some considerable number in the seventeenth and eighteenth centuries and exhibit the unsettlement of the country during these centuries. Such disturbances and settlements in reparation are under reference even under the successors of Achyutarāya, that is, the rulers of the last dynasty of Vijayanagar. But it is hardly necessary to pursue the subject any further.

Almost from the middle of the fifteenth century when the invasions from the north by the kings of Orissa on the one side and the Sultans of the Bahmani kingdom on the other had become fairly frequent, the unsettlement and disorganisation became more or less common, and efforts had to be made to remedy the disorganisation then and there. These invasions alone were not the only unsettling cause. There were other disturbances besides, both internal and external, such as the rebellion within as in the case of the great Sāḷuva-nāyaka in the heart of the Tamil country, and, what followed as a consequence, the war against external rulers as in the case of the great invasion of the Tiruvaḍirājya, varied occasionally by raids and expeditions even by the Portuguese. The rulers were anxious that the unsettlement ought not to be allowed to persist as much in the interests of the state, and the welfare of the people, as in their selfish interest, enlightened interest though that be. The prevalence of the confusion and the breaking up of the rural life would have resulted in the fall of revenue, which would have been quite detrimental to the welfare of the state and the maintenance of its position as such. The pursuit of an enlightened policy like that is in evidence not merely in the kind of reparation work such as had been referred to above, but in the abolition of the ordinarily prevalent imposts and duties that for one reason or another had become unpopular in process of time. Returning victorious from his northern invasion, king Krishnadēvarāya is said to have made a very large remission of taxes amounting to 10,000 pieces of gold, the benefit of which was to extend to all the temples of South India, those of Vishṇu and Śiva alike, for one thing. Almost simultaneously and in the following years, there are numbers of references to his having abolished taxes and imposts of various kinds, such as the tax on barbers.[1]

[1] Nos. 210 and 235 of 1917.

He also abolished the tax on marriages in the Ghanagiri-rājya (that is, the province of Penugonḍa), Kandanavolu (Kurnool), Ganḍikoṭa *Sthala* Siddhavaṭṭa (Sidhout), Siddhapurasima, Chandragiri Rājyam, Nāgamangala Śima, Mūla Rājya and Rāyadurga Rājya. These remissions were made in the second year after his accession, and as the enumeration shows this remission was granted for not one division or another, but to a very considerable part of the territory included in the empire of Vijayanagar. There are other records relating to this remission in other divisions of the empire as well, so that these remissions are not merely local and sporadic remedies, but were of a far more general character. The enlightened policy, of which such an example was set by Krishnadēvarāya was followed even by his warlike successor Aḷiya Rāmarāja, the Kāryakarta (agent) of the whole empire of Sadāśivarāya Mahārāya, by remitting the taxes on barbers. This exemption was granted in the first instance to barbers of one city, and the concession was extended by Ramaraja's agent to fifty other villages in the Konḍavīḍu country. That was again followed by similar remissions in other divisions, such as those dependent upon Vinikonḍa, Bellamkonḍa, Addanki, Ammanabrolu all in the eastern division. This is the more remarkable as Ramaraja's time was one of expensive wars against the neighbouring Sultans of the Bahmani kingdom, and the remission of taxes, vexatious taxes though they be and all of a comparatively minor character, still exhibits an interest in the administration and an appreciation of the value of remedies such as those under reference.

We thus see that, in the course of the history of the empire of Vijayanagar, notwithstanding the successful resistance made by the new foundation against the incursions of Islamic rulers from the north into the Tamil country, the constant wars and even harrying invasions had the effect of unsettling to a very considerable extent the administrative organisation of the times immediately preceding. The whole organisation of Hindu kingdoms in pre-Muslim India, whether it applied to the north or south, was one essentially of peace. Wars there were, and we might even say, pretty frequent wars. But then so long as these wars were among the Hindu rulers and conducted on the recognised practice of Hindu warfare, the work of destruction actually brought about by the war was kept at a minimum. War was frankly regarded as an evil to be avoided, and when inevitable, carried only so far as to bring about the desired object, without carrying it to the uttermost till the political extinction of the one or the other party had been brought about. Usually wars among the Hindus were either wars for reparation, or wars undertaken in assertion of superiority with a view to achieving a hegemony. There was no object in carrying the war farther than was necessary to gain either of these objects, and wars ceased as soon as the one or the other came about. In that case the wars for reparation of injustice the first crushing defeat put an end to the war and the defeated party was made to consent to make the reparation for his previous action demanded; and in the case of a war of hegemony and not conquest, which is a misnomer applied to Hindu wars the war ceased immediately the weaker power acknowledged or showed an inclination to acknowledge the hegemony of the other. It is just like the war described in the *Dig-vijaya* of the Mahābhārata where, after having fought a whole day against Sahadeva's forces, the ruler of Māhishmati sent his ambassadors to tell him that they were satisfied that Sahadēva had the strength to make good the claim to the imperial title on behalf of his brother, and therefore they offered him the usual presents and sent through him the message to Yudhishṭira, his brother, that the good work undertaken by him of celebrating the Rājasūya may go through without interruption, and that he may enjoy the merit of the beneficent sacrifice he intended to celebrate. The wars between the Muhammadans and the Hindus were of a different character, and, in the early wars at any rate, the Muhammadans carried on the war with needless cruelty and unnecessary destruction, the object of which seems to have been to terrorise not merely the inhabitants of the region where they were fighting, but terrorising the Hindu inhabitants of the country generally. We have it on record in the pages of the Muhammadan historian Firishta that in one of the early wars that Vijayanagar had to wage against the Muhammadans, the war was concluded by a treaty that the two parties agreed to enter into; and almost the first condition of the treaty stipulated for by the Hindus was that the Muhammadans might not carry on their work of killing and destroying beyond the people actually engaged in war, and that, as far as possible, the peaceful agriculturists and the ordinary inhabitants might be left unmolested in their various pursuits. It may be set down to the credit of Muhammad Shah Bahmani that he readily fell in with the proposal, and undertook that, in the wars that he might be under necessity to carry on ever after, he would observe the solemn pledge given them of not molesting the civil population except to the extent of the very minimum necessitated by the operations of war. The seventeenth and the eighteenth centuries, however, as was remarked already, give evidence of a neglect of this pledge in the considerable amount of unsettlement, as the direct result of the invasions and counter invasions by the one party and another. The so-called battle of Talikota, the battle which ought really to be called by another name, Rākshasatangaḍi, if the battle is to be named after the locality in which it was actually fought—resulted merely in the abandoning of the famous capital of Vijayanagar. The rulers of the empire fell back upon the second line of defence in the fortress of Penugonḍa. It seems Tirumalarāja, the successor of Rama, who died in battle, was more anxious to save the treasure and secure the sinews of war thereby, and retired in consequence from Vijayanagar for safety to the walls of Penugonḍa, wherefrom he continued to exercise, if not to the same degree, the same kind of influence even in the affairs of the inter-relation between the five states of the Bahmani kingdom. In the latter years of his reign, his intervention was called for and sometimes proved decisive. But a change took place, not many years after the battle, when the empire of the Mughals under Akbar showed an inclination to extend that empire across the Vindhya mountains. This divided the attention of the five Bahmani Sultans; the northern ones, particularly Ahmadnagar and Berar had to face about and prevent if possible the extinction of the local authority in their kingdoms. Bidar, the middle one, was, as compared with the other four, a comparatively ineffective power; but the two southern powers Bijapur and Golkonda enjoyed freedom from this preoccupation and become more aggressive on the southern frontier and actively cooperated to dismember the empire. The wars on the northern frontier of Vijayanagar therefore assumed a different character, and became more frequent and more unsettling in regard to the internal administration of the country. It is these invasions that were ultimately responsible for the dismemberment and ultimate destruction of the Vijayanagar empire, and it is these wars that gave the character to the seventeenth and eighteenth centuries, which may not inappropriately be described as a period more or less of anarchy, and which brought about ultimately a change of rulers. The efforts of Bijapur and Golkonda, however, were resisted with comparative success. The fall of these successively before the great Mughal, Auranga-zeb, and his occupation of the kingdoms introduced a little more vigour in the operations of the Muhammadans in this region. The fall of Gingee in 1698 sets the high watermark of this Mughal advance towards the south. The death of the great emperor which followed, and the disturbance in the empire itself brought about a relaxation, and it is a question of the wars between the Nizam of the Dakhan and his lieutenants, the Nawabs of Arcot and the Hindus. The struggle was over at the end of the third quarter of the seventeenth century and the Muhammadan power established itself more or less. The culmination of this new Muhammadan viceroyalty of the south, the Nawabship of Arcot was reached with the abolition of the Nayakship of Madura at Trichinopoly in 1739; and the struggle between the Companies, the French and the English, began soon after, and terminated in the acquisition of an ascendency over the Nawab of Arcot by the British in the middle of the eighteenth century; and the fifty years of struggle for the establishment of one power laid the foundations of the British Madras Presidency and the period of Muhammadan rule actually is less than a century. But anything like an actual organisation of Muhammadan administration could hardly be brought about in the half century of their actual rule at the outside. When therefore the British administrative organisation was about to be introduced, the first organisers found that anything like a system based upon what they found prevailing at the time would have been to the great disadvantage of the agricultural inhabitants of the region, and they therefore found that the better way to proceed in bringing about a permanent organisation of the region under British rule, would be to go back to a period two or three generations behind their times, and revert to the condition of the territory under Hindu rule. That was what exactly was done and the adoption of a revenue settlement for South Kanara which was the district to come first under the British organisation, and subsequently the Baramahals. To some extent therefore the British organisation of the Madras Presidency may be regarded as the inheritance of the administrative organisation, which we have been trying to picture in the pages above.

APPENDIX

(The following translation of No. 202 of 1912 at Tiruvottiyūr differs in some important particulars from the summary given in the Epigraphist's report. Hence it is appended.)

In accordance with the royal orders by word of mouth;—In the year 35 of the emperor of the three worlds, Tirubhuvana Vīra Dēva, who had the annointment of heroes and the annointment of victors, in the month when the sun was in Leo (*Simha,*) the former fortnight, the 12th day, Friday, Uttiraṭṭādi, this sale deed was made, under the hand of the Sabha of Punnavāyil, otherwise Raja Nārayaṇa Chaturvēdi Mangalam, belonging to the sub-division Puḻalnāḍu in the division Puḻal Koṭṭam, otherwise Vikramaśoḻa Vaḻanāḍu, in the province of Kulottunga Śoḻa Manḍalam. In the year 34 of this king, prince Yādavarāyar imposed a tax called *Ponvari,* at the rate of a quarter of a *Māḍai* per *vēli* of land, without excluding from this impost land lying abandoned and uncultivated. He imposed the tax, as though it was occupied country and appointed, under authority (Tīṭṭu-konḍu) as collector thereof, Valaiyam Aḻahiyān, otherwise Kulottunga Chola Paiyūr Nāḍāḻvān. He then insisted upon the payment of the gold tax. In lieu of the payment due from those who held the lands, he collected the amount to the extent due from the owners of the land such sums as we held in a capitalised form, and for the balances, he held us under destraint by tying us up together and putting us in confinement. We the following members of the Sabha including Vaṭṭamaṇi

Tiruvēngaḍa Bhaṭṭa, the residents: Tōlayya Bhaṭṭa, Padmanada Bhaṭṭa, Śiva Dēva Bhaṭṭa, Arulāla Bhaṭṭa; as also the outsider Udayāditta Bhaṭṭa, Ōḍapurai Malaikuniya Ninrān Bhaṭṭa, residents Śrī Krishna Bhaṭṭa, Kandayya Bhaṭṭa, Uḍali Tiruvēngaḍa Bhaṭṭa, residents, Kanḍayya Bhaṭṭa, Aiyan Bhaṭṭa, Sēndram Karumāṇikka Bhaṭṭa, residents, Āḷkonḍa Villi Bhaṭṭa, Kārāmbiśēṭṭu Droṇayya Bhaṭṭa. These members constituting the Sabha put up for sale eighty *vēlis* of land (with the boundaries defined in detail) which are classed as cultivable lands, including in it the lands unclassified, such as *nattam* (village site), the tank, the water spread of the tank, its banks, and the pools of water close to the banks, gardens, roads, channels for irrigation, sites for assembly, unoccupied land for the calves, forests and waste lands together with the trees above ground, the wells below ground with the privilege of leading water from the tank of Punnavāyil by the sluice Pullandi as of old, and called for a bid. The response came from Kāvanur Kiḻavan, Pichchan Duggaiyāḷvān, a resident of Māḷikai Kāvanūr in the sub-division Polikai in the division Maṇavirkoṭṭam that he was prepared to purchase the lands thus defined. Having heard this, the Sabha of Punnavāyil (Rajanārāyaṇa Chaturvēdi Mangalam) above described agreed to sell to the said Kāvanūr Kiḻavan Pichchan Duggaiyāḷvān the land as defined above for 200 *kāśu* of the current coin that was in circulation. These 200 good coins having been received exclusive of all expenses, we executed this deed of sale. The buyer shall have the right of sale, hypothecation, gift of this land. He shall also have the right to separate the village from the register of Punnavāyil and get it registered in "the register of taxes collected" in his own name. We shall not show it in our register of lands liable to taxes in this village, or of minor dues. The water for the tank at Punnavāyil shall be taken from the canal running westwards on the northern side of the tank at Kuḷattūr. On this channel the eastward flow shall be shut up and water led by a westward channel into the tank at Punnavāyil. The water of the tank at Kuḷattūr shall not be led away till after the tank at Punnavāyil is full. The fields of Kuḷattūr which by long usage had irrigation water from the tank at Punnavāyil through the sluice Pullandi shall continue as heretofore. We have duly received the current old coin of 200 *kāśu* exclusive of all expenses and in lieu thereof sold this and executed this deed of sale. We shall not demand in exchange for this land any other amount and shall regard this amount as satisfying all conditions of sale. We shall not claim any rights because of defect in the document, in the writing or in the language. We thus declare, once, twice and thrice.

Given under the hand of (the same names as above)

Under the orders of these, this deed was put in writing by the *Madhyasta* Aruḷāḷa Perumāḷ Udayam Śeydān of Punnavāyil, otherwise Raja Nārāyaṇa Chaturvēdi Mangalam, followed by the signatures of the above said members of the Sabha.

From out of this land, the following dispositions were made. 3 *vēlis* were set apart for the temple of Tiru Agattīśvaram of Punnaivāyil; 1 *veli* was set a art for the temple of Vinayaka Piḷḷaiyar (Gaṇapati or Vignesvara); 2 *vēlis* for the Narpatteṇṇayira Viṇṇagar Aḷvar Vishṇu temple in the village; 1 *vēli* for the Narpatteṇṇayira Perumpaḷḷi; ½ *veli* for the temple of Piḍāri as Pidaripaṭṭi; 2 *vēlis* were distributed as *Bhaṭṭavritti* (gift to learned Brahmans); ½ a *vēli* was set apart for the owner of this village, Kavanur Kiḻavan Pichchan Duggaiaḷvan for the purpose of a backyard to his house and a garden; 5 *velis* were set apart as tax free land for this Kāvanūr Kiḻavan Pichchan Duggaiāḷvan and his descendants for the donation of public benefit to the Tiruvottiyūr temple that he made out of this land. Including those, the tax free lands given as temple gifts, etc., totalling up to 15 *vēlis,* from out of the 80 *vēlis,* the remaining 65 *vēlis* were set apart for the following purposes, namely the fourteeen days' festival in the temple at Tiruvottiyūr celebrating the grant of the 14 Māhēśvara Sutras of Vyākaraṇa to Pāṇini by Śiva. This fourteen days' festival used to be celebrated in a special hall (*Manṭapa*); the lands now set apart were to be applied for the repairs of this *Manṭapa* and for the maintenance of the staff and students of a school of Vyakaraṇa in this hall. This arrangement of Pichchan Duggaiāḷvan was to be duly intimated to Kulottunga. The 5 *vēlis* of gift to his descendants were in gratitude thereof. The 65 *vēlis* of land were to constitute the capital, the income from which was to be applied for the expenses of the festival on the fourteen days and for the maintenance of the school. This charity is intended to last as long as the sun and the moon. Those that "obstruct this charity will commit a sin like that of killing a good cow on the bam of the Ganges and of the sin of killing a good Brahman." The whole charity is placed under the direction of the Māhēśvaras.

CONCLUSION.

The elaborate survey of Hindu administrative institutions in South India made above, from such material as has come down to us, gives a more or less complete picture of the administration as it must have worked in the centuries down to the foundation of the empire of Vijayanagar. During the period of this empire, which set itself up as a bulwark against the incursions of the Islamic power into the Dravidian south, the organisation of the administration continued practically unaltered except for the exigencies of the unremitting war that this wardenship of the marches imposed upon the new-born state. We have seen in the course of our previous study that a very high degree of the genuine spirit of co-operation prevailed not only as between the various castes and the communities which constituted the Hindu population and which strikes the modern observer as almost impossible of satisfactory management; but the spirit of genuine co-operation pervaded the very sympathetic relation between the rulers and the ruled. It cannot be said of this administration, as in fact it cannot be, of the most perfectly organised of the administrations for government, that the institutions such as they were did not exhibit any hitch in the working. Complicated as the organisation was, there must have been misunderstandings, unanticipated difficulties and even difficulties arising out of the shortcomings of the agents who had to carry out the details of the administration. These were met as they arose, satisfactory solutions were found and those than differed even violently accepted the final arrangements cheerfully, and attempted to carry them out to the best of their ability. It is that spirit of goodwill to accept a bad position and labour to get out of it the best way that human ingenuity can devise satisfactorily to all concerned, that really constituted the secret of the success of these institutions. Wars there were in plenty. Frontier forays were not altogether absent and wanton devastation even cannot be said to have been absent. Wanton destruction had always met with the strongest disapproval. Wars were carried on generally, there were no doubt exceptions and those exceptions only prove the rule, as between the fighting folk only, but the peaceful pursuit of the average agriculturists, and the other folk being deliberately exempt as a matter of principle from the operations of war. It is this that is the secret of the success, generally the financial success, of Hindu administrations which caught the eye of even shrewed Muhammadan observers such as the emperor Allauddin who could not be regarded as wanting in the practical knowledge of administration to make pennies multiply into pounds. It was one of the instructions that he gave to his general going to the south not to aim at abolishing all Hindu rule or the carrying out of the war completely crippling the Hindus down. His definite instructions were to carry the war only so far as to strike terror and put the administrators of Hindu governments in fear of the Islamic power, so that, as he cynically observed, the Hindu rulers may go on accumulating like the busy bee to admit of the Muhamhadan conqueror drawing largely from the accumulated supplies occasionally. It was not only the observation of Allauddin Khilji, whose testimony in this particular is of undoubted importance; but even the travellers that came and passed through the country when these administrations were at their very best have left it on record that the condition of the country was one of great prosperity and wealth. On the whole therefore, it would not be far wrong to say that the institutions such as they were, were devised to meet the needs of the administration satisfactorily, so satisfactorily as to promote the prosperity of the people of the land of all classes.

If that is so, the interesting question would arise as to what exactly was the general character of the administration that made for the happiness of the people in such a satisfactory degree. It consisted in this. In every department of the administration that touched the people intimately, the people were allowed to carry on the administration in the best way that appealed to them to achieve the end. Civil administration as such in all departments seems to have been entirely in the hands of the people subject no doubt to the control and regulation both of the subordinate governments of the provinces and the headquarters government of the monarch, and his council. Except to the degree of interference, when interference was actually called for by misfeasance or maladministration, the rulers seem to have been content to allow the people to carry on the administration as they thought best. This devolution of power in the people, practically in all the departments of a modern administration with the exception of a few matters regulating inter-state relations, matters affecting the army and the development of the military resources of the state, matters relating to the maintenance of peace in the interior in regard to that part of it which fell outside the bounds of capacity of the local authorities, and the exercise of a general healthy control over the administration in all its details, these and these alone seem to have been the departments reserved for the central governments. A kingdom of the Hindus therefore showed the king and his councillors and a comparatively large body of officials at headquarters discharging these responsible duties with as much efficiency as could normally be expected, having regard to the means of communication possible at the time. It would be futile to institute any useful comparison between the administration of the first fifteen hundred years of the Christian era with the British or any other administration of to-day for the simple reason that the common basis necessary for comparison does not exist at all. If any useful comparison is to be made at all, the comparison to be valid ought to be comparison with civilised organisations contemporary with the times in other parts of the world. While here and there we may find particulars of institutions perhaps more useful for achieving particular ends, than corresponding institutions that may obtain at the time, it may prove futile to press the comparison further than that for any useful purpose. The ultimate end of the state is the maintenance of the people constituting the state in substantial happiness and freedom, to pursue life in the best manner that that life appealed to the communities denerally, and governments are good or bad according as they contributed to this great end. We ought therefore to judge of Hindu administration by that standard and by no other.

It would be interesting in this connection to note the end that those good people have in view who are making serious attempts at what is generally termed rural reconstruction. The aims and objects that this body of administrative reformers set before themselves, and the tests by which they wish that an administration should be considered satisfactory or otherwise would apply in this case aptly. Dr. Butterfield, who early in the year lectured on the building and maintenance of an adequate rural civilisation suggested the following tests as providing a practical rule by which administrations may be judged in respect of their being good or bad. "He was of the view that an adequate rural civilisation ought to be sufficiently social. *The farmers ought to be considered as the trustees of the soil.* It was incumbent upon the agriculturists to utilise the soil to the very best advantage of not merely themselves but of the society as well. They should make the best of each acre of land. Land was to be thought of and treated in terms of public interest, because society had got more stake in land than on anything else. For an adequate rural civilisation, another test was that *the cultivator should have just reward for the work.* But Dr. Butterfield had never heard of a formula by which they could guarantee a farmer an equivalent to a real wage. It was more difficult to determine the wage of the cultivator than the wage of the industrial worker. There were the exigencies of weather, and the difficulty about determining the cost of production. But as researches progressed, as education became more widespread, as critics grew more and more, and as the call for good became even more insistent than it was now, the difficulties in determining the just reward for the farmer's work would become easier of solution. The third test was the *satisfying quality of rural life.* Some used to say that if people were satisfied why should they be disturbed. The answer to that is that it is against the character of human nature. They had all the passion for progress. Therefore satisfying country life meant a rise in the general level of intelligence of the people, and intelligence which could grasp new things and ideas. Till now tradition and experience had been the teacher to the tiller of the soil. But now science had come on the field and the cultivator must have that type of intelligence which would be able to grasp what science had to teach. Literacy was not the same as intelligence. He did not hold the view at all that a group of people must be literate in order to be intelligent and educated. Nevertheless, they must not take up this attitude and remain inactive. The demands of modern life and modern civilisation were being heaped upon them, and they could not but try to abolish illiteracy as easily as possible. *There must also be a measure of culture* in an adequate rural civilisation. By culture he meant an appreciation of the social and economic environments in which the rural life was cast. He also thought that in an adequate rural life there must be an opportunity for those who were competent to change their status. The last test he desired to lay stress on was that *the people of the rural areas should participate politically* and contribute their peculiar share to the common civilisation of the times."

Judged by these modern tests, the ordinary administration under the Hindus in this part of the country, of which a picture had been drawn from such glimpses of information that we could get, the arrangements for the administration of rural localities as well as the urban, seem to have been devised with an eye to these modern requirements. The first point to which attention is drawn by Dr. Butterfield is that the farmers should have sufficient interest in the land that they cultivate, and feel that they must make the most of this invaluable source of production—it may be in the first instance for their own benefit, but ultimately for the benefit of society. That refers to land as a source of production. The more the labour, the more the useful and intelligent labour that is applied to it, the more it is capable of producing. The more that is produced, the greater the number of people benefited by it. In fact the underlying idea is the ploughman plies his trade for the benefit of humanity, at least of that section of humanity constituting the society in which he lives. That that idea was not absent from the minds of the Hindus is vouched for by verses in the Kural which exalt the peasant perhaps even higher than Dr. Butterfield's statement would imply, so that the farmer was there in the Hindu political organisation, a man whose occupation was regarded as at the very root of social well-being. He received the consideration due to that position that he occupied in society. If the organisation, socio-political organisation—admitted of that position even theoretically, the organisation stands justified so far as that test goes.

The second test is that the cultivator should have the reward of his labour. From the information that is available to us, not ony is the share of the sovereign strictly limited, but even the division of produce between the actual owners of the land and the cultivators was so well regulated, and withal so equitable, that what was left to the farmer must have been quite a reasonable portion of the produce of his labour upon the land. The arrangement of the *mēlvāram* and the *kuḍivāram*, and the various nice grades of regulating their proportion that we come across with, is a clear indication that this principle was not lost sight of. The third is a little more difficult of defining in a categorical statement, viz., that the rural life lived by the farmer must have been a satisfying life. A satisfying life is a variable quantity, and certainly would vary from time to time and according to circumstances. Without going into the question whether we should leave people that may be satisfied with their satisfaction without trying to improve life according to our superior lights, we may say at once the life that these people led was a satisfying life in the sense that it gave them undoubtedly adequate reward for their labour, which enabled them to live their life in comfort and perhaps even to indulge in some little enjoyment of life. It is after all a question of means to do this. We have indicated above that the means that the farmers enjoyed as their share was adequate and reasonable to live in comfort and to admit even of a certain amount of enjoyment of life. But then that is not enough. Did it really admit of that intelligent life and appreciation of the occupation, which would be wide awake to possible improvements and their active adoption? This would involve naturally education and development of intelligence not necessarily in the matter of mere literacy, but perhaps otherwise where universal literacy was not possible of attainment. It would be well if we could have had more information on the subject, but such as we have seems to suggest that the farmer was very far from being a mere predial slave, but was capable of intelligent thinking regarding his work and ready to adopt improvements either of his own or of others' suggestion. The evidence that may be available is not perhaps quite positive, but negative scraps of information that we have seem clearly to indicate that the cultivating farmer was really capable of understanding and of applying these, and in the doing exhibited a certain amount of intelligence, cultivated intelligence, though he might have been perhaps illiterate. The means of education and the method adopted were such as to convey all kinds of information direct to the masses usually in the form of story-telling of various kinds. Of course modern life and modern civilisation may demand more by the fact that all parts of the world have come very near together by the almost complete abolition of distances by steam and electricity. But the Indian of the first millenium, and even the first half of the second, was while in touch with the outside world to a far higher degree than we are prepared to recognise, was still in a position to pursue his life in his own way.

Coming to the next point, the same investigator

lays it down that they must be possessed of a certain measure of culture in an adequate rural civilisation. He takes care to define culture as an appreciation of the social and economic environments in which rural life is cast. This culture we may say the Indian possessed, and the cultured Indian has not forgotten that as yet, although perhaps he is doing so very rapidly on account of the vast inrushing changes of modern times. He surely knew where he was and what his actual surroundings happened to be. He knew his duties and he could even stick out for his rights. Not only could he appreciate his position, but he could appreciate the position of other communities in society, and render unto them his duties and his assistance whenever required, exhibiting a spirit of co-operation which is perhaps the very soul of rural life. The alacrity with which they did their work in the common interests of the village—may be for the village temple or even for the Brahman folk of the village—is a clear evidence of their appreciation and realisation of this spirit.

The last of these modern tests is that the people of the rural areas should participate politically in the government of the country, and contribute their peculiar share to the common civilisation of the times. In the rural administration that is pictured above, the farmer certainly had his own part, and exercised a substantial influence in the shaping of the arrangements under which he lived, and therefore we might even say he took an active part in the administration, though perhaps he had not much part in the active executive carrying on of the administration. As far as the mere external conditions of life would admit of it, the farmer had free scope for much that made his influence far from negligible in the rural life of the locality.

Having said so much about the mere rural side of the administration, we may try and gather together what the other side of the administration had been. Above this administration of the rural units was the administration of the larger division, which perhaps need not exactly be called provincial, though somewhat analogous to it. This divisional administration had general oversight and control, and powers of audit on the financial side. Their powers were generally powers of report to headquarters and these had the full plenary authority of the government of the king for royal intervention to set matters right where there was any suspicion of their going seriously wrong. In as much as these divisional administrations were merely carrying out the duties of control and supervision that the government of the king and his council should exercise, they were mere intermediary officials with no particular powers of their own. Such as these were, they were large and were to some extent capable of even admitting some degree of discretion on the part of the divisional authorities, and powers of rectification, so long as they could bring this about with the co-operation of the rural authorities concerned. They were ready, and had the means, to render assistance, whenever they might be called upon by the rural authorities under their supervision, and on the whole this supervisory administration seems to have exercised its authority as intermediaries between the rural and the royal administrations with a sense of responsibility and moderation.

Coming to the administration of the king himself, it is generally described as an autocracy, oriental despotism at that, as though it were altogether a term of abuse. Autocratic in appearance it seems to have been to the superficial observer, but the essence of autocracy consists in the capacity to make laws at the pleasure of the governing authority or the sovereign. But the law-making power was not there for one thing. The king was no more than the administrator of the law, such as it was understood to be, and even in matters of doubt, delicacy and importance, he was not exactly the ultimate arbiter of law; this power lay in a body or person quite aside of the king. In addition to this limitation, the king was certainly bound by the advice of his council, and as far as we are enabled to see, he carried out no act of administration without consulting his council. While therefore the king exercised a very considerable authority, and far more influence than authority, on the administration, and was even looked upon as almost a god on earth, the powers that he could exercise were carefully limited, and the limitations were understood by him as well as by those that he governed. He could administer justice only according to law and not according to his pleasure. He could prescribe punishments under the law, and not as it suited his individual taste.

The character of the administration and the body of officials that surrounded the king may perhaps for convenience be described as beaurocratic. There were departments well divided and demarcated in respect of their powers, and they had to co-operate where their co-operation was called for. It is the joint report of various departments concerned that led to a final decision by the king and the promulgation of orders of a general character in the executive departments of his administration. In the matter of the army, in interstate relations, in the conduct of war, the king's power reached the highest, and even there it was not by himself alone that he did anything of importance. He usually took counsel and often-times his own individual resolution was made to give place to the more deliberate resolutions of the council, so that on the whole, we may characterise Hindu administration, such as we have been trying to describe as monarchy, limited in regard to law-making and even in the carrying out of the actual administration.

According to modern notions of government the end of Government is not merely "the efficiency of its results, but really the education of its own process." It may be useful in this connection to quote a few sentences from a lecture delivered before the Aberdeen University by Mr. Ernest Barker, who in one part of the lecture quotes a passage from General Smutts, a statesman engaged in the actual rough and tumble of the carrying on of the administration of a difficult dominion. He takes the passage from a lecture delivered by the General to the Cambridge University. In the course of the lecture, General Smutts said:—"The end of government is not merely good government, but the education of people in good government, which is self-education in running its own affairs. Even at the price of less efficient government, let the people go on by all means gaining its own experience and develop its own capacty for self-government." Applying this dictum, Mr. Barker proceeded to observe "that we should be false to ourselves if we applied to India the test of efficiency only, at a time when, as our whole system of democracy shows, we are applying to ourselves the other test of self-development of capacity." He proceeds further to modify the statement by bringing to bear upon this general position the notion of responsibility and the possibility of difficulties, etc., which is not our concern at present If what is stated above by these two eminent authorities in regard to current notions of what a government ought to be, we may judge of the Hindu Government of India in the centuries long gone, by this standard, and consider whether that Hindu administration did not make as close an approach to this as the circumstances of the times admitted of it. If, without sacrificing efficiency as one of the main objects of administration, that efficiency could be obtained along with the education of the people in governing themselves, perhaps it may be said, that on the whole, the administrative system devised by the Hindus served this end in a measure beyond ordinary expectation. Of course it must be borne in mind that the study made above applies only to a part of India, as far as the details of it go, and from the available details other blocks of a distinct character have to be similarly studied, and then a synthesis made as to what the general character of Hindu administration of India must have been before anything like a final and historically sound characterisation of that administration could be undertaken. But so far as we have been able to carry on the investigation under the limitations imposed by the partial character of the material at our disposal, we may flatter ourselves that the administration seems to have made a clear, but close approach to these ideals which modern democracy is making an effort at realising.

INDEX.